The Unemployme

MW01107429

High unemployment and the pervasive economic insecurity created by lay-offs, cutbacks, and corporate downsizings during the 1990–93 recession dominate the Canadian social reality of the 1990s. *The Unemployment Crisis*, a collection of essays based on the first annual economic policy conference held at Laurentian University in Sudbury, Ontario, explores the severity of the 1990–93 recession, the reasons for the crisis, and what governments can do to make low unemployment a reality.

Arguing that the unemployment crisis could have been avoided by better government policies, particularly less restrictive monetary control, the contributors examine the effect of the zero-inflation policy adopted by the Bank of Canada and the role of unemployment insurance on the unemployment crisis of recent years. Their analysis includes comparative discussions of various facets of unemployment in France, Germany, and Japan.

Both critical of past performance and optimistic about future possibilities, *The Unemployment Crisis* is a timely and valuable addition to current literature on economic policy.

BRIAN K. MacLEAN is associate professor of economics, Hokkaido University, Japan.
LARS OSBERG is McCulloch Professor of Economics, Dalhousie University.

CRITICAL PERSPECTIVES ON PUBLIC AFFAIRS
Series Editors: Duncan Cameron, Bruce Campbell, and Daniel Drache

This series, sponsored by the Canadian Centre for Policy Alternatives
and co-published by McGill-Queen's University Press, is intended to
present important research on Canadian policy and public affairs.
Books are by leading economic and social critics in the Canadian
academic community and will be useful for classroom texts and the
informed reader as well as for the academic specialist.

The Canadian Centre for Policy Alternatives promotes research on
economic and social issues facing Canada. Through its research
reports, studies, conferences, and briefing sessions, the CCPA provides
thoughtful alternatives to the proposals of business research institutes and many government agencies. Founded in 1980, the CCPA
holds that economic and social research should contribute to building
a better society. The centre is committed to publishing research that
reflects the concerns of women as well as men; labour as well as
business; churches, cooperatives, and voluntary agencies as well as
governments; disadvantaged individuals as well as those more
fortunate. Critical Perspectives on Public Affairs will reflect this
tradition through the publication of scholarly monographs and
collections.

Getting on Track
Social Democratic Strategies for Ontario
Daniel Drache, Editor

The Political Economy of North American Free Trade
Ricardo Grinspun and Maxwell A. Cameron, Editors

Poverty Reform in Canada, 1958–1978
State and Class Influences on Policy Making
Rodney S. Haddow

Women, Work, and Coping
A Multidisciplinary Approach to Workplace Stress
Bonita C. Long and Sharon E. Kahn, Editors

Trials of Labour
The Re-emergence of Midwifery
Brian Burtch

The Unemployment Crisis
All for Nought?
Brian K. MacLean and Lars Osberg, Editors

The Unemployment Crisis: All for Nought?

BRIAN K. MacLEAN AND
LARS OSBERG, EDITORS

McGill-Queen's University Press
Montreal & Kingston • London • Buffalo

© McGill-Queen's University Press 1996
ISBN 0-7735-1417-1 (cloth)
ISBN 0-7735-1418-X (paper)

Legal deposit fourth quarter 1996
Bibliothèque nationale du Québec

Printed in Canada on acid-free paper

Publication of this book has been assisted by a grant
from the Douglas-Coldwell Foundation.

McGill-Queen's University Press is grateful to the
Canada Council for support of its publishing program.

Canadian Cataloguing in Publication Data

Main entry under title:
The unemployment crisis : all for nought?
(Critical perspectives on public affairs)
Includes bibliographical references and index.
ISBN 0-7735-1417-1 (bound) –
ISBN 0-7735-1418-X (pbk.)
1. Unemployment – Canada. 2. Manpower policy –
Canada. 3. Canada – Economic policy – 1991–
I. MacLean, Brian Kenneth, 1957–   II. Osberg, Lars
III. Series.
HD5707.5.U58 1996   331.13'7971   C96-900372-2

Typeset in Palatino 10/12
by Caractéra inc., Quebec City

Contents

Acknowledgments

This volume consists of selected papers presented at a conference in the Annual Economic Policy Conference series organized by Brian K. MacLean at Laurentian University since 1993. We would like to acknowledge our debt to all of the participants in the "Unemployment: What is to be done?" conference. Claude Vincent of Laurentian University not only helped to run the conference, but also assisted with proofreading all the chapters of this volume, and he deserves our special thanks.

Funding for the unemployment conference was provided by the Laurentian University Research Fund; Human Resources Development Canada; Industry Canada; and the Academic Vice-President, Dean of Social Sciences, Director of Graduate Studies, and Department of Economics of Laurentian University. Sources of funding for the conference are, of course, not responsible for the contents of this volume.

The publication of this book has been assisted by financial support from the Douglas-Coldwell Foundation, and we would like to thank the officers for their support. We would also like to thank Lynn Lethbridge for her work in preparing the index. We have appreciated the support of our project by Critical Perspectives on Current Affairs series editors Duncan Cameron and Daniel Drache and by McGill-Queen's Executive Director Philip Cercone.

Finally, it should be noted that the ideas expressed in each of the chapters are those of the authors. We are grateful for the promptness with which they carried out their revisions.

Contributors

BRIAN MacLEAN is a visiting associate professor with the Department of Economics, Hokkaido University, Sapporo, Japan, where he is on leave from his position at Laurentian University until mid-1997. He has published articles in the *Cambridge Journal of Economics*, *Review of Income and Wealth*, *Canadian Business Economics*, and other journals, and is the organizer of the Annual Economic Policy Conference series from which this volume has arisen.

LARS OSBERG is McCulloch Professor of Economics at Dalhousie University. In addition to contributing numerous scholarly articles to learned journals such as *European Economic Review*, *Canadian Journal of Economics*, *Oxford Economic Papers*, and the *Cambridge Journal of Economics*, he has published several works for a broader audience, including *Economic Inequality in Canada*, *Vanishing Jobs: Canada's Changing Workplaces*, and (with Pierre Fortin) *Unnecessary Debts*.

PIERRE FORTIN is a professor of economics at the Université du Québec à Montréal, a member of the Economic Growth Programme of the Canadian Institute for Advanced Research, and president of the Canadian Economics Association (1995–96). He has published in such journals as the *European Economic Review* and the *Atlantic Economic Journal*. At recent meetings of the Canadian Economics Association (CEA) he has delivered the Innis Lecture and a lecture for the twenty-fifth CEA anniversary symposium.

JOHN SMITHIN is an associate professor of economics with the Department of Economics and the Faculty of Administrative Studies, York University. He has published in journals such as the *Economic Journal*, the *Review of Political Economy*, and the *Journal of Macroeconomics* and is the author of *Macroeconomics After Thatcher and Reagan* and *Controversies in Monetary Economics*.

MARK SETTERFIELD is a graduate of Cambridge and Dalhousie universities, and is currently an assistant professor in the Department of Economics, Trinity College in Connecticut. He has published in such journals as the *European Economic Review, Canadian Business Economics*, and the *Journal of Post Keynesian Economics*.

TONY MYATT is a professor of economics at the University of New Brunswick. He has contributed articles to the *Canadian Journal of Economics, Journal of Macroeconomics, Canadian Journal of Regional Science, Canadian Business Economics*, and other journals.

SHELLEY PHIPPS is an associate professor of economics at Dalhousie University. Her publications include articles in the *Economic Journal, Canadian Journal of Economics, Journal of Human Resources*, and other journals. She is actively involved with the Luxembourg Income Study group.

ANDREW SHARPE is executive director of the Ottawa-based Centre for the Study of Living Standards, past president of the Canadian Association for Business Economics, and co-editor of the journal *Canadian Business Economics*. He was co-editor with Duncan Cameron of a volume of essays on unemployment published in 1988.

HELMAR DROST is professor of economics and social and political thought at York University. He has published in such journals as *Canadian Public Policy, Review of Economics and Statistics*, and *Review of Income and Wealth*.

DOMINIQUE GROSS is an assistant professor in the Department of Economics at Simon Fraser University and is the author of articles in European journals and in the *Journal of Macroeconomics* and *Applied Economics*. She has experience as a research economist with the Swiss National Bank and recently spent a year at Charles University in Prague.

PATRICE DE BROUCKER is a senior economist with the Analytical Studies Branch of Statistics Canada and has years of experience at the Canadian Labour Force Development Board, the Organization for Economic Cooperation and Development, and the former Economic Council of Canada. This paper derives from a lengthy stay in Japan during which he was affiliated with the Japan Institute of Labour.

MIKE McCRACKEN is chairman and CEO of Informetrica Limited, a leading Canadian economic research and forecasting firm. He participates regularly in policy debates and comments on economic events for the national media. He is past president of the Canadian Association for Business Economics, past chair of the Conference of Business Economists in the United States, and active on a number of advisory groups.

Introduction
The Unemployment Crisis:
All for Nought?

BRIAN K. MacLEAN and
LARS OSBERG

High unemployment dominates Canadian social reality in the 1990s. Economic insecurity has become pervasive as waves of lay-offs, cutbacks, and corporate "downsizings" have swept across the country. Mired in double-digit unemployment until 1994, the economy is predicted to register close to 10-percent unemployment rates for the balance of the decade – barring substantial changes in government policies (or exceptionally good fortune). Once a society where good jobs and rising wages meant that each generation could pass on a better life to their children, Canada in the 1990s has become a country where many citizens have begun to question whether such aspirations are still realistic. Why has all of this happened? Does the high unemployment of the 1990s represent a structural change in the economy, or is it the unfortunate consequence of a misguided adventure in federal macroeconomic decision making? How can we reduce both the cyclical and structural components of our unemployment rate? The chapters that follow provide some answers to these and other questions surrounding the unemployment crisis.

The chapters are a selection of papers from "Unemployment: What is to be done?," a conference in the Annual Economic Policy Conference series that has been held at Laurentian University in Sudbury, Ontario since 1993. The contributors to this volume share the perspective that high unemployment is extremely important, both because of the income loss it causes and because of the psychological and social costs it imposes. In this respect, and in the shared perspective that macroeconomic policy has seriously worsened the unemployment rate, the contributors differ with the "established consensus" of Ottawa policy-makers.

For the past decade, the twin imperatives of federal macroeconomic decision making have been the elimination of inflation and the reduction of the federal deficit. Of these, fighting inflation has been assigned top priority. In 1988, when inflation in Canada had been averaging 4.1 percent for the previous four years, the Bank of Canada embarked on an unprecedented policy adventure, using tighter monetary policy to eliminate inflation entirely. The resulting surge in real interest rates peaked in 1990 when short-term interest rates were 10.3 percent higher than the rate of inflation. This precipitated a 21-percent appreciation of the Canadian dollar relative to its United States' counterpart. Simultaneous declines in net exports, investment, and consumer confidence produced a collapse in employment, income, and output. The recession of the early 1990s has left behind massive government debt (due to decreased tax revenues and increased expenditures on unemployment insurance and social assistance) and a legacy of long-term unemployment. For years to come, Canadians will be picking up the pieces.

Although most Canadians voted in the 1993 election for a shift to job creation, the incoming government has followed a policy of continuity rather than change. In part, this is undoubtedly because the government gets its economic advice from the same old sources, who continue to function within the intellectual framework that produced the policy adventure of 1988–93.

The "established consensus" of the Ottawa policy-making community has been that unemployment is largely a *microeconomic* problem. Both under the Conservative regime of 1984–93 and in the emerging Liberal "reform" of the social policy framework, the rhetoric of policy analysis has emphasized the importance of "incentives," primarily those embodied in unemployment insurance, to the decisions of the unemployed. In a tidy (but ineffective) division of bureaucratic responsibilities, the Bank of Canada is responsible for inflation, the Department of Finance deals with federal deficit reduction, and Human Resources Development oversees changes in training and work incentives to reduce the rate of unemployment. Except for inflation control, this division of responsibilities has failed.

The idea that each objective can be pursued in isolation makes sense only within a particular intellectual framework. Only if the determinants of unemployment lie primarily on the supply side of labour markets – in the job-search decisions and skills training of individual workers – does it make sense to ignore the role played by the demand side of the labour market (the availability of jobs). The contributors to this volume share a perspective that the demand side of the labour market is crucially important, both in the short and in the long term.

Part one deals with macroeconomic theory and evidence related to the unemployment crisis, and leads off with chapters by Lars Osberg and Pierre Fortin. In chapter 1, Osberg argues there are huge costs to the total elimination of inflation. The decision to incur these costs cannot be justified by the Bank of Canada's legal mandate, the pressures of public opinion, or the empirical evidence on the supposed benefits of zero inflation. Although there is little doubt about the huge costs of the 1990s' recession, there is great uncertainty surrounding estimates of the eventual benefits of inflation reduction, as both Osberg and Fortin argue. Osberg further argues that it is reasonable to expect that the Canadian economy will experience external inflationary shocks over the next thirty years at a rate not unlike that of the past thirty years. Hence, the cost of future price-level certainty will be uncertainty in future output and employment. In addition, Fortin presents econometric evidence that the Canadian economy is characterized by "hysteresis" – i.e., that high unemployment today plays a causal role in creating higher unemployment in future years.

In economic theorizing associated with the intellectual framework guiding federal macroeconomic policy making, there exist "natural rates" for both unemployment and interest. The natural rate of unemployment is said to be set uniquely by social institutions, national customs, and the demographic composition of the labour force. The natural rate of interest is said to be determined by the underlying savings preferences of potential investors and the marginal productivity of capital. Those who believe that deviations from these natural rates will be temporary tend to believe that the monetary authorities should concentrate on stabilizing prices by stabilizing the money supply.

In their contributions, John Smithin and Mark Setterfield examine the natural rate perspective from different angles. Smithin points out that, in a monetary economy, the central bank will necessarily have a substantial influence on real interest rates and, therefore, a substantial impact on the level of economic activity. Indeed, he notes that the substitutability of monetary instruments makes it extremely difficult (and somewhat pointless) to control "the money supply"; hence, fluctuations in real interest rates are in fact the means by which the central bank influences the rate of inflation. By restricting the growth of credit, the central bank can raise real interest rates, depress output, and lessen the rate of inflation – but there should be no pretence that this does not involve substantial costs in output and employment. As Setterfield argues in chapter 4, there is little reason for believing that, following such a decline in activity, the economy will return naturally to a unique NAIRU (non-accelerating inflation rate of unemployment) – and a good deal of evidence that the costs of unemployment are often long-term in nature.

In the supply-side perspective on unemployment, macroeconomic policy is de-emphasized, while unemployment insurance is assigned a major causal role. Unemployment insurance may have been established to decrease the financial hardships and economic insecurities caused by unemployment, but the supply-side perspective reverses the direction of causation, arguing that unemployment insurance "generosity" is a major cause of high unemployment. In Part two, Shelley Phipps, Tony Myatt, and Lars Osberg address the empirical evidence on whether unemployment insurance can legitimately be blamed for high unemployment in the 1990s.

Lars Osberg in chapter 5 notes that the evidence on the impact of unemployment insurance on unemployment comes at three levels – case studies, econometric analysis of micro-data, and macroeconomic time series. All three types of evidence are, however, far more ambiguous than is commonly realized.

Tony Myatt begins by noting that the fourteen published studies of the impact of the 1971 unemployment insurance reforms on aggregate unemployment have split evenly between those that found some effect and those that found none. Macroeconomic time-series evidence is extraordinarily sensitive to the exact form of econometric specification, as Myatt demonstrates. He suggests that researchers need to combine cross-sectional evidence on interprovincial variations in unemployment rates with time-series evidence on unemployment insurance revisions and unemployment rates over time. However, although there are many ambiguities in the statistical evidence on the impact of unemployment insurance and unemployment, the public debate is often characterized by confident assertions of direct causality.

While Myatt surveys econometric work based upon macroeconomic time series, Shelley Phipps focuses on the evidence from microeconomic analyses. She begins chapter 6 by examining the basic "incentives" argument that unemployment insurance represents a subsidy to "leisure" and that lowering unemployment insurance benefits would decrease the unemployment rate. For the sake of argument, Phipps first assumes, as the critics of unemployment insurance are wont to do, that jobs are readily available, and then asks the question: "Given the evidence on the wage elasticity of labour supply, what would be the predicted impact on employment of a cut in the unemployment insurance earnings replacement rate?" The econometric evidence indicates that the increase in the labour supply of unconstrained workers will at best be minuscule, since the overwhelming consensus of the labour-supply literature is that the wage elasticity of labour supply is almost zero. Second, she examines the assumption of job availability, providing plenty of evidence that workers cannot get all the hours of employment they desire. For those who are already constrained in labour supply, increased incentives are irrelevant.

Although parts one and two suggest that unemployment determination is heavily dependent upon the state of aggregate demand in the economy, they imply neither that other factors are irrelevant nor that disaggregated analysis is unwarranted. Part three looks at unemployment in comparative perspective and considers factors besides aggregate demand policies. Whereas the chapters in part one imply that aggregate demand policy could be used to reduce the Canadian unemployment rate substantially (say, to the 7 percent range), the chapters in part three provide clues about dealing with that portion of unemployment that is not due to aggregate demand deficiency.

The most recent Canadian recession was exceptional in many respects – for example, in that the rise in unemployment was especially pronounced in the industrial heartland of Southern Ontario. In chapter 8, Andrew Sharpe dissects the rise of unemployment in Ontario, pointing to the importance of increased unemployment of workers, especially middle-aged and older blue-collar workers who were formerly employed in interest rate sensitive industries such as construction. Sharpe's industry-level analysis provides further confirmation of the macroeconomic conclusions advanced in part one. It also points to the role of overbuilding during the real estate speculation and construction boom of the late 1980s in setting the stage for a "correction" that deepened the recession in Ontario and has hampered the recovery.

Aggregate demand conditions have a significant impact on the labour-market experience of all labour-force groups. While cyclical fluctuations in economic activity may help to explain the unemployment patterns of different groups over time, they provide little help in understanding the differences between the unemployment levels at any point in time. Helmar Drost shows in chapter 9 that Aboriginals bear a disproportionate share of unemployment in Canada. Using census data, Drost seeks to quantify the relative importance of demand-side versus supply-side variables in explaining exceptionally high Aboriginal unemployment rates. The results suggest that large gains in lowering Aboriginal unemployment rates could be achieved by raising school completion rates.

Chapters 10 and 11 bring cross-national perspectives to bear on thinking about unemployment reduction. The European unemployment experience in the 1980s, particularly the historically high unemployment rates in France and Germany and the high shares of unemployment accounted for by the long-term unemployed, gave rise to hypotheses such as "hysteresis" that have put advocates of the conservative "natural rate" hypothesis on the defensive. In chapter 10, after providing a clear discussion of developments in French and German unemployment, Dominique Gross employs a "flow approach" to assess various hypotheses about the incidence and average duration of unemployment in France and Germany. Policies suggested by the European experience – such as policies to combat the tendency of employers to use workers' length of unemployment as a signalling device about workers' "quality" – will not necessarily be as effective in Canada as they might be in Europe. The flow approach, however, correctly views the level of unemployment as the product of the incidence and the duration of unemployment (and not merely as a stock, as is it commonly viewed by non-specialists) and should inform policy judgments in Canada as elsewhere.

Whereas the Canadian unemployment rate for the 1980s averaged 9.5 percent, the Japanese rate averaged a mere 2.5 percent. Patrice de Broucker notes in chapter 11 that only a small part of the gap between the Canadian and Japanese rates relates to "hidden" unemployment in Japan. Moreover, there is no evidence that Canadian and Japanese unemployment rates differ because of different degrees of structural change, as the "sectoral shifts" hypothesis might suggest. Some would argue that low Japanese unemployment rates are due to unique cultural characteristics of the Japanese. De Broucker, however, suggests that low Japanese rates result from a coherent combination of macro-policies and micro-practices. Canada, too, would benefit from such "coherence."

In the closing chapter of the book, Mike McCracken gathers together the "clues" to unemployment reduction provided by earlier chapters and presents a macroeconomic policy package for Canada in the 1990s. McCracken's policy package includes: (1) aiming for real interest rates less than 3 percent and a lower exchange rate; (2) increased infrastructure spending, social employment programs, and tax cuts until full employment is approached; (3) emphasis on non-monetary means of inflation control, including the use of a net Consumer Price Index that omits effects of indirect taxes, exchange rate fluctuations, and international commodity price shocks; and (4) education, training, and

Research and Development measures to improve productivity growth. These recommendations are forwarded with due recognition of Canadian institutional realities.

In closing we would like to explain the double meaning of this volume's subtitle: "All for Nought?" In one sense, "all for nought" points to the key role of the zero- (i.e., "nought-") inflation strategy in bringing about the unemployment crisis. In the more obvious sense, "all for nought" suggests that the crisis could have been avoided. The phrase is at once critical of past performance and optimistic about future possibilities.

Brian K. MacLean
Lars Osberg

PART ONE

The Macroeconomics of Unemployment

1 Digging a Hole or Laying the Foundation? The Objectives of Macroeconomic Policy in Canada

LARS OSBERG

Despite widespread disagreement on the wisdom of current macro-economic policy in Canada, there is broad agreement on the analysis of many important aspects of the real economy.

1 The output gap in Canada today is huge. Although precise esti-mates of the gap between potential output and actual output depend on one's precise estimate of "full employment," it is rea-sonable to think of the output gap in Canada in January 1995 as being of the order of 8 to 10 percent of Gross Domestic Product (GDP) – i.e., $60 billion to $70 billion.[1]
2 Since the rate of growth of output is now only slightly greater than the rate of growth of potential output (i.e., trend labour-force growth plus trend growth in productivity), the output gap is decreasing very slowly.
3 With current policies, there is little probability of a major reduction in aggregate unemployment within the next couple of years.
4 The long-duration unemployed are an increasing fraction of total unemployment. Long-duration unemployment has very severe personal costs to the unemployed, as well as introducing a signif-icant degree of persistence into aggregate unemployment, since long spells of unemployment tend to decrease the employability of the unemployed.

However, all these points of agreement have not produced agree-ment on the wisdom of a monetary policy aimed at zero inflation.

And in the debates on this issue, it is interesting to observe that, despite the change in government, Bank of Canada and Ministry of Finance economists continue to use the same language in private discussions as in the public rhetoric of political statements – they refer repeatedly to the macroeconomic policies of 1988 to 1993 as "laying the foundations for sustainable growth."

FAITH AND SALVATION

Differences of opinion about macroeconomic policy are really about faith, or more precisely, about lack of faith. After all, if one observes people digging, and the hole they are digging is getting deeper and deeper, how is one to know whether this is an ordinary hole, or the hole for the foundation of a building? How can one, empirically, tell the difference? If they are asked what they are doing, and they say, "We are not digging a hole, we are digging the excavation for a *big* foundation for a *beautiful* building," how can an impartial observer know if this is true? One can ask, "Who will build this building?" but if the answer received is, "The market will build the building," how can one know whether this reveals justifiable faith in the private sector, or wishful thinking?

Faith provides both a particular interpretation of past events and a particular expectation of future events. In the case of the Bank of Canada, faith in the virtues of zero inflation was stronger than the law, more powerful than democratic sentiment, and unsupported by empirical evidence. The problem for Canada is that those who held this faith continue to have great power over the Canadian economy and many personal and professional incentives to avoid recognizing any evidence inconsistent with their faith.

The religion of salvation through zero inflation was clearly evident during the constitutional discussions of 1991–92, when the federal government made the proposal to limit forever the mandate of the Bank of Canada to the target of attaining a zero rate of price inflation. The doctrines of the faith, as enumerated in these discussions, were that (1) the *only* contribution that the Bank of Canada can make to the well-being of Canadians in the long run is to maintain a constant price level; (2) other economic objectives such as mitigating the fluctuations of production, trade, and unemployment either cannot be achieved or can be achieved only through price stability; and (3) the long-run gains from maintaining a constant price level in Canada exceed the short-run costs of the massive unemployment necessary to eliminate inflation permanently.[2]

These propositions can be fairly described as a religion, because although there is a well-elaborated theology, there is only fragile evidence to support such assertions. And as a religion, the doctrine of zero inflation has many familiar characteristics – a single deity, the promise of inevitable damnation to non-believers, and "pie in the sky" (bye and bye) for believers.

Faith in the doctrine of zero inflation is clearly stronger than law – the Bank of Canada Act explicitly enjoins the Bank of Canada to a *multiplicity* of objectives. The law requires the Bank of Canada "to regulate credit and currency in the best interest of the economic life of the nation, to control and protect the external value of the national monetary unit and to mitigate by its influence fluctuations in the general level of production, trade, prices and employment, so far as may be possible in the scope of monetary action, and generally to promote the economic and financial welfare of Canada."[3] However, despite the multiplicity of objectives specified in legislation, the operational objective of the Bank of Canada has become price constancy, and nothing else.

One might have thought that in a democracy, public opinion would be powerful, but the doctrine of zero inflation is stronger than that as well. Public opinion in Canada was clearly hostile to the acceleration of inflation in the late 1970s, and during this period public opinion polls consistently showed that a large number of Canadians wanted to "get inflation under control." However, getting inflation under control is a very different thing from getting it to zero. The long-run (sixty-year) average inflation rate in Canada is about 3.5 percent per annum, and by the mid-1980s inflation in Canada had returned to that historic range. Between 1984 and 1988 inflation in the Consumer Price Index averaged 4.1 percent per annum in Canada.

ZERO INFLATION FOR ETERNITY?

However, the Bank of Canada in 1988 aimed at something far more fundamental than keeping inflation under control. In that year the Bank of Canada decided to aim at "price stability," which, taken literally, means an inflation rate of *zero*. As a conscious strategy, the Bank of Canada implemented a restrictive monetary policy that produced historically high real interest rates and a long and severe recession. Although Canada was joined in recession misery by the United States and the United Kingdom, one must not forget that recession in Canada predated recession in both these countries – it was, in a very real sense, "made in Canada." Furthermore, Canada remained in recession much longer than either of these countries because the major levers of macroeconomic policy were locked in reverse. Federal and provincial governments tried to cut expenditures to keep up with the decline in their revenues, thereby perpetuating the decline in economic activity. In real terms, interest rates remain high by the conscious decision of the Bank of Canada, which remains reluctant to stimulate economic activity.

When inflation is "under control" at its long-run trend rate of 3.5 percent to 4 percent, there is some remaining uncertainty in the exact level of inflation one can expect and some costs to occasionally changing prices to reflect inflation. There is no evidence that Canadians wanted to trade off the remaining uncertainty in low, but fairly stable, inflation for continual insecurity in job availability. And there is no reason to believe it would be rational for them to want to do so – after all, economists tend to emphasize that markets have both price *and* quantity dimensions.

One of the most surprising aspects of discussions with colleagues from the Bank of Canada and the Ministry of Finance is learning that they are much more "academic" than most academics. Although models of stable, long-run, "steady-state" growth can be fascinating, most academics know that these are theoretical models and they cannot imagine that the real world will, in fact, be as stable and predictable as the models of economic theory. It strains credulity to imagine that Canada's economy will not be subject, in the next twenty-five or thirty years, to shocks that are at least as large as the external shocks we have experienced over the last thirty years. The real world always brings us surprises, such as the acceleration of United States' inflation in the late 1960s, the price shocks of the Organization of Petroleum Exporting Countries in the 1970s, and the commodity price collapse in the 1980s.

In the real world, such external shocks have an impact both on relative prices and on the aggregate price level: if the aggregate price level is to be frozen forever, all future external shocks to the Canadian economic system must be absorbed by variations in aggregate quantities of production and employment. Since we can be sure that future shocks *will* exist in the real world, a policy of maintaining a constant price level is necessarily a policy of greater quantity instability. If price "stability" is to be maintained, any future short-run shock to the economy that produces a short-run general increase in the price level *must also* be followed by a period of generally declining prices (enforced, if necessary, by restrictive monetary policy) in order to keep the long-run average inflation rate at approximately zero.[4]

There is no reason to believe that Canadians ever wanted this policy shift.

EMPIRICAL EVIDENCE

One must also stress that there is no empirical evidence on the long-run pay-off to maintaining zero inflation, for the simple reason that no country has done it for very long in modern times. There *is* a great deal of evidence on the costs of high unemployment. When one adds the output lost in 1995 to the output lost in between 1990 and 1994, as well as the output that will be lost in 1996 and in successive years, one is clearly talking about hundreds of billions of dollars of foregone output (see, for example, Fortin 1996). There is also a substantial literature in sociology and social psychology on the human costs of unemployment – in mental and physical illness, family violence, suicide, and crime.[5]

What empirical evidence exists on the benefits of a constant price level? What does Canadian society get if the Bank of Canada succeeds in maintaining a near-zero rate of price inflation in the long term?

Clearly, *hyperinflation* has many negative implications for economic equity and efficiency. For *moderate inflation*, the evidence is less clear. Levine and Zervos (1993: 428) conclude that "inflation is not significantly negatively correlated with long-run growth. More impressively, we could not find a combination of variables that produced a significant negative association between growth and average inflation over the 1960 to 1989 period." As Pierre Fortin has demonstrated, econometric estimates of the relationship between rates of inflation and productivity growth are extremely fragile, since a few high-inflation countries will inevitably dominate an ordinary-least-squares regression, just as a few anecdotes from Latin American hyperinflation clearly dominate journalistic discussions of inflation. However, since most of the developed countries have, since the 1960s, had average inflation rates within a fairly narrow range (4 percent to 11 percent), the inclusion or exclusion of a few high-inflation countries such as Peru and Turkey can easily dominate regression results. As well, the inclusion or exclusion of other variables such as population size can significantly influence estimates of the relationship between inflation and growth rates. Nevertheless, despite the difficulties of estimation, many economists believe that high and unstable rates of inflation are undesirable, for both social and economic reasons.

However, the issue in Canada is *not* the evils of 400-percent inflation, or 40-percent inflation, or 10-percent inflation. The issue in

Canada is the benefits, and the costs, of the Bank of Canada's decision in 1988 to try to go from 4-percent inflation to 0-percent inflation. Since it is agreed by all that there are high short-run costs to this decision, the decision makes sense only if inflation goes to zero and can be kept there for the very long time that is required in order to recoup the costs of the current recession. The Bank of Canada's decision makes sense only if inflation is reduced to zero, *and stays there* for the next twenty-five to thirty years.

One recent discussion of the relationship between inflation and macroeconomic performance is a Bank of Canada discussion paper, authored by Cozier and Selody (1992). In it they note that the lowest average inflation rate in their sample of sixty-two countries between 1960 and 1985 is 3.6 percent per annum. In other words, *no country* attained a long-run rate of inflation that is even approximately equal to zero. Paragons of financial virtue such as Germany and Switzerland had average inflation rates for this period of 3.8 percent and 4.1 percent respectively. Japan (a notoriously poor performer) had an average inflation rate of 6.2 percent yearly. Canada was well below the sample mean, with an average inflation rate of 5.6 percent, while the long-term inflation winner was Malaysia with 3.6 percent.

In econometrics classes, we teach our students that it is statistically invalid to make predictions that are well out of the range of observed data. Yet zero inflation is well out of the range of historically observed data. Indeed, the relationship estimated by Cozier and Selody between output growth and inflation breaks down, in a bizarre way, at very low rates of inflation. Over the sample as a whole, estimating a relationship in which the logarithm of output growth is regressed on the logarithm of the inflation rate implies that the estimated regression coefficient is an *elasticity* (in this case, −0.6). However, this specification also implies that a 1-percentage-point drop in inflation represents a much smaller proportionate change when one is moving from 20-percent inflation to 19-percent inflation, than when one is going from 2-percent to 1-percent inflation. Taken literally, the log-log specification implies that the benefit of going from 4-percent inflation to 2-percent inflation (a 50-percent decline) would be a 30-percent increase in the growth rate. The benefits of moving from 2-percent inflation to zero percent would be an infinitely large increase in output![6]

Clearly, if there is a relationship between inflation and macroeconomic performance, the relationship that is estimated over the range of historically observed data (i.e., 4 percent plus, as a long-term average) *cannot* be extrapolated to the historically unobserved range of a long-term average inflation rate of 0 percent to 2 percent. However, the bank's policy decisions were not, in fact, based on empirical research. The Cozier and Selody regressions of 1992 did not in fact influence the policy decisions of the Bank of Canada, since these were taken in 1988. The publication dates of almost all the empirical research on the inflation-growth relationship make it clear that a 1988 decision to go for zero inflation could only have been based on faith.[7]

A policy of focusing on zero inflation in the long run *above all other* goals is not consistent with the legislated goals of the Bank of Canada, nor is it supported by public opinion or based on empirical evidence. This policy can be based only on faith, since no country has, in modern times, succeeded in maintaining a rate of inflation approximately equal to zero for anything like the length of time necessary for this policy to pay off. But although it may not be easy to predict why a person will choose a particular faith, history does provide many examples of the proposition that faith *combined with self-interest* makes a potent brew. If we think of the incentives that the different sides of this debate face, we will recognize that it was next to impossible for the governor of the Bank of Canada to admit the possibility of error, once the decision was made.

INCENTIVES AND OBJECTIVITY

If I look at my personal incentives for accepting or rejecting new evidence on the relationship between inflation, productivity, and unemployment, I recognize that my past arguments against the policy of zero inflation create a barrier for my ego – the same barrier that we all face in admitting that we have been wrong. This barrier may colour my judgments in assessing the strength of new arguments and new evidence on the issue. On the other hand, as a professor of economics, I am expected to examine the evidence dispassionately. If I were to convert to monetarism, I would gain new friends (and lose old ones), but I could expect to receive increased status, as someone who is scientifically objective in their consideration of the evidence. Financially, I could probably expect an increase in my consulting income, since the Fraser Institute or the Business Council on National Issues likes nothing better than a "lapsed lefty." But whatever happens, I have tenure. My current job will always be there, and nothing very important in my personal life will change.

The incentives to deny new evidence, and to persist in the pursuit of previously announced policy, are entirely different for the governor of the Bank of Canada and his most senior advisers. After inducing the most severe recession in fifty years in the pursuit of zero inflation, they could not conceivably appear before the Commons

Committee on Finance and say, "We got it wrong." All incentives – personal, professional, and financial – point to refusing to admit error.

Most individuals would find it inconsistent with their sense of fundamental decency to admit that they have been responsible for a policy that has caused enormous pain to thousands of people, to no good purpose. To the ordinary barriers of ego, senior Bank of Canada officials must add the sense of personal responsibility that goes with the power of the bank. It is inconceivable that the governor could admit error on such a fundamental policy and expect to retain his job; therefore, income, prestige, and power have been on the line, over and above the personal psychological impediments to admitting error. It is thus probably just about impossible for the governor and senior staff of the Bank of Canada to admit the error of their faith and their policy – and it is always possible for them to see the benefits that are "just around the corner, if only we stay the course, for just a little bit longer."

THE POLICY PROBLEM

Canada has, therefore, a very big policy problem. The policy of high real interest rates that the Bank of Canada followed over the period 1988 to 1993 produced a huge inflow of foreign capital and an over-valued foreign exchange rate. As a consequence, there is a very large overhang of foreign debt and current account deficit. Canada quickly became far more dependent on the vagaries of opinion of international capital markets than it was previously.

Furthermore, if the policies of the Bank of Canada become personalized in the governor of the Bank of Canada, the fate of the governor becomes an important public issue. If he were to fall under a bus, or face removal from office, capital markets would not know what to expect. The governor of the Bank of Canada therefore possesses immense power, since the threat of his resignation (or even a hint of disagreement with the elected government of the day) could well spark an extremely serious foreign exchange crisis.

In December 1993, it was announced that Governor Crow would not be reappointed, and Assistant Governor Thiessen was promoted to fill his place. In a careful mix of signals, it was stated that the inflation-reduction targets would be extended to 1998 *and* the incoming governor stated the bank's interest in promoting growth in output and employment. Despite widespread predictions of a foreign exchange crisis if Governor Crow were not reappointed, the Canadian dollar did not fall (and indeed rose slightly on the news).

Financial markets were reassured by the fact that the new governor had been a party to the policy making of the previous five years, but there were, at the same time, hints to the media that he was more "pragmatic" in his opinions.

However, for a country as large as Canada, it is bizarre that so much should depend on the opinions of a single unelected person. It is surely undesirable that, despite the need of financial markets for continuity in policy, the administration of the Bank of Canada can change in discrete jumps at infrequent intervals. In a democratic society, it is also highly undesirable that the elected representatives of the people should have, in practice, so little real influence on the decisions of such an important agency. I would, therefore, suggest that Canada would be well served by adopting the operational model of the Federal Reserve Board in the United States, whose crucial characteristic is that monetary policy is made by the majority vote of a committee, and whose members serve fixed, overlapping terms. If, for example, the board of directors of the Bank of Canada had real operational power over monetary policy and if one-seventh of the directors of the bank were replaced each year, one would have an institutional arrangement that would guarantee both continuity in monetary policy *and* the possibility that empirical evidence could shape the policy decisions of the day. If there was a rotating chairmanship, and the requirement that directors be full-time, each supported by a small research staff and resident in the different regions of the country, the result might well be a more balanced input of perspectives on the real economy and better monetary policy decisions.

CONCLUSION

This essay has argued that although there may be widespread agreement about the severity of the recent recession, there is little agreement as to the wisdom of the policies that produced it. Since the policy goal of a constant price level, for the long term, is not based on the legislated mandate to the Bank of Canada, is not supported by public opinion, and is not derived from an empirical analysis of the costs and benefits of monetary policy, such a policy goal can be supported only by faith. The Bank of Canada has taken us into unknown territory, and it remains an article of faith as to whether it is "digging a hole or laying the foundation."

Personally, I do not have the gift of faith. Although Mike McCracken (1996) has suggested that holes can be graves, I profoundly hope that the continued high unemployment of the 1990s, and the zero-inflation policy that has produced it, will not be a mass grave for the hopes and aspirations of hundreds of thousands of Canadians.

ACKNOWLEDGMENTS

I would like to thank Brian MacLean for helpful comments; errors remaining are my own.

NOTES

1 For an estimate of the output gap in Canada, see Fortin (1996) or McCracken (1996). An output gap of $70 billion is unimaginably large, representing about six to eight times the amount of money necessary to eliminate poverty in Canada for this year. The poverty gap in 1981 was 1.3 percent of GDP, rising to 1.6 percent in 1990 – see National Council of Welfare (1992: 45) or Osberg (1992: 46).
2 See Minister of Supply and Services (1991: 37).
3 Ibid. (38).
4 If price shocks are accommodated, there will necessarily be *some* inflation; hence there will be uncertainty as to the value of money. The whole argument for zero inflation is based on the supposed benefits of "sound money" – i.e., accommodating shocks would negate the policy.
5 See, for example, Hayes and Nutman (1981) or Kelvin and Jarrett (1985).
6 Cozier and Selody argue that since they also estimate a linear inflation-productivity relationship, readers should not worry about the specifics of the log-log specification. However, the implications of a linear specification are even more unattractive, since such a specification implies that if going from 6-percent inflation to 2-percent inflation increases the growth rate, going from +2-percent inflation to −2-percent inflation (i.e., deflation) would increase the growth rate even further. Clearly, however, deflation is likely to have substantially different impacts on the real economy than slower inflation. The point is that one cannot estimate valid "out-of-sample" results.
7 See the references in Selody (1993) for evidence on the empirical content and date of publication of support for the zero-inflation argument. The only then existing empirical study of the productivity benefits to Canada of zero inflation (Cozier and Selody 1982) was widely referred to by advocates of the zero-inflation initiative at the time (e.g. Howitt 1990) but has since been largely discredited (see MacLean and Setterfield 1993).

REFERENCES

Cozier, B., and J. Selody. 1992. "Inflation and Macroeconomic Performance: Some Cross-Country Evidence." Bank of Canada Working Paper No. 92–6.

Fortin, P. 1996. "The Unbearable Lightness of Zero-Inflation Optimism." This volume.

Hayes, J., and P. Nutman. 1981. *Understanding the Unemployed: The Psychological Effects of Unemployment*. London: Tavistock Publications.

Howitt, P. 1990. "Zero Inflation as a Long-run Target for Monetary Policy." In R.G. Lipsey, ed., *Zero Inflation: The Goal of Price Stability,* 67–108. Toronto: C.D. Howe Institute.

Jarrett, J.P., and J.G. Selody. 1982. "The Productivity-Inflation Nexus in Canada, 1963–1979." *The Review of Economics and Statistics* 44, No. 3: 361–7.

Kelvin, P., and J. Jarrett. 1985. *Unemployment: Its Social Psychological Effects*. Cambridge: Cambridge University Press.

Levine, R., and S. Zervos. 1993. "What We Have Learned about Policy and Growth from Cross-Country Regressions?" *American Economic Review,* Papers and Proceedings (May): 426–30.

MacLean, B., and M. Setterfield. 1993. "Nexus or Not? Productivity and Inflation in Canada." *Canadian Business Economics* 1, No. 2 (Winter): 44–52.

McCracken, M. 1996. "A Macroeconomic Policy Package for the 1990s." This volume.

Minister of Supply and Services. 1991. *Canadian Federalism and Economic Union: Partnership for Prosperity.* Ottawa: Minister of Supply and Services.

National Council of Welfare. 1992. *Poverty Profile (1980–1990).* National Council of Welfare: Minister of Supply and Services, Autumn.

Osberg, L. 1992. "Canada's Economic Performance: Inequality, Poverty and Growth." In G. R.C. Allen and G. Rosenbluth, eds., *False Promises: The Failure of Conservative Economics*. Vancouver: New Star Books.

Selody, J. 1993. "Comment on 'Nexus or Not?: Productivity and Inflation in Canada'." *Canadian Business Economics* 1, No. 2 (Winter): 53–60.

2 The Unbearable Lightness of Zero-Inflation Optimism

PIERRE FORTIN

In 1988, the governor of the Bank of Canada announced that he was determined not only to prevent demand-pull and cost-push factors from raising inflation, but also to reduce permanently the inflation rate to near zero, a state he termed "price stability" (Crow 1988). Later, in February 1991, the governor and the minister of finance agreed to set an inflation target of 2 percent by the end of 1995 (Bank of Canada 1991). That target was in fact reached by the end of 1992.

But success on the inflation front has come with the worst recession Canada has experienced since the Great Depression. The drop in output from peak to trough was initially less severe in the 1990–92 recession than in the 1981–82 recession. But the current recession has been so protracted that, overall, the cumulative output loss has been larger this time.[1] Moreover, the Canadian slowdown has been the worst among G-7 countries, with the ratio of actual-to-potential output being the smallest in 1992 (OECD 1992).

By pursuing its goal of price stability, the Bank of Canada was a major contributor to the severity of the recession. Between 1987 and 1990, the annual average of real short-term interest rates increased steadily from 3.5 percent to 9.5 percent and the Canadian-American exchange rate appreciated by almost 20 percent. Central bank restriction is the obvious source of tightened monetary conditions because soft commodity prices, tight fiscal policy (by measures of the Organization for Co-operation and Economic Development [OECD] and the International Monetary Fund), and eventually the United States' recession exerted downward pressure on interest rates and the exchange rate during the period. With the usual nine-month lag behind the onset of tightened monetary conditions, annual real growth in the Gross Domestic Product (GDP) declined steadily from a positive rate of 5 percent to a negative rate of 2 percent.

The economic literature is clear that inflation has increased marginal costs. But to infer from this that zero or near-zero inflation is optimal requires the further empirical judgment that the marginal benefits of reducing inflation exceed the marginal unemployment costs of doing so even at very low levels of inflation. The Bank of Canada has consistently argued that this is indeed the case. As one bank official recently put it: "The available evidence does suggest that the benefits of price stability are many and large while the costs are transitory and small by comparison" (Selody 1990: 47).

In my view, such statements are quite premature. The empirical issue of whether the benefits of eliminating moderate inflation are quantitatively larger than the costs of doing so is far from settled. The next two sections of this chapter look at the evidence on benefits and costs. The first argues that the only warranted conclusion from international cross-section and Canadian time-series evidence is that the magnitude of the macroeconomic benefits from eliminating moderate inflation is very uncertain at best.

Proper measurement of the unemployment costs of disinflation must rest on some theory of determination of equilibrium (or natural) unemployment. Accordingly, the following section begins by comparing the implications of two competing theories of the *natural rate* of unemployment. Standard natural rate theory (the "Friedman" view) acknowledges that natural unemployment depends on structural factors such as demography, social policy, institutions, and the like. *Hysteresis* theory (the "Tobin" view) argues that, in addition to structural factors, the path of actual unemployment could exert a determinant influence on natural unemployment. Although further confirmation and interpretation of the facts is required, Canadian and American macroeconomic evidence is shown to be consistent with a strong degree of hysteresis (that is, with the natural rate of unemployment depending strongly on the actual rate). On that basis, the unemployment costs of disinflation would be substantially higher than previously thought.

I conclude that, if the "strong hysteresis" view of the unemployment process is confirmed and no alternative, recession-free method of controlling inflation is adopted, the prospects for reconciling the objectives of price stability and full employment in Canada look rather bleak.

EVIDENCE ON THE MACROECONOMIC
BENEFITS OF ELIMINATING INFLATION

The Harmful Effects of Moderate Inflation

Casual observation and theoretical arguments make the case that inflation is costly, even when it does not exceed the upper limit of 20 percent generally observed in advanced industrial countries.[2] Our accounting practices and institutions, such as the tax system, the fixed-instalment mortgage, or unindexed private pensions, are based on the assumption that the value of money will remain stable. They adjust less than perfectly even to well-anticipated inflation. Inflation pushes people to use up real resources in order to reduce their holdings of currency ("shoe-leather" costs), to change posted prices more frequently ("menu" costs), and to constantly adjust the money yardstick ("accounting" costs). Uncertain and volatile inflation causes unpredictable transfers that generate conflicts between individuals and groups. It also distorts relative-price signals, particularly inter-temporal signals, leading to sub-optimal saving and investment decisions, and hence to slower growth.[3]

It is easy enough to put out long lists of the harmful consequences of inflation for the economy. But such *qualitative* descriptions do not indicate how significant the listed costs really are for economic performance. Only *quantitative* information across countries and over time for Canada can provide the required evidence. In this section, I concentrate on the macroeconomic benefits of lower (and less volatile) inflation in the form of a higher level or rate of growth of output than would have otherwise occurred. I do not deal here with allocational and distributional benefits, but most would agree that without global income benefits, the case for price stability would at any event be considerably weaker.

Cross-country Evidence

What does the evidence across countries say? Averaging over the thirty-year period 1960 to 1989 or the shorter ten-year period 1980 to 1989, inflation among the seventeen most advanced industrial countries is not correlated at all with either unemployment or productivity growth (OECD 1991).[4] Macroeconomic experiences are extremely diverse. In particular, there are countries with low inflation and high unemployment (Belgium) or slow growth (Switzerland), and there are others with high inflation and low unemployment (Scandinavia) or rapid growth (Italy).

But simple correlations can be misleading because they disregard the many other influences on employment or productivity growth besides inflation. No serious investigation of the impact of inflation on growth can escape controlling for these other factors.

Mankiw, Romer, and Weil (1992) recently analysed the determinants of cumulative real growth in ninety-eight non-oil countries over the twenty-five-year period 1960 to 1985. They explained growth à la Solow (1956) with the help of four basic variables: (1) the starting level of GDP per working-age person in 1960, which allows testing for international convergence of productivity levels; (2) the average fraction of GDP allocated to physical investment; (3) the average percentage of the working-age population in secondary school; and (4) the sum of the population growth rate and a flat 5-percent allowance to account uniformly for technological progress and capital depreciation.

Equation 1.1 of Table 1 adds three potential determinants of cumulative real growth to the list already used by Mankiw, Romer, and Weil: average population size over the sample period, which is meant to capture market scale effects, and (following Cozier and Selody 1992) measures of the average rate of inflation and of inflation volatility.[5] The only acceptable procedure here is to restrict the observations of ninety-eight countries to the sample of twenty-two OECD countries (tiny Iceland and Luxembourg are omitted) whose institutions and level of development are similar to Canada's. Severe unobserved heterogeneity problems arise whenever advanced and less-developed countries are mixed together in the same cross section.[6]

The outcome is clear enough: none of the short- and long-run coefficients of any of the two inflation variables is statistically different from zero.[7] The hypothesis that the level and volatility of inflation are without effect on the level or on the rate of growth of output over a twenty-five-year horizon or longer is not rejected by the country data. The proper conclusion is not that moderate inflation is absolutely harmless for growth, but that the global experience of industrial countries over the quarter-century 1960 to 1985 offers no convincing evidence that the macroeconomic benefits from reducing inflation are "large."

Historical Evidence for Canada

What about the historical evidence for Canada? Some ten years ago, Jarrett and Selody (1982) examined the Canadian macroeconomic evidence over the period 1963 to 1979. They concluded that each percentage-point increase in the inflation rate reduced the annual

Table 1
Estimated Equation for Cumulative Growth of Real GDP per Working-age Person
in Twenty-two OECD Countries, 1960–85

RIGHT-HAND VARIABLE	Equation No. 1.1
Constant	3.954
	(1.482)
Real GDP per working-age person in 1960	0.498
	(0.098)
Average investment/GDP ratio for 1960–85	0.352
	(0.181)
Average annual population growth rate (adjusted) for 1960–85	−0.600
	(0.362)
Average percentage of the working-age population in secondary school, 1960–85	0.213
	(0.128)
Average population size, 1960–85	0.062
	(0.027)
Average annual rate of CPI inflation, 1960–85	−0.090
	(0.147)
Volatility of CPI inflation, 1960–85	−0.250
	(0.185)
SUMMARY STATISTICS	
Adjusted R^2	0.75
Sum of squared residuals	0.22
Standard error of regression	0.13
Long-run coefficient for average CPI inflation	−0.182
	(0.271)
Long-run coefficient for volatility of inflation	−0.502
	(0.371)

Sources: Mankiw, Romer, and Weil (1992); OECD (1991); Cozier and Selody (1992); author's calculations.
Notes: Ordinary-least-squares regression. The sample includes all OECD countries, except Iceland and Luxembourg. The left-hand variable is the log difference between real GDP per working-age person in 1985 and in 1960. A flat allowance of 5 percent is added to all population growth rates to account uniformly for technological progress and capital depreciation. Inflation volatility is the coefficient of variation of CPI inflation over the period 1960–85. All right-hand variables are in logs. The two long-run coefficients for the inflation variables are equal to the ratios between the corresponding "impact" coefficients and the coefficient of real GDP per working-age person in 1960. Standard errors appear in parentheses below the estimated coefficients.

growth rate of labour productivity permanently by 0.23 points. Recently, Novin (1991) extended the study and confirmed the results with data for the period 1969 to 1988.

Equation 2.1 of Table 2 presents a regression showing how the Jarrett-Selody conclusion can be obtained with annual data for the 1964 to 1991 period. The sum of the two coefficients on one- and two-

Table 2
Estimated Equations for Annual Growth Rate of Labour Productivity in the Private Sector, Canada, 1964 to 1991

	Equation Number	
	2.1	2.2
RIGHT-HAND VARIABLE		
Constant	3.002	3.168
	(0.809)	(0.718)
GDP-deflator inflation, lagged one year	−0.476	−0.100
	(0.191)	(0.191)
GDP-deflator inflation, lagged two years	0.334	−0.067
	(0.185)	(0.184)
Capacity utilization rate, current change		0.325
		(0.106)
Capacity utilization rate, one-year-lagged change		−0.295
		(0.103)
SUMMARY STATISTICS		
Adjusted R^2	0.14	0.42
Standard error of regression	1.89	1.55
Durbin-Watson statistic	1.56	1.54

Sources: Statistics Canada's CANSIM data base; author's calculations.

Notes: Ordinary-least-squares regressions. The left-hand variable is the annual log change in Statistics Canada's measure of labour productivity (real GDP per person-hour) in the private sector. Inflation is the annual log change of the GDP deflator. The capacity utilization rate is the Bank of Canada's measure of capacity utilization for total non-farm goods-producing industries. Standard errors appear in parentheses below the estimated coefficients.

year-lagged inflation, which is the estimated permanent effect of a one-point increase in the inflation rate on the growth rate of labour productivity is −0.14 percentage points, somewhat lower than the estimate from the shorter Jarrett-Selody sample. The new twist here is that with the longer span of data one cannot reject the hypothesis that inflation has no permanent effect on productivity growth.[8]

But why should higher inflation reduce the level of productivity after a while? There are many possible conjectures, but a simple one is that the central bank will not accommodate the higher inflation permanently. It will let a monetary contraction occur, which will bring about an economic slowdown, with a lag. Capacity utilization will decline, the unemployment rate will rise, and measured labour productivity will fall. As we all know, productivity is a pro-cyclical variable. On this account, the negative correlation between current productivity and past inflation would be largely spurious, an example of the post hoc, ergo propter hoc fallacy.[9]

. The story would imply that, once the change in the aggregate capacity utilization rate is introduced explicitly into the labour-productivity equation, the measured impact of inflation on productivity would lose much of its strength. Equation 2.2 of Table 2 reports the results of adding the current and one-year-lagged changes in capacity utilization into the regression. A persistent fall of one per-centage point in utilization is estimated to induce a contemporaneous productivity decrease of 0.3 points, which is just about reversed the following year (as has been observed, say, in the present slow-down).[10]

As expected, the estimated coefficients of the two inflation vari-ables are smaller. Not only is their sum statistically negligible (no permanent effect of inflation on productivity *growth*), but the two coefficients are individually and jointly insignificant too (no tempo-rary or permanent effect of inflation on the *level* of productivity).[11] Just as the OECD cross-section regression, the Canadian time-series regression is entirely consistent with the hypothesis that the level and growth of productivity are insensitive to changes in the rate of infla-tion within the moderate range observed in the postwar period.[12]

The above evidence for OECD economies and for Canada in partic-ular is based on models of productivity that could be improved upon. It does suggest, however, that strong claims that there are large macroeconomic benefits to be reaped from a zero-inflation monetary strategy are not presently founded on robust quantitative evidence. They are premature.

THE NATURAL RATE, HYSTERESIS, AND THE COST OF DISINFLATION

Natural Rate Theory

I now turn to the unemployment costs of reducing inflation. The first step is to have a theory of the determinants of inflation. The modern version of the Phillips curve readily provides such a theory, often called "natural rate" theory. It is summarized by the following equation:

$$(1) \qquad \Delta I = -a(U - U_n) + S \, ,$$

which states that the annual change in the inflation rate (ΔI) broadly depends on two sets of influences: demand and supply.

The first term on the right-hand side of the equation reflects demand pressure. With $a > 0$, it stipulates that inflation (I) will decline more, the higher actual unemployment (U) is above some critical or "natural" rate of unemployment (U_n). The unemployment gap ($U - U_n$) varies inversely with aggregate demand pressure ("demand-pull" factors).

Friedman (1968: 8) defined the natural rate U_n as "the level that would be ground out by the Walrasian system of general equilibrium equations, provided there is embedded in them the actual character-istics of the labor and commodity markets, including market imper-fections, stochastic variability in demands and supplies, the cost of gathering information about job vacancies and labor availabilities, the costs of mobility, and so on." The empirical literature has identi-fied several possible structural influences on the natural rate of unemployment. They include demographic changes, sectoral shifts, unemployment insurance and other welfare policies, minimum-wage regulations, union density and militancy, and the tax structure (e.g., Rose 1988).

The second term on the right-hand side of equation (1) is a *zero-mean* variable S that lumps together the supply-side ("cost-push") influences on inflation, such as food, energy, and import prices; indi-rect tax shocks; and wage-and-price controls.

The Size and Duration of the Income Sacrifice

Canadian studies in the natural rate tradition have estimated the marginal impact of the unemployment gap on the change in inflation (the slope a of the equation (1) Phillips curve) to be of the order of 0.5 per year.[13]

With $a = 0.5$, lowering the annual inflation rate permanently by one percentage point from a given year onward would require maintain-ing a temporary two-percentage-point unemployment gap in that year (or a one-point gap two years in a row). Since each point-year of excess unemployment has in turn been associated historically with a 2.5 percent decline in annual real GDP,[14] the one-point inflation reduction would finally force a loss of 5 percent of annual national income, termed the *sacrifice ratio*. This figure is the estimate reported by lead-ing textbooks for the United States (Gordon 1990a; Mankiw 1992), and by Howitt (1990) and Ball (1993) for Canada.[15] A sacrifice ratio of 5 would mean that the recent campaign to reduce the inflation rate by 3 points (from 5 percent to 2 percent) in Canada has cost approxi-mately $105 billion (15 percent of our $700 billion annual GDP).[16]

A crucial implication of natural rate theory is that the income sacrifice required by disinflation is only temporary. This follows from the *change* in inflation depending on the *level* of the unemployment gap in the Phillips equation (1). Assume, for simplicity, a stable level of natural unemployment U_n and a calm supply side ($S = 0$). Inflation will then keep declining as long as actual unemployment exceeds the fixed natural level. But this means that, once the disinflation job is done, the unemployment rate can return to its natural value safely without rekindling inflation.

The reason is that, as U decreases toward U_n, the unemployment gap is made smaller and smaller, but remains positive and, therefore, disinflationary all along. Then, once U is back to U_n, inflation is stabilized ($\Delta I = 0$) at its new, lower level. Correspondingly, real GDP climbs back onto its trend growth path determined by demography, technology, and time preference. There is no further income sacrifice. The gain is lasting, and the pain, short-lived.

Recent Unemployment Persistence in Europe and North America

The basic problem with natural rate theory is that it has trouble explaining recent history. Consider the four post-recession years, 1984 to 1987, in Canada. The national unemployment rate was 10 percent on average, or 2 percentage points higher than the 8-percent natural rate estimated by Bank of Canada researchers for that period (e.g., Rose 1988). With $a = 0.5$ for the slope of the Phillips relation, one would have expected the inflation rate to fall by 1 percentage point per year on average, or 4 points cumulatively over 1984 to 1987. Instead, observed inflation declined by 1.3 points only, from 5.7 percent in 1984 to 4.4 percent in 1987. This occurred in (1) a favourable demographic context, since the falling youth population was exerting downward pressure on U_n, and in (2) a generally deflationary supply-side environment, where plummeting commodity prices made S negative.[17]

These inflation-unemployment developments in Canada in the 1980s were similar to what happened simultaneously in a number of European countries. In Belgium, France, Italy, and the United Kingdom, where the natural rate was thought to be in the 6-percent range, inflation also stopped falling while unemployment was still in the double digits. Inflation then moved up again whenever unemployment began to decline.

In the United States, inflation behaviour displayed a similar, albeit less-pronounced, pattern over the 1984 to 1987 period. The aggregate unemployment rate averaged 7 percent, exceeding by 1 point the most widely quoted estimate for the United States' natural rate (Gordon 1990a, A3). However, Consumer Price Index (CPI) inflation (excluding food and energy) remained steady at around 4 percent throughout the period. Later, there was only a limited tendency for inflation to trend upward when unemployment fell below 6 percent at the end of the decade.

The North American and European experiences of the 1980s call the Friedman view into serious question. While Friedman stated that the level of natural unemployment was influenced by structural factors such as demography, labour-market policies, institutions, and the like, he did not view natural unemployment as depending also systematically on the historical path of actual unemployment. No *path dependence*, or "hysteresis" as the physicists would say, was implied by his story.

Could Natural Unemployment Follow Actual Unemployment?

The apparent tendency of the natural rate of unemployment to follow the actual rate upward in the 1980s led several researchers to ask whether standard natural rate theory was drawing too sharp a dichotomy between natural unemployment and actual unemployment. They echoed the warning by Tobin (1972: 17) that "we have no license to assume that the natural rate of unemployment is independent of the history of actual unemployment" and the earlier fear of Samuelson and Solow (1960: 193) that "a low-pressure economy might build up within itself over the years larger and larger amounts of structural unemployment." The key intuition is that a sustained period of high actual unemployment would raise equilibrium unemployment temporarily, and perhaps even permanently.[18]

Why would actual unemployment pull the natural rate along with it? Four main potential channels of hysteresis have been proposed so far in the economic literature – capital decumulation, "insider" bargaining power, duration effects, and unemployment insurance:[19]

1 Prolonged recessions lead to capital decumulation. Marginal costs increase, the demand for labour declines, and equilibrium unemployment rises unless workers accept real wage cuts, which they sometimes stiffly resist. The leading proponents of this theory have been Malinvaud (1986), and Drèze and Sneessens (1986).
2 Employed workers will at any time use their "insider" bargaining power to protect their membership and to escape the threat that increased unemployment represents for their jobs. The more successful they are in these two respects, the stronger unemployment persistence will be. Solow (1985), Blanchard and Summers (1986),

and Lindbeck and Snower (1988) have explored this channel based on insider power, but with mixed results (see Blanchard 1991 for an appraisal).

3 The anti-inflationary pressure exerted against wages by sustained high unemployment could weaken over time. For example, a long period of unemployment can lead to actual or perceived skill deterioration, which in turn may induce firms to rank workers inversely by duration of unemployment (see, e.g., Gross 1996). Or, as unemployment duration increases, the unemployed may eventually give up their search activity altogether. Thus, ranking behaviour on the part of firms, or the search behaviour of the long-term unemployed, could weaken the negative effect of persistent unemployment on wages, leading to even more persistence. These duration effects were tested by Layard and Nickell (1987), who found that British long-term unemployment had no significant effect on wage outcomes.

4 Regionally extended unemployment insurance benefits that are triggered when actual unemployment is high could in turn raise natural unemployment. In Canada, unemployment insurance regulations provide for shorter minimum qualifying periods and longer maximum-benefit duration as regional unemployment rates increase, which could lead to higher natural unemployment in a sort of vicious circle. Canadian researchers Milbourne, Purvis, and Scoones (1991) recently found this potential source of unemployment persistence to be significant, but their results have been questioned by others (Storer 1992, Corak and Jones 1993, Osberg 1996).

Full Hysteresis: Economic and Policy Implications

The idea of unemployment hysteresis, or that the natural rate of unemployment tracks the actual rate (with a lag), has profound implications for our understanding of economic facts and for macroeconomic policy. Let us assume, for clarity, that there is *complete path dependence*, so that this year's natural rate (U_n) is just last year's actual rate (U_{-1}):

$$(2) \qquad U_n = U_{-1} .$$

It then follows that $U - U_n = U - U_{-1} = \Delta U$. Demand pressure in the Phillips equation (1) is now measured by the simple annual *change* in the unemployment rate, not by the *level* of the gap between the actual unemployment rate and some fixed natural value. Therefore, the Phillips curve takes the form:

$$(3) \qquad \Delta I = -a\Delta U + S .$$

This brings both bad news and good news. The bad news is that, once unemployment has been raised to reduce inflation, it can no longer be returned to its initial level without rekindling inflation, because the very process of reducing unemployment (having ΔU negative) increases the inflation rate (makes ΔI positive), and simply undoes the initial disinflation.

The stark implication for anti-inflation policy is that a permanent reduction in the inflation rate can be achieved only at the cost of a permanent increase in the unemployment rate. The gain may be lasting, but since it entails an annual cost that is repeated forever, the (undiscounted) sacrifice ratio is infinite. A standard real discount rate of $r = 2$ percent would make the unemployment costs of disinflation $1/r = 1/0.02 = 50$ times larger than they would be if experienced only one year, as the fixed natural rate theory implies. They would be far more likely to exceed the benefits of eliminating inflation.

The good news is that a permanent reduction of unemployment raises inflation permanently, but only by a finite amount. By contrast, Friedman believed that maintaining unemployment permanently below the fixed natural rate would lead to ever-rising inflation. Hysteresis theory would rehabilitate the now "old-fashioned" notion that the policy authorities face a permanent trade-off between inflation and unemployment.[20]

What would complete path dependence combined with a zero-inflation monetary strategy imply for the behaviour of the unemployment rate? If the price level is stable, the inflation rate is also stable (at zero level) so that $\Delta I = 0$. From the "hysteretic" Phillips equation (3), it then follows that:

$$(4) \qquad \Delta U = S/a \text{ or } U = U_{-1} + S/a .$$

Depending on how quickly the zero-inflation target is established and maintained, unemployment would essentially follow a "random walk" driven by the history of supply-side influences. Deflation on the supply side ($S < 0$), as observed in 1964 to 1971 or in 1983 to 1990, would have unemployment trend downward, while inflationary supply-side pressure ($S > 0$), as experienced in 1972 to 1982, would have it trend upward. A calm supply-side environment ($S = 0$) would leave unemployment essentially unchanged.

Partial Hysteresis and the Sacrifice Ratio

The assumption of complete path dependence (i.e., that this year's natural rate of unemployment is just last year's actual rate) that I have just made for expository purposes, brings the implications of unemployment hysteresis into sharp focus. It could be true, but it is extreme. It is perhaps more realistic to consider cases whereby the natural rate rises temporarily, not permanently, following an increase in the actual rate. A simple characterization would set the short-term natural unemployment rate (U_n) equal to a weighted average of some fundamental long-term natural or equilibrium rate à la Friedman (U_e) and of last year's actual rate (U_{-1}) à la Tobin:

$$(5) \qquad U_n = (1 - h)U_e + hU_{-1} .$$

As the weight h increases toward 1, the influence of the historical path of actual unemployment on the natural rate rises in relative importance. If $h = 0$, there is no hysteresis at all. Natural unemployment is completely independent from past actual unemployment; U_n is simply anchored at the fixed point U_e, as in Friedman's natural rate theory. If $h = 1$, we have full hysteresis as in equations (2) and (3). In between, where there is partial path dependence, substitution of equation (5) into equation (1) yields:

$$(6) \qquad \Delta I = -a[(1 - h)(U - U_e) + h\Delta U] + S .$$

This equation is a weighted average of the Friedman and Tobin views. The weight or degree of hysteresis h plays a crucial role in the measurement of the unemployment costs of anti-inflation policy. It is indeed immediately apparent from equation (6) that a temporary (one-year) increase of one percentage point in the unemployment gap $U - U_e$ lowers inflation by an amount a on impact, but only $a(1 - h)$ in the long run. The value of h is the fraction of the first-year negative impact on inflation that disappears in the following years. Alternatively, a permanent one-point reduction of inflation requires a cumulative sacrifice of $1/[a(1 - h)]$ point-years of unemployment and a commensurate sacrifice of national income.

If the value of the short-run slope a is given, as h increases toward 1 the lasting effect of unemployment on inflation, $a(1 - h)$, becomes a smaller and smaller quantity and the undiscounted sacrifice ratio $1/[a(1 - h)]$ rises to infinity. As mentioned earlier, in that limiting case of full hysteresis, no temporary rise in unemployment can actually do the disinflation job. It is, of course, for empirical research to determine what the value of h is for actual economies.

Empirical Evidence for Canada and the United States

High values of h have been estimated for several European labour markets (e.g., Blanchard and Summers 1986; Gordon 1988; Drèze and

Bean 1990). But what does the existing evidence say on the degree of unemployment hysteresis in North America?

Equations 3.1 and 3.2 of Table 3 report regression results obtained with annual Canadian data for 1973 to 1990 and annual American data for 1966 to 1990. The Phillips equations estimated there explain the changes in "core" CPI inflation (excluding food and energy) with the list of regressors suggested by equation (6) above: (1) the current *level* of the unemployment rate (U); (2) current (and lagged) *changes* in the unemployment rate (ΔU); and (3) various measures of supply-side pressure (S): food-energy price shocks, import price shocks, indirect tax changes, and wage-and-price controls.[21] The Canadian equation is similar to the one I reported in Fortin (1991), while the American results are new.

The point estimates for the degrees of hysteresis (h) reported in Table 3 are quite high: 77 percent for Canada, and 81 percent for the United States.[22] Given the estimated standard errors, the hypothesis of complete absence of hysteresis $(h = 0)$ is rejected for both countries, and the hypothesis of full hysteresis $(h = 1)$ cannot be rejected in either case.[23] According to the estimated coefficients on the level of unemployment (−0.10 in both cases), it would take ten point-years of unemployment to reduce inflation permanently by one percentage point, compared to only two point-years for the previous Canadian estimates of Fortin (1989) and Cozier and Wilkinson (1991). This would imply much larger sacrifice ratios (and other costs of unemployment) than those to which we have grown accustomed. With an Okun coefficient of 1.5 to 2.0,[24] gaining a one-percentage-point decrease in the inflation rate would require the sacrifice of 15 percent to 20 percent of one year's GDP (currently $105 to $140 billion). The cost of the Bank of Canada's campaign to reduce inflation by three points (from 5 percent to 2 percent) would, of course, be three times as large ($315 to $420 billion).

These results raise the possibility that previous research has vastly underestimated the costs of the traditional recession method of reducing inflation in the two countries. It is easiest to understand their implications in an economy subjected to full hysteresis $(h = 1)$. Under that assumption, the trend increase in Canadian unemployment from the late 1960s to the late 1980s would be the permanent consequence of macroeconomic policy struggling to eliminate the inflation generated by the supply-side shocks of the 1970s, which were only partially offset by the deflationary commodity shocks of the 1980s. Under strong (rather than full) hysteresis, that story needs to be amended only in the sense that the increase in unemployment will eventually reverse itself in some long run instead of literally persisting forever.

Table 3
Estimated Equations for Annual Change in CPI Inflation (excluding Food and Energy):
Canada, 1973–90 and United States, 1966–90

	Canada, 1973–90		United States, 1966–90	
	Equation 3.1		Equation 3.2	
RIGHT-HAND VARIABLE				
Constant	0.677	(0.370)	0.696	(0.510)
Unemployment rate, current level	−0.098	(0.058)	−0.099	(0.102)
Unemployment rate, current change	−0.322	(0.089)	−0.422	(0.168)
Unemployment rate, one-year-lagged change	−0.955	(0.084)	−0.505	(0.130)
Unemployment rate, two-year-lagged change	−0.303	(0.080)	−0.133	(0.132)
Real food and energy prices, one-year-lagged change	0.100	(0.015)	0.031	(0.022)
Real import prices, current change	0.085	(0.022)	0.152	(0.028)
Indirect tax rate, current change	0.254	(0.064)	0.800	(0.460)
Wage-and-price controls, current level	−1.326	(0.229)	−1.864	(0.807)
SUMMARY STATISTICS				
Adjusted R^2	0.98		0.86	
Standard error of regression	0.24		0.64	
Durbin-Watson statistic	2.60		2.32	
Degree of hysteresis	0.77	(0.13)	0.81	(0.19)

Sources: CANSIM data base and Fortin (1991) for Canada; CITIBASE data base, Office of the President (1992), and Gordon (1990b: 1167) for the United States.

Notes: Ordinary-least-squares regressions. The left-hand variable is the change in the annual log change of the CPI excluding food and energy. The unemployment rate is that of adult males (twenty-five and over in Canada, twenty and over in the United States). The real food and energy price-change variable is the sum of the annual log changes of the CPIs for food and energy, minus the annual log change of the CPI excluding food and energy, all lagged one year. The real import price-change variable is the current annual log change of an import-price index, minus the one-year-lagged annual log change of the CPI excluding food and energy. For Canada, the import price index is a price index for all merchandise imports except food and energy; for the United States, it is the National Income and Product Accounts (NIPA) import-price deflator. The indirect tax rate for Canada is the effective indirect tax rate on non-food non-energy consumption; for the United States, it is the ratio of NIPA indirect business taxes to GNP. The wage-and-price controls variable for Canada reflects the operation of the Anti-Inflation Board in 1976–78; it is equal to 0.5 in 1976, 1.0 in 1977 and 1978, and 0.0 in other years. For the United States, the variable reflects Nixon controls; it is equal to 0.5 in 1972 and 1973, −0.3 in 1974, −0.7 in 1975, and 0.0 in other years. The degree of hysteresis is the ratio $b_2/(b_1 + b_2)$, where b_1 is the coefficient of the current level of the unemployment rate and b_2 is the coefficient of its current change. Standard errors appear in parentheses below the estimated coefficients.

Criticism and Interpretation

The idea that the degree of unemployment hysteresis is strong and that, consequently, the sacrifice ratio could be much larger than what everyone once believed, say in excess of 15 to 20 percent of one year's GDP per percentage-point decline of inflation, goes against conventional wisdom and understandably meets with some resistance. There are two reasons for this.

First, there remains some uncertainty about the robustness of the econometric results. The degrees of freedom are still few. Estimates and tests based on models with a small number of degrees of freedom necessarily have larger variances and lower statistical power. Using quarterly instead of annual data to increase the number of degrees of freedom is not going to improve the situation. The natural periodicity for wage-and-price adjustment is the year, not the quarter. Quarterly data are inherently more "noisy" than annual data. With quarterly data, large numbers of degrees of freedom must be used up anyway for proper identification of seasonal factors and distributed lags. For all those reasons, unless there is an intrinsic interest in the fine timing of economic relationships, going quarterly does not obviously improve estimation efficiency and testing power.

The main challenge against the hysteresis result of Table 3 for Canada has come from the rejection of hysteresis by Cozier and Wilkinson (1991). These authors estimate a quarterly Canadian Phillips curve, with some measure of the output gap (the difference between actual and potential output, say $Y - Y_p$) to capture demand pressure. Its specification is quite restrictive, though, with indirect tax, exchange rate, or foreign price variables (other than commodity prices) all omitted from the equation, and only two quarterly lags allowed for the output gap to affect the inflation rate. Accordingly, its goodness-of-fit properties are poor (its R^2 is around 0.35 in the sample period 1973 to 1990), and it is so temporally unstable that it can be saved only by assuming away ten quarters of data (Poloz and Wilkinson 1992).

Cozier and Wilkinson find that the change in inflation (ΔI) depends mainly on the *level* of the output gap ($Y - Y_p$), which they interpret as consistent with standard natural rate theory and against hysteresis theory. However, even if their result was correct, a different interpretation is possible. We know from the *accelerator mechanism* that potential output Y_p should adjust to actual output Y with a lag. The Cozier-Wilkinson result is therefore consistent with the change in inflation depending on current and past *changes* in actual output, a pure hysteretical result. For example, if there is a recession, Y declines below Y_p, which generates disinflation. But if it is long enough, the recession inhibits capital formation, which in turn slowly reduces Y_p. When the recovery comes, Y catches up with the lower Y_p before the latter has had time to pick up speed again, and hence before the unemployment rate corresponding to Y in the labour market has had time to return to its starting level. Inflationary pressure thus reappears prematurely, monetary policy tightens up again, and unemployment goes up to another peak. There is hysteresis.

The foregoing argument assumes no real wage response to rising or falling unemployment, and so it is extreme. But if real wages are slow to adjust, as we know they are, it can be seen that the apparently anti-hysteretic result of Cozier and Wilkinson can provide a plausible hysteretic interpretation of the medium term.

Another challenge to the results of Table 3 for Canada has come from the review of the debate by Poloz and Wilkinson (1992). They show that the evidence in favour of hysteresis often disappears when the adult male unemployment rate used in Table 3 is replaced by alternative measures of market slack, such as the adult female or youth unemployment rates, or the unadjusted or demographic-weighted unemployment rates. However, it is well known that all these measures were seriously distorted by the major demographic and other structural changes of the last twenty years. They are clearly inferior measures of slack, as indeed several past Bank of Canada studies have shown (e.g., Rose 1988). Another measure suggested by Poloz and Wilkinson, the Bank of Canada in-house measure of the unemployment gap, is also suspect because it was constructed from the bank's macroeconometric model RDXF after *assuming* that standard natural rate theory is correct. This is not a claim that the adult male unemployment rate has not been affected at all by structural change and is an ideal measure of market slack, but only that the other measures were more affected and are worse gauges of slack.

In any event, the behaviour of the aggregate unemployment rate in the coming years will no doubt help reduce part of the econometric uncertainty. If Canadian unemployment averages 10 percent over the period 1993 to 1996 while the supply side remains calm, then standard Phillips curves such as those estimated by Fortin (1989) or Cozier and Wilkinson (1991), which assume a natural rate of 8 percent or less, forecast a *deflation* rate of 3 percent by 1996. The revisionist equation of Table 3 above predicts, on the contrary, that inflation will remain positive and will rise again, with a lag, if and when unemployment begins to decline.

The second reason why the idea of unemployment hysteresis meets with some resistance is that the true underlying causes of strong hysteresis have not so far been satisfactorily identified at the macro- or micro-levels. We do not know which of the popular explanations listed earlier fits the facts best or, indeed, if any one does. The credibility of the strong hysteresis story hinges crucially on identifying a convincing causal explanation for the phenomenon. This is clearly the most pressing issue on the research agenda.

Meanwhile, one should recognize that recent macroeconomic history and a number of theoretical and empirical findings on unemployment persistence seem to imply that, within the range of moderate-to-high unemployment rates, Phillips curves are flatter, and sacrifice ratios larger, than was earlier thought. Serious questions are raised about the validity of standard natural rate theory. Model uncertainty about the inflation-unemployment trade-off is therefore greater now than at any point since the late 1960s. One would hope that this would at least induce greater prudence in future manipulation of macro-policy instruments, as implied by the normative theory of economic policy (Brainard 1967).

CONCLUSION

I have shown that the optimistic view that the recession method for eliminating moderate inflation carries large benefits and small costs rests on very fragile empirical evidence. The second and third sections have presented arguments and evidence respectively suggesting that the benefits of (near) zero inflation are more uncertain, and its costs larger, than recently stated by Canadian policy authorities.

Zero Inflation is Sub-optimal

Two broad implications follow from the analysis. First, *if* imposing recessions is the only available means of reducing inflation (and the recent recession only added to the evidence that a game plan based on central bank "credibility" does not reduce the costs of disinflation), then, as a matter of sheer logic, achieving zero inflation is sub-optimal.

As the inflation rate is progressively brought down to zero, the marginal benefits of further inflation reduction decrease toward zero. They could even become negative (Summers 1991). However, the marginal unemployment costs of reducing inflation are always positive, even if the natural rate of unemployment is not moved at all by changes in the actual rate. The optimal inflation rate, at which marginal costs and benefits are equated, must therefore be greater than zero.[25] Cost-benefit analysis implies not that zero inflation should be approached slowly (as is often heard), but that it is the wrong target. Naturally, the presence of unemployment hysteresis increases the marginal unemployment costs of disinflation, and raises the optimal inflation rate further.

The present state of knowledge does not allow anyone to hold a firm view on what the optimal inflation rate is for Canada, whether 3 percent, 5 percent, or 10 percent. The third section has presented evidence that the sacrifice ratio is such that a percentage-point decrease in the inflation rate is associated with the loss of 15 percent to 20 percent of one year's GDP, three to four times the previous standard estimate. However, the evidence of the second section on the macroeconomic benefits of inflation reduction has been inconclusive. For moderate levels of inflation, the marginal benefits could range from negligible to important, but we do not know how important.

The minimal implication of these results is that the present monetary strategy in Canada is probably much more costly than the policy authorities are ready to admit, and that its benefits are much more uncertain than they want to acknowledge. In other words, the problem with the strategy is not that it is so hard to sell to the Canadian public, but that it is an imprudent strategy to start with.

Recession-free Alternatives Are Needed

On the more constructive side, the second broad implication of the analysis is that, better than learning to live with inflation, we should explore alternative, recession-free, methods of controlling inflation. What would be required is an effective institutional mechanism (other than wage-and-price controls) that could "shock down" inflation through coordinated wage-and-price guidelines. Formally, this would amount to attacking inflation directly through the supply-side variable S of equation (6). The degree of unemployment hysteresis need not be very strong to make this type of policy strategy economically attractive, but stronger hysteresis makes it even more so.

A number of countries have successfully controlled inflation through various types of cooperative institutional arrangements. The cases of Austria, Germany, Japan, and Switzerland, which have experienced the lowest combined levels of inflation and unemployment of all industrial countries in the last thirty years, are well known. The necessary ingredients for success in all four countries have been a strong degree of social consensus on the importance of achieving both price stability *and* full employment, as well as a clear understanding of the relevant socio-economic trade-offs, and willingness to act upon them for the collective good.

One need not be overly pessimistic to believe that Canada will not satisfy anyone of these conditions soon. The logical implication is that our prospects for reconciling the objectives of price stability and full employment are not good. *If* (near) zero inflation remains the overriding objective of macroeconomic policy, if it turns out that our unemployment rate is indeed strongly "hysteretic," and if our supply-side inflationary bias remains, we will likely continue to experience Japanese inflation rates and British unemployment rates in the foreseeable future.

ACKNOWLEDGMENTS

I am indebted to Vickie Miller, Pierre Mohnen, Michel Normandin, Erik Poole, Andrew Sharpe, and two anonymous referees for very helpful comments and suggestions; to Nathalie Noreau for research assistance; and to Milan Kundera for title assistance. The financial support of the Fonds FCAR and the former Economic Council of Canada is gratefully acknowledged. This paper incorporates minor corrections to the version published in *Canadian Business Economics* 1, No. 3 (Spring 1993): 3–18.

NOTES

1 Assuming for simplicity that real GDP was at potential in the peak quarters of 1981 (second quarter) and 1990 (first quarter) and that the annual potential growth rate is 3 percent, it follows at once that the sum of the percentage output gaps for the twelve following quarters cumulated to 17.9 percent of one year's GDP for 1981 (third quarter) to 1984 (second quarter), but to 19.1 percent for 1990 (second quarter) to 1993 (first quarter).

2 Important references are Fischer and Modigliani (1978), Fischer (1981), and Howitt (1990). Exceptions to the 20-percent ceiling were Italy in 1980 (21 percent), the United Kingdom in 1975 (24 percent), and Japan in 1974 (25 percent).

3 The foregoing arguments militate for low inflation, but not necessarily near-zero inflation. One potential cost of zero inflation is that it introduces downward inflexibility in real interest rates and real wages. Since nominal interest rates cannot be negative, real interest rates cannot be negative when expected inflation is zero. If productivity growth is slow (as it is now, relative to the 1950s and 1960s) and nominal wages stiffly resist taking absolute cuts, zero inflation will make real wages more difficult to adjust downward. As a result, the real economy is made more resistant to change, at a cost for output and employment (Summers 1991).

4 Seven of the twenty-four OECD members are excluded: the five "less-advanced" countries (Ireland, Greece, Portugal, Spain, and Turkey), and the two smallest (Iceland and Luxembourg).

5 Other variables were tried without success: the overall tax burden, long-term strike activity (as a proxy for social consensus), and early membership in the European Economic Community.

6 One potentially important bias arises from forgetting about the weak capabilities for administering taxation, the thin domestic capital markets, and the limited access to foreign capital that are characteristic of less-developed countries. Government budgets are then biased toward money-financed deficits. Stong correlations are found, but it could be slow growth causing inflation as well as inflation causing slow growth.

7 For average inflation, the t-statistics for the nullity of the short- and long-run coefficients are -0.62 and -0.67, respectively. For inflation volatility, they are both -1.35. The p-value for the F-test of joint nullity of the two short-run coefficients is 0.24.

8 The t-statistic for the nullity of the sum of the coefficients of the two inflation variables is 1.10.

9 As most first-year economics textbooks explain, *post hoc, ergo propter hoc* is translated from the Latin as "after this, therefore necessarily because of this."

10 The t-statistic for the nullity of the sum of the coefficients of the two capacity utilization variables is 0.23.

11 The t-statistic for the nullity of the sum of the coefficients of the two inflation variables is -1.4. The p-value for the F-test of their joint nullity is 0.38.

12 The conclusion remains unchanged if total factor productivity is substituted for labour productivity and if other measures of market slack are used.

13 Recent examples of this tradition are Fortin (1989) and Cozier and Wilkinson (1991). Fortin reported a coefficient of 0.45 on the adult male unemployment rate. Cozier and Wilkinson obtained an annualized steady-state coefficient of -0.57 on a Bank of Canada in-house measure of the unemployment gap.

14 Regressing the change in the aggregate unemployment rate on the log change in real GDP with annual data for the 1974–91 period yields an estimated coefficient of about 0.4 on the latter variable. This empirical regularity is known as "Okun's Law," and the inverse coefficient $2.5 = 1/0.4$, as "Okun's coefficient" (Okun 1962).

15 By contrast, Cozier and Wilkinson (1991) arrived at a low estimate of 2 for the sacrifice ratio. This followed from the surprisingly low value (1.3) they attributed to Okun's coefficient, based on previous work at

the Bank of Canada. However, the standard error around that estimate was very large (Ford and Rose 1989: 21).

16 The sacrifice ratio only measures the short-term macroeconomic cost of unemployment. Other costs include the associated mental, family, and social pathologies, the unevenness of incidence across social classes, and the retardation of long-term growth due to destruction of young promising firms, and more generally to delayed investment in physical and human capital.

17 The persistence of high unemployment in 1984 to 1987 can be largely attributed to the unfavourable terms-of-trade shocks on the western provincial economies. But there is no *a priori* reason to discount these sectoral-regional shocks and the related excess unemployment as more "structural" and less disinflationary than other types of shocks. There is, in fact, a strong negative correlation over time between interregional inflation differentials and unemployment differentials. Over the period 1982 to 1991, the correlation coefficients were −0.77 and −0.87 for the Ontario-Alberta and Ontario-British Columbia comparisons, respectively.

18 Phelps is also widely cited as the father of the two ideas of hysteresis (Phelps 1972: 77–80) *and* natural unemployment (Phelps 1967). This precludes using his name to identify either camp!

19 Most of them were actually suggested by Tobin (1980: 61)

20 Since the unemployment rate cannot be negative, there should of course exist a minimum unemployment rate below which the hysteresis story would break down, no trade-off with inflation would be feasible, and natural rate theory would hold again.

21 The United States' import price and indirect tax variables are not exclusive of food and energy, which could explain the looser fit of the estimated American equation.

22 Franz and Gordon (1993) have recently obtained an estimate of 0.46 for the degree of hysteresis in the United States which, given the standard errors, is not inconsistent with my own estimate.

23 Equation (6) indicates that the coefficient of the level and change variables (U and ΔU) are $b_1 = -a(1 - h)$ and $b_2 = -ah$, respectively. Therefore, the point estimate for h is calculated as $b_2/(b_1 + b_2)$. The tests of the hypotheses that $h = 0$ and $h = 1$ are based on the asymptotic standard errors for the estimates of h reported in Table 3. The t-statistics for $h = 0$ are 5.7 for Canada and 4.4 for the United States; the t-statistics for $h = 1$ are 1.7 for Canada and 1.0 for the United States.

24 Since the unemployment costs must be spread over a number of years, the Okun coefficient used must in this case be lower than the short-run value of 2.5 referred to in note 14. The longer the horizon, the

more complete the adjustment of employment to output, and therefore the smaller the reduction of output associated with any given increase in unemployment.

25 This should be taken to mean that the optimal *measured* inflation rate must exceed the positive rate actually corresponding to price stability. Reviewing the evidence in 1990 (Fortin 1990), I concluded that CPI inflation could overestimate the true rate of inflation by up to 1 percent per year. Recent research by Gordon (1992) indicates that the bias could be somewhat higher.

REFERENCES

Ball, L. 1993. "What Determines the Sacrifice Ratio?" National Bureau of Economic Research Working Paper No. 4306.

Bank of Canada. 1991. "Targets for Reducing Inflation." *Bank of Canada Review*, March: 3–21.

Blanchard, O.J. 1991. "Wage Bargaining and Unemployment Persistence." *Journal of Money, Credit, and Banking* 23 (August): 277–92.

Blanchard, O.J., and L.H. Summers. 1986. "Hysteresis and the European Unemployment Problem." In S. Fischer, ed., NBER *Macroeconomics Annual*, 15–78. Cambridge, Mass.: MIT Press.

Brainard, W.C. 1967. "Uncertainty and the Effectiveness of Policy." *American Economic Review* 57 (May): 411–25.

Corak, M., and S.R.G. Jones. 1993. "The Persistence of Unemployment: How Important Were Regionally Extended Unemployment Insurance Benefits?" Statistics Canada Analytical Studies Branch Research Paper No. 53.

Cozier, B., and J. Selody. 1992. "Inflation and Macroeconomic Performance." Bank of Canada Working Paper 92-6.

Cozier, B., and G. Wilkinson. 1991. "Some Evidence on Hysteresis and the Costs of Disinflation in Canada." Bank of Canada Technical Report No. 55.

Crow, J.W. 1988. "The Work of Canadian Monetary Policy." *Bank of Canada Review*, February: 3–17.

Drèze, J.H., and C.R. Bean (eds.). 1990. *Europe's Unemployment Problem*. Cambridge, Mass.: MIT Press.

Drèze, J.H., and H.R. Sneessens. 1986. "A Discussion of Belgian Unemployment, Combining Traditional Concepts and Disequilibrium Econometrics." *Economica* 53, Supplement, s89–s119.

Fischer, S. 1981. "Towards an Understanding of the Costs of Inflation: II." In K. Brunner and A.H. Meltzer, eds., *The Costs and Consequences of Inflation*, 5–42. Carnegie-Rochester Conference Series on Public Policy 15. Amsterdam: North-Holland.

Fischer, S., and F. Modigliani. 1978. "Towards an Understanding of the Real Effects and Costs of Inflation." *Weltwirtschaftliches Archiv* 104, No. 4: 810–33.

Ford, R., and D. Rose. 1989. "Estimates of the NAIRU Using an Extended Okun's Law." Bank of Canada Working Paper 89-3.

Fortin, P. 1989. "How 'Natural' is Canada's High Unemployment Rate?" *European Economic Review* 33 (January): 89–110.

– 1990. "Do We Measure Inflation Correctly?" In R.G. Lipsey, ed., *Zero Inflation: The Goal of Price Stability,* 109–30. Toronto: C.D. Howe Institute.

– 1991. "The Phillips Curve, Macroeconomic Policy, and the Welfare of Canadians." *Canadian Journal of Economics* 24 (November): 774–803.

Franz, W., and R.J. Gordon. 1993. "German and American Wage and Price Dynamics: Differences and Common Themes." National Bureau of Economic Research Working Paper No. 4292.

Friedman, M. 1968. "The Role of Monetary Policy." *American Economic Review* 58 (March): 1–17.

Gordon, R.J. 1988. "Back to the Future: European Unemployment Today Viewed from America in 1939." *Brookings Papers on Economic Activity* 1: 271–304.

– 1990a. *Macroeconomics.* 5th ed. Glenview, Ill.: Scott Foresman.

– 1990b. "What is New Keynesian Economics?" *Journal of Economic Literature* 28 (September): 1115–71.

– 1992. "Measuring the Aggregate Price Level: Implications for Economic Performance and Policy." National Bureau of Economic Research Working Paper No. 3969.

Gross, D. 1996. "Unemployment Persistence in France and Germany." This volume.

Howitt, P. 1990. "Zero Inflation as a Long-term Target for Monetary Policy." In R.G. Lipsey, ed., *Zero Inflation: The Goal of Price Stability,* 67–108. Toronto: C.D. Howe Institute.

Jarrett, J.P., and J. Selody. 1982. "The Productivity-inflation Nexus in Canada, 1963–1979." *Review of Economics and Statistics* 64 (August): 361–7.

Layard, R., and S. Nickell. 1987. "The Labour Market." In R. Layard and R. Dornbusch, eds., *The Performance of the British Economy,* 131–79. Oxford: Clarendon Press.

Lindbeck, A., and D.J. Snower. 1988. *The Insider-Outsider Theory of Employment and Unemployment.* Cambridge, Mass.: MIT Press.

Malinvaud, E. 1986. "The Rise of Unemployment in France." *Economica* 53, Supplement, s197–s217.

Mankiw, N.G. 1992. *Macroeconomics.* New York: Worth Publishers.

Mankiw, N.G., D. Romer, and D.N. Weil. 1992. "A Contribution to the Empirics of Economic Growth." *Quarterly Journal of Economics* 107 (May): 407–37.

Milbourne, R.D., D.D. Purvis, and W.D. Scoones. 1991. "Unemployment Insurance and Unemployment Dynamics." *Canadian Journal of Economics* 24 (November): 804–26.

Novin, F. 1991. "The Productivity-inflation Nexus Revisited: Canada, 1969–1988." Bank of Canada Working Paper 91–1.

Office of the President. 1992. *Economic Report of the President*. Washington, DC: Government Printing Office.

Okun, A.M. 1962. "Potential GNP: Its Measurement and Significance." In American Statistical Association, *Proceedings of the Business and Economic Statistics Section*, 98–103. Washington, DC: American Statistical Association.

OECD (Organisation for Co-operation and Economic Development). 1991. *Historical Statistics 1960–1989*. Paris: OECD.

– 1992. *OECD Economic Outlook*. Paris: OECD.

Osberg, L. 1996. "Unemployment Insurance and Unemployment – Revisited." This volume.

Phelps, E.S. 1967. "Phillips Curves, Expectations of Inflation, and Optimal Unemployment over Time." *Economica* 34 (August): 254–81.

– 1972. *Inflation Policy and Unemployment Theory*. New York: Norton.

Poloz, S.S., and G. Wilkinson. 1992. "Is Hysteresis a Characteristic of the Canadian Labour Market? A Tale of Two Studies." Bank of Canada Working Paper 92–3.

Rose, D.E. 1988. "The NAIRU in Canada: Concepts, Determinants and Estimates." Bank of Canada Technical Report No. 50.

Samuelson, P.A., and R.M. Solow. 1960. "Analytical Aspects of Anti-inflation Policy." *American Economic Review* 50 (May): 177–94.

Selody, J. 1990. "The Goal of Price Stability: A Review of the Issues." Bank of Canada Technical Report No. 54.

Solow, R.M. 1956. "A Contribution to the Theory of Economic Growth." *Quarterly Journal of Economics* 70 (February): 65–94.

– 1985. "Insiders and Outsiders in Wage Determination." *Scandinavian Journal of Economics* 87, No. 2: 411–28.

Storer, P. 1992. "Persistent Unemployment and Sectoral Shocks in the Wake of the 1982 Recession." Cahier 1, Centre de recherche sur l'emploi et les fluctuations économiques, Université du Québec à Montréal.

Summers, L. 1991. "How Should Long-term Monetary Policy Be Determined?" *Journal of Money, Credit, and Banking* 23, Part 2 (August): 625–31.

Tobin, J. 1972. "Inflation and Unemployment." *American Economic Review* 62 (March): 1–18.

– 1980. "Stabilization Policy Ten Years After." *Brookings Papers on Economic Activity* 1: 19–71.

3 Real Interest Rates, Inflation, and Unemployment

JOHN SMITHIN

An obvious explanation for economy-wide employment and unemployment outcomes in Canada over the past two decades would seem to be found in the conduct of monetary policy by the Bank of Canada. As suggested by Smithin and Wolf (1993), one of the more destabilizing elements in the world economy in recent years has been substantial variations in real interest rates. These have been largely the by-product of the pursuit of "monetarist" policies by key central banks, which have been willing to drive up real interest rates and provoke recessions and unemployment in order to reduce inflationary pressures. A more stable and sensible monetary policy would be to stabilize real financial interest rates at low but still positive levels, recognizing that this would only be possible in the case of an individual national central bank, such as the Bank of Canada, if real exchange rates were also free to adjust. Such a policy would likely improve the growth and employment experience in the jurisdiction concerned. It would be unlikely to produce literal price stability, but might be capable of at least stabilizing the inflation rate at a moderate level, and certainly of avoiding the inflationary extremes that occur when real rates are allowed to become negative as in the 1970s.

In the Canadian context, two specific episodes in which the conduct of monetary policy apparently destabilized the real economy immediately come to mind. The first is the later years of the monetary targeting experiment of 1975–82, when the original policy of "gradualism" was drastically intensified by an attempted defence of the exchange rate at a time when the United States Federal Reserve was itself pursuing a policy of disinflation (Courchene 1982). This did lead to a lower inflation rate in the mid-1980s, but at the cost of a severe recession in 1981–82, and an annual unemployment rate that remained in double figures through 1985. The second episode is the "zero-inflation" policy announced by the governor of the Bank of Canada in 1988 (Lipsey 1990). Once again, high real interest rates were the means for inducing disinflation, and as early as 1992 the policy might have been judged a "success" in that the inflation rate had dropped below 2 percent.[1] However, the cost of the reduction in the inflation rate was yet another recession in 1990–91, and a national unemployment rate that had already climbed back into double figures by 1991 and remained in that range until late 1994.

The conventional calculus of costs and benefits assumes that it is worthwhile to bear the rigours of a short-term recession for the supposed benefits of a permanently lower rate of inflation. However, this is dubious on a number of grounds, not least because the economics profession has been notoriously unclear in specifying precisely what the benefits of "zero inflation," rather than some other number, exactly are (Smithin 1990). Also, experience seems to show that the economic slowdowns required to reduce inflation to a low figure are much more severe and long-lasting, particularly in their impact on unemployment, than the public was originally led to believe. In technical language, the processes involved seem to be subject to "hysteresis" or "persistence." Recovery from these situations does not come about "automatically," but only after an explicit reversal of policy when the authorities have judged that the downturn has gone far enough. Moreover, as illustrated by the Canadian experience of the late 1980s, whatever effect the bouts of recession may have on inflation in the short term, they are unlikely to be "permanent."

The purpose of this chapter is to relate the bitter practical experience of Canada in recent years (described in detail elsewhere in this volume) to the broader changes in the intellectual climate that have made such apparently destructive policies seem both necessary and desirable to contemporary policy-makers and academics. In particular, it will discuss some of the developments at the level of economic doctrine or theory which have so altered the current consensus about the ultimate objectives of macroeconomic policy.

Obviously, the main point at issue is the age-old debate about the impact of central bank activities and policy on economic variables other than those directly under their control, and, in particular, on the "real" variables such as output and employment that are significant for economic welfare. Historically, the most popular answer has been that monetary policy can have only a transitory influence on such real variables, and that ultimately central bank activities affect only inflation rates. The present era seems to be characterized by a particularly strong revival of the doctrine of the long-run "neutrality" of money. This would explain why professional opinion is apparently so unconcerned about the consequences of deliberately deflationary policy and also why alternative policy prescriptions such as the suggestion that central banks stabilize real interest rates are ruled out. The argument would simply be that it is not in their power to do this.

However, this chapter will suggest that both practical experience and certain heterodox views in monetary theory provide reasons to question this conventional analysis. Given the importance of the money/credit network for the effective operation of production and exchange in the market economy, it is unlikely, in fact, that central bank interest rate policy, even if primarily directed at inflation, will be neutral in either the short or the long term. In the "monetary production" economy (Keynes 1936), the policy of the central bank remains one of the most important determinants, if not the most important determinant, of the prosperity or otherwise of the entire system.[2] This explains why the various policy "experiments" of the monetary authorities, designed to cure inflation, seem also to have had a dramatic impact on the real economy.

THE INFLUENCE OF THE QUANTITY THEORY OF MONEY AND MONETARISM

Central to the development of current attitudes was the resurgence, in the second half of the twentieth century, of the ancient quantity theory of money in its modern guise of monetarism. This theory asserts that an increase in the quantity of money (somehow defined) will increase the level of money prices in the same proportion. Similarly, that an increase in the rate of growth of the money supply, allowing for changes in the rate of growth of the real economy and adjustments to the *velocity of circulation*, will lead to an increase in inflation. The standard prescription for a reduction in inflation immediately follows.

The contribution of the monetarists was to persuade both academic economists and policy-makers that, appearances to the contrary, it was possible to apply the logic of the quantity theory even in the context of a contemporary "credit economy" in which the bulk of the money supply consists of the liabilities of financial intermediaries such as banks. The most obvious feature of this environment, as compared with a situation in which "money" consists only of coins or fiat currency, is that the money supply will expand when bank lending increases and contract when the loans are repaid. Hence, if the authorities are to conduct monetary policy according to the principles of the quantity theory, the question immediately arises as to how the central bank can exert control over this process.

According to monetarist theory, the answer was that the commercial banks would continue to need to hold reserves of the *monetary base* of the system, which in essence means the note and deposit liabilities of the central bank. Hence, the rate of growth of the money supply can supposedly be controlled by controlling the rate of growth of the base, which feeds through to the published monetary aggregates via the *money multiplier*. This in turn will control inflation. These ideas provided the basic inspiration, in Canada and elsewhere, for the *monetary targeting* experiments of the late 1970s and early 1980s and, albeit at one remove, for the "zero-inflation" policies of the late 1980s and early 1990s.

As is well known, however, *base control* has not worked well in practice, because for institutional reasons most central banks are unable to conduct monetary policy in the textbook monetarist fashion. Central banks can and do make use of their monopoly supply of base money to enforce a desired level of short-term interest rates in their respective jurisdictions (Goodhart 1989; Goodfriend 1993) but, in practice, do not actually refuse *accommodation* on those terms because of their responsibility for the liquidity of the system and the *lender-of-last-resort* function.[3] The short-term rate of interest is then the effective monetary policy instrument, and the central bank will have only indirect control over the monetary base or the monetary aggregates, as these adjust endogenously to different settings of the interest rate. Also, in a period of rapid financial innovation, the information content of the traditional monetary aggregates is drastically reduced, and it becomes unclear which of the statistically defined aggregates, if any, corresponds to the theoretical concept of the quantity of money. Therefore, what "tight money" has actually meant in practice is simply increases in short-term real interest rates, to whatever extent is necessary to provoke an economic slowdown and then to feed through to reductions in the inflation rate.

It was usually recognized by both monetarists and earlier quantity theorists that a negative side-effect of attempts to reduce inflation rates from established levels would be a recession, at least in the short term. In the quantity-theory tradition however, this would be due only to either short-run nominal wage or price rigidity, or to inertia in inflationary expectations, and would be explicitly temporary. Over a somewhat longer time horizon, wage bargains would be revised and/or expectations would adjust, and full employment would be quickly restored at a lower level of inflation. One of the more startling claims of the "rational expectations" school of the 1970s was that even this degree of disruption could be avoided in the case of a "tight-money" policy which was pre-announced and "credible." This argument was certainly influential politically at the time of the "Volcker disinflation" in North America in 1979–82. A more moderate view, however, is expressed in the popular slogan "short-term pain for long-term gain," which has often been the publicly stated justification for severe monetary policy-induced recessions. The argument is simply that for society as a whole, it is worth undergoing the rigours of a short-term recession in order to enjoy the (presumably) long-lasting benefits of a lower inflation rate.

It has been of crucial importance, both from the theoretical and practical point of view, that although the non-neutrality of central bank activity is usually conceded for the short run, it is adamantly denied that monetary policy as such can have any impact on real economic variables over a longer time horizon. As in Friedman (1974: 36–7, 41), the idea is that the economy converges to the equilibrium or "permanent" growth rate, which is independent of any monetary influence, and reflects only the "real" forces of "productivity and thrift." In particular, the rate of interest itself is believed to be pre-eminently a "real" phenomenon determined only by the forces of supply and demand in the capital markets. In the terminology of Wicksell (1898), the assumption is that there is a unique "natural" real rate of interest that can never be permanently altered by monetary policy. This is view that has a long history in monetary economics, going back at least to Thornton and Ricardo (Smithin 1994a), and it essentially predisposes the resulting theory to come to what are now described as long-run monetarist conclusions. It is also very closely connected to the other famous "natural rate" associated with Milton Friedman (1968: 7–11), the natural rate of unemployment.

The assumption that monetary policy cannot permanently affect the real rate of interest has been taken very seriously in many influential analyses of inflation (Friedman 1968; McCallum 1991). At one point Fama (1975) went so far as to present evidence from the post-war American data that supported the conclusion that the real rate of interest was effectively constant. This, however, obviously seems much less plausible today in the light of the experience of more recent years. Later work (e.g., Mishkin 1984) suggests that this result does not hold in periods other than the relatively tranquil postwar years. The key issue then becomes whether the volatility of real interest rates observed in practice can be explained away in Wicksellian fashion as changes in the natural rate (caused, for example, by supply shocks, or large budget deficits) or whether it has been the change in central bank policy itself that has been the main causal factor. Certainly the era of very high real interest rates, beginning in the late 1970s and early 1980s, has coincided with the apparent shift of central bank priorities at around that time, placing more emphasis on fighting inflation and less on outcomes in the real economy.

IS THE CONCEPT OF A "NATURAL RATE" OF INTEREST PLAUSIBLE?

The concept of a unique "natural rate" of interest, impervious to monetary manipulation, is therefore the cornerstone of the contemporary conventional wisdom on monetary policy, even if this is not often made explicit. However, as argued in some detail by Smithin (1994a), in spite of its widespread acceptance by both academics and policy-makers, this assumption is not particularly plausible in a genuine "credit" or "monetary production" economy.

The natural rate concept amounts to assuming that a unique real rate of interest is determined on barter capital markets in which savings are somehow embodied in heterogenous concrete physical commodities and can be traded to investors for use in specific production processes. We are asked to imagine that, in principle, a rate of interest exists which represents the outcome of the "true" motives of borrowers and lenders *if* they could interact in a capital market operating without the intervention of money, banks, or other financial intermediaries. The next step in the argument is to assert that the real world complications caused by the actual existence of money and banks do not, in fact, ultimately have any impact on the motives of those engaged in the supposedly more fundamental barter transactions. The natural rate established by these imaginary capital transactions is then taken to be the most basic determinant of the complex of interest rates actually observed in reality. Given these premises, if follows that central bank influence over the level and term structure of interest rates can only be temporary at best, and that in the long run, money must be neutral.

These ideas, in one version or another, have a history as long as the quantity theory of money itself. However, in continuing to provide the intellectual foundation for the conduct of monetary policy by contemporary central banks, including the Bank of Canada, they have also had definite practical consequences in our own time. In particular, they are responsible for the confident assertions that repeated bouts of "tight money" can do no permanent damage to the real economy.

An obvious response to the natural rate doctrine, however, would simply be that the idea of interest rates being somehow determined on (non-existent) barter capital markets is as much a theoretical fiction as commodity exchange taking place in Walrasian barter commodity markets with the aid of an "auctioneer." The concept takes no account of the actual historical evolution of the monetary market economy or of the internal logic of the system.

A more reasonable conception for the monetary production economy would be that the rate of interest is determined in the first instance in the monetary or financial sector, and that rates of return elsewhere must adjust to this standard rather than vice versa. If an economy based on the "exchange of debts" is to flourish, the financial system must generate a basic monetary asset which unambiguously represents final payment of debt and hence serves as both the standard of value and the ultimate means of payment (Hicks 1989). The business of borrowing and lending, and hence also the formation of physical capital and real economic activity in general, could hardly get off the ground without the assistance of the monetary system in this sense. The rate of interest charged on loans of the basic monetary asset, in practice the rate set by the central bank, therefore plays a key part in determining the overall pace of expansion. In a monetary production economy, production itself cannot proceed unless adequate financial resources are made available at the *start* of the process. Therefore, the real cost of borrowing the funds necessary to get production under way must have a major effect on the scale of production entrepreneurs find it worthwhile to undertake, and central bank policy over interest rates, whether aimed at curing inflation or any other target, inevitably makes itself felt in the real economy.

These commonsense notions may be contrasted with the idea that precisely the same economic interactions could take place in barter-type capital markets as in systems with sophisticated monetary and financial markets, independently of the stage of evolution that these institutional arrangements have reached. Yet the latter is what the natural rate doctrine quite clearly implies. The existence of money and financial markets literally makes no difference to the economy in these formulations.

ALTERNATIVE THEORIES OF THE RATE OF INTEREST

In an earlier era, Keynes (1936) was one major economist who did attempt to take a crucial step in the development of monetary theory and abandon the natural rate of interest. According to Keynes's theory of "liquidity preference," interest rates are determined not by flow demand and supply in barter capital markets but by the relative demands for a given quantity of money and the existing stock of alternative financial assets ("bonds"). For Keynes, interest rates were essentially a monetary phenomenon, determined in the money markets, and the direction of causality between the monetary economy and the real economy was explicitly reversed. However, if a critique of the accepted theory of interest rates was one of Keynes's main intended messages, it is obvious that the so-called Keynesian revolution did not succeed. The pre-Keynesian view of the determination of interest rates is once again a key component of the contemporary approach to monetary theory and policy. Most economists today believe that Keynes's main argument was that nominal wages can be "sticky" and pay little or no attention to Keynesian interest-rate theory.

A second post-Keynesian monetary theory, however, which is more straightforward, is simply that the short rate of interest is an exogenous policy-determined variable set by the central bank (Moore 1988, Kaldor 1986, Lavoie 1992a). In this case, both the monetary base and the money supply adjust endogenously, the "money supply function" being horizontal at the given interest rate.

Some of the "horizontalist" authors are critical of the original Keynesian liquidity preference theory on the grounds that it assumes a fixed exogenous quantity of money, somewhat similar to the monetarist view (Kaldor 1986: 21–4; Moore 1988: 171–208). As suggested earlier, the contrary view is that the endogeneity of money arises because central banks, committed to preserve the liquidity of the financial system, are obliged to provide the necessary reserves to support increases in the demand for credit, albeit at a price of their own choosing. Moreover, although some economists (such as Wray 1992: 13–21), in an attempt to reconcile endogenous money with Keynesian liquidity preference, have suggested that the supply curve of money should be taken as positively sloped rather than as horizontal, the latter position is persuasively defended by Lavoie (1992a: 197–203).[4]

Of the two "monetary" theories of the rate of interest, it is clearly the argument that the interest rate is an exogenous policy-determined variable that is most directly relevant to the interpretation of the actual conduct of Canadian monetary policy in recent years as sketched out above.

THE POWER OF THE CENTRAL BANK

Even granted central bank control over nominal short rates in their own national jurisdictions, however, this still leaves plenty of room for debate as to how extensive central bank control over the whole structure of rates, including long rates, might be. There is room for debate also about precisely how interest rate changes do affect inflation, output, employment, exchange rates, and other key economic variables. If there is no natural rate of interest, and the central bank can control the short rate of interest because of its monopoly in the provision of the basic monetary asset, the possibility immediately arises that monetary policy will be profoundly non-neutral. However, the full implications of this for the conduct of monetary policy may still be resisted, on the grounds that even if there is no natural rate per se, there must still be some fundamentals, operating either at the level of the domestic economy or the international economy, which put limits on how far central bank manipulation of interest rates is feasible.

In contemporary conditions, a preliminary point that can obviously be made is that central bank power to control short rates of interest should be thought of as control over real rates. Although the proximate monetary policy instrument will be changes in the nominal rate, central bank officials can and do form expectations about inflation. For any given setting of the nominal rate, they will be well aware of the implications for the ex-ante real short rate as defined on the inflationary expectations derived from the estimates of their forecasting departments.

Moreover, in the absence of a natural rate of interest, it can also be argued that central bank policy over short real rates must ultimately influence the entire structure of interest rates in the economy, including long rates. According to the expectations theory of the term structure, the long rate is simply a reflection of the expected future time path of short rates. Although, in practice, this obviously allows for a wide range of outcomes for the yield curve (depending on what expectations actually are, and also on liquidity preference considerations which may periodically insert a "wedge" between interest rates directly under central bank control and those elsewhere in the system), the implication is nonetheless that a sufficiently determined and consistent policy by the central bank regarding the general level of real interest rates will eventually achieve its objective, whatever that happens to be.[5] The real economy must adjust to the policy-determined interest rate, rather than vice versa. This is therefore the precise opposite of the natural rate doctrine.

The reason that central banks possess an extraordinary degree of power is inherent in the nature of a monetary production economy. Such a system has far greater productive power than a implausible barter mechanism. However, the logic of the credit system inevitably confers great power on the institution responsible for issuing the key monetary asset, whether the central position is achieved by governmental legislation or otherwise. Essentially, at least within a closed monetary network, the central institution can dictate the terms on which production is permitted to expand. The set of ideas and doctrines which influence central bankers and shift their perceptions of the scope and objectives of monetary policy therefore have serious consequences for the economic well-being of the whole society.

COMPETING MONETARY NETWORKS IN THE INTERNATIONAL ECONOMY

In the case of a small open economy such as Canada, there is also always the further argument that the hands of the domestic monetary authorities are tied by international economic conditions, and that domestic policy decisions are in effect subject to a veto by international bondholders. The Canadian economy is often described as actually the classic textbook case of the "small open economy," with the implication that domestic interest rates are primarily determined, in practice, by what is happening in financial markets in the United States.

These considerations lead directly to the question of how interest rates are actually determined in an international system in which the balance of payments, capital flows, and exchange rates must be taken into account.

The international economy can be seen as the interaction of a number of competing monetary networks, not necessarily confined to the boundaries of political nation states, each centred on a particular central bank. Within each network, the central banks set interest rates, provide reserves, and generally dictate the terms on which monetary production can be undertaken. In general, each central bank has at least some degree of independent power, if only because promises-to-pay denominated in different currencies will never be perfect substitutes. Naturally, the degree of power possessed by each central bank will vary and it is likely that there will be a hierarchy of central banks in the international sphere just as there is between financial institutions within a given national network (Dow and Smithin 1991). Whatever the degree of independence in each individual case, this will be abandoned if there is commitment either to join a fixed exchange rate regime, or, obviously, a common currency area.

The key question for present purposes is whether, in the context of the "managed" or "dirty" float that has been in place since the breakdown of the Bretton Woods system in 1971–73, it is possible for the "small" or "medium-sized" open economy to pursue an independent monetary policy in the sense of lower real rates of interest than those prevailing elsewhere. If not, it would hardly be reasonable either to praise or blame the Bank of Canada for interest rate outcomes in the domestic economy, as these would be simply a reflection of what is happening elsewhere.

The usual answer has been that a "made-in-Canada" interest policy is not realistic, given the relative sizes of the economies of Canada and the United States. In support of this point of view, moreover, it is obviously true that interest rate changes (and economic events in general) in the two countries are often highly correlated, and also that the capital markets of Canada and the United States are highly integrated and satisfy most tests of "perfect capital mobility." There remains a serious question, nonetheless, as to whether the similarities in the conduct of economic policy always occur from economic necessity or simply from shared ideas at particular junctures of history, and hence ultimately from deliberate decisions on the part of Canadian policy-makers to follow the lead of the United States.

There is now also the argument that contemporary structural changes in the world economy, particularly in financial markets, are conspiring to make the constraints ever more binding. Particular stress is laid on contemporary technological or regulatory changes in financial markets that have vastly increased and facilitated international capital movements. These trends have supposedly established an effective "global capital market" which undermines any attempt by an individual jurisdiction at an independent policy. Interestingly enough, it is not usually made clear just who does set monetary policy and interest rates in this environment. Presumably the idea is that there is some kind of global "natural rate" fixed by demand and supply for capital at the world level.

There are, however, a number of alternative arguments which suggest reasons for questioning the conventional view. One point that can immediately be made is that the growth of capital mobility in the modern era does *not* seem to have equalized real interest rates through the world (Frankel 1992). In a regime of a "managed" or "dirty" float, expected exchange rate changes and the uncovered interest differential provide the necessary degrees of freedom for this to occur.[6] Furthermore the era of "globalization" in capital markets has coincided with a period in which central bank policy on interest rates in the separate jurisdictions has apparently been more decisive than ever in its impact on their respective economies. What the changes in capital markets have done, of course, is to greatly increase the *responsiveness* of capital movements to changes in interest rates and other policy indicators, ensuring that it is developments in the capital account that are the driving force for the evolution of the national balance of payments rather than the current account. If anything, however, this would tend to reinforce the view that domestic monetary policy is of crucial importance rather than the reverse.

In a paper that allows for perfect capital mobility but does not treat claims denominated in different currencies as perfect substitutes, Paschakis and Smithin (1992) have shown that, in fact, it *is* theoretically feasible for a small- or medium-sized open economy to pursue an independent policy on real interest rates, even in modern conditions. If the national monetary authorities do succeed in depressing real interest rates to a lower level than that which prevails elsewhere, then this will certainly imply a real depreciation of the currency and an increase in the real net foreign credit position. The key point, however, is that the process is *not* necessarily unstable. The increase in the foreign credit position may actually have a beneficial impact on the risk premium demanded by foreign investors to hold assets denominated in the domestic currency (Branson 1988) and this enables the gap between foreign and domestic real interest rates to be maintained. The analysis applies in reverse for a nation that pushes real interest rates up to higher levels than those elsewhere.

If this analysis is correct, statements by the domestic monetary authorities to the effect that they should not be blamed for high interest rates because these are determined on "world markets" would not be valid. Even if, in practice, high real rates do emerge from (say) a defence of the exchange rate, the authorities do have a choice in the matter. It would be feasible to have a lower domestic real rate of interest than prevails elsewhere, as long as the authorities are willing to live with a depreciated real exchange rate (which in any event will be good for exports) and a higher proportion of foreign assets in the portfolios of domestic residents.

INTEREST RATE CHANGES, OUTPUT, INFLATION, AND EMPLOYMENT

It has been taken for granted in this chapter that high real interest rates are bad for the economy, in the sense that high real rates cause a reduction in output and employment, and that lower real rates are conducive to prosperity. There is unquestionably a strong correlation between ex-post real interest rates in Canada and the unemployment rate over the past two decades (Smithin 1994b).

However, it must be admitted that this prediction that high real interest rates reduce output is obviously not unassailable at the theoretical level (Lavoie 1992b). For example, some economists have used arguments from capital theory to suggest that there is no predictable relationship between changes in real interest rates and real investment expenditures, and hence no predictable relationship between interest rates and output. At the other extreme, supply-side models based on intertemporal substitution in labour supply actually predict a *positive* relation between interest rate and output, as higher interest rates are believed to stimulate work effort.

It should therefore be stressed that the view taken here that high real interest rates will tend to reduce output and employment, is ultimately based essentially on recent historical experience, and specifically on the monetary-policy-induced recessions that have occurred in Canada and other jurisdictions over the past twenty years. Whenever real interest rates have been driven up in the pursuit of what have been thought to be "monetarist" or stringent anti-inflation policies, recession and mass unemployment have been the result. The straightforward conclusion that emerges is that much of this could have been avoided by a commitment to stabilize real interest rates at more moderate levels.

Recent experience has also made clear the basic channel by which monetary policy can affect the inflation rate. High real interest rates reduce output and employment and hence lower inflationary pressures by increasing economic insecurity and undermining the bargaining position, in negotiating wage and price contracts, of groups other than rentiers. This mechanism hardly offers a permanent solution to the problem of inflation, however. In the immediate aftermath of a "tight money" recession, it may be possible to achieve non-inflationary growth for a few years while memories of the debacle are still fresh in the minds of those involved in the price-setting and wage-bargaining process. However, it is inevitable that, as the years pass, this restraining element will weaken, unless periodic doses of high real interest rate "discipline" are reapplied.

Instead of deliberately inducing this type of destabilizing cycle, the most sensible "rule" for central banks to follow would be to attempt to stabilize real interest rates at low but still positive levels. This would eliminate the damage to the real economy that central banks can currently inflict by driving real rates up to very high levels. On the inflation front, even though this rule would obviously not squeeze all inflationary pressures out of the system, it would at least avoid the severe inflationary episodes that ensue when real interest rates are allowed to become negative, as in the 1970s.

Although this policy advice would no doubt be considered heterodox in many quarters, during 1994 there was actually some evidence that the United States Federal Reserve itself was starting to think in terms of real interest rate targets. The public justification for nominal interest rate hikes during that year was the need to restore *real* short rates to their "historic average" of around 2 percent (*Economist* 1994). It is true that the motivation in this case was the fear of the inflation that might result with a real rate below that level, rather than the unemployment that might be caused if they rose much above it. Nonetheless, from the point of view taken in this chapter, the mere mention of real interest rates in this context was a significant development.

Exactly what a reasonable real interest rate target might be in other jurisdictions would obviously depend on the concrete circumstances in each case. However, historical precedent (for example, the experience of the quarter-century after World War II in the developed industrial nations) does seem to suggest that short real rates in the 2-percent to 3-percent range have been consistent with healthy economic growth, high employment, and moderate inflation.

CONCLUSION

In a monetary production economy, money is non-neutral almost by definition. Monetary policy, in the sense of central bank control over real financial interest rates is an important determinant of the terms on which production can be undertaken.

As illustrated by recent Canadian experience, the implication is that aggressive anti-inflation or "disinflation" policies, involving central bank action that drives real interest rates to very high levels, are potentially much more dangerous for the real economy than their protagonists may have realized. Their willingness to conduct this type of policy must rest on the widespread acceptance of theories that focus on the impact of central bank activity on inflation and downplay or ignore the impact on employment and growth. The experiences of the 1980s and early 1990s show that it is always possible to "cure" inflation by provoking a sufficiently severe recession in real economic activity. What they also show, however, is that recovery of the real economy from such episodes can be painfully slow, particularly if the adequacy of that recovery is measured by the impact on the national unemployment rate.

A more sensible course of action for the central bank to follow would be to stabilize real interest rates at low but still positive levels. This would represent a more viable "monetary policy rule" than many which have been suggested in the past, including both quantitative rules over the rate of growth of base money and the attempted pegging of nominal rates.

In order for the central bank in a separate jurisdiction to retain some independent control over interest rate policy, there would have to be a "managed" or "dirty" floating regime for exchange rates. It would be necessary to avoid a strategy that places too much weight on short-run exchange rate behaviour and hence allows real interest rates to be determined elsewhere.

ACKNOWLEDGMENTS

I am grateful to the editors for a number of comments and suggestions which have improved this paper.

NOTES

1 As measured by either the Consumer Price Index (CPI) or the GDP deflator.
2 This is not to deny the obvious fact that there have been many other serious economic problems facing Canada in addition to the conduct of monetary policy. These include supply-side problems and microeconomic inefficiency in many sectors, a heavy burden of taxation, and the impact of political uncertainty on investment. However, it is implied that many of these difficulties are more likely to show up in the erosion of living standards over time than in the aggregate employment picture.
3 A recent issue of the *Bank of Canada Review* (1992/93: 3–4) states that "monetary policy operations during 1992 were designed to guide short-term rates lower." This language would seem to indicate that Bank of Canada officials also concede that the bank can control short-term interest rates.
4 The basic argument is that although there may be subjective limits to bank lending, reflected in higher interest charges or credit rationing, at the microeconomic level of the individual bank and client, the same restrictions do not apply to the overall system expanding in concert.
5 Everyday experience confirms that long rates often stay high when short rates fall or vice versa. Nonetheless, over the long haul, most interest rates in the system do move together.
6 In the specific case of Canada, Murray and Khemani (1990) have concluded that increased international capital mobility has not affected the Bank of Canada's ability to conduct monetary policy along traditional lines. In their paper, the exposition of the way in which monetary

policy works is the traditional one, and the authors take long-run neutrality for granted. Nonetheless, the transmission mechanism that is envisaged explicitly includes changes in Canadian real interest rates, relative to those in the United States, in the short to medium term.

REFERENCES

Bank of Canada. 1992/93. "Recent Economic and Financial Developments," *Bank of Canada Review*, Winter: 3–21.

Branson, W.M. 1988. "Sources of Misalignment in the 1980s." In R.C. Marston, ed., *Misalignment of Exchange Rates: Effects on Trade and Industry* (Chicago: University of Chicago Press).

Courchene, T.J. 1982. "Recent Canadian Monetary Policy 1975–81: Reflections of a Monetary Gradualist." Queens University Discussion Paper No. 505.

Dow, S.C., and J.N. Smithin. 1991. "Change in Financial Markets and the 'First Principles' of Monetary Economics." University of Stirling Discussion Paper in Economics.

Economist. 1994. "America's Bond Market: Much Ado About Nothing." March 20: 92–4.

Fama, E.F. 1975. "Short-term Interest Rates as Predictors of Inflation." *American Economic Review* 65: 269–82.

Frankel, J.A. 1992. "International Capital Mobility: A Review." *American Economic Review* 82, May: 197–202.

Friedman, M. 1968. "The Role of Monetary Policy." *American Economic Review* 58, March: 1–17.

– 1974. "A Theoretical Framework for Monetary Analysis." In R.J. Gordon, ed., *Milton Friedman's Monetary Framework: A Debate with his Critics*. Chicago: University of Chicago Press.

Goodfriend, M. 1993. "Interest Rate Policy and the Inflation Scare Problem: 1979–92." *Federal Reserve Banka of Richmond Economic Quarterly* 79, No. 1: 1–24.

Goodhart, C.A.E. 1989. "Monetary Base." In J. Eatwell, M. Milgate, and P. Newman, eds., *The New Palgrave: Money*. London: Macmillan.

Hicks, J.R. 1989. *A Market Theory of Money*. Oxford: Oxford University Press.

Kaldor, N. 1986. *The Scourge of Monetarism*, 2nd ed. Oxford: Oxford University Press.

Keynes, J.M. 1936. *The General Theory of Employment Interest and Money*. London: Macmillan.

Lavoie, M. 1984. "The Endogenous Flow of Credit and the Post Keynesian Theory of Money." *Journal of Economic Issues* 18 (September): 771–97.

– 1992a. *Foundations of Post-Keynesian Economic Analysis*. Aldershot: Edward Elgar.

– 1992b. "Interest Rates and Kaleckian Growth Models." University of Ottawa Working Paper No. 9214E.

Lipsey, R.G., ed. 1990. *Zero Inflation: The Goal of Price Stability.* Toronto: C.D. Howe Institute.

McCallum, B.T. 1991. "Inflation: Theory and Evidence." NBER Reprint No. 1581.

Mishkin, F.S. 1984. "The Real Rate of Interest: A Multi-country Empirical Study." *Canadian Journal of Economics* 17 (May): 283–311.

Moore, B.J. 1988. *Horizontalists and Verticalists: The Macroeconomics of Credit Money.* Cambridge: Cambridge University Press.

Murray, J., and R. Khemani. 1990. "International Interest Rate Linkages and Monetary Policy: A Canadian Perspective," Bank of Canada Technical Report No. 52.

Paschakis, J., and J.N. Smithin. 1992. "Is an Independent Monetary Policy an Option for the Medium-sized Open Economy?" Paper presented at the International Conference on Economic Integration between Unequal Partners, Athens, Greece, August.

Smithin, J.N. 1990. *Macroeconomics after Thatcher and Reagan: The Conservative Policy Revolution in Retrospect.* Aldershot: Edward Elgar.

– 1994a. *Controversies in Monetary Economics: Ideas, Issues and Policy.* Aldershot: Edward Elgar.

– 1994b. "Cause and Effect in the Relationship Between Budget Deficits and the Rate of Interest." *Economies et Sociétés, Monnaie et Production* 28, Nos. 1–2: 151–69.

Smithin, J.N., and B.M. Wolf. 1993. "What Would be a 'Keynesian' Approach to Currency and Exchange Rate Issues?" *Review of Political Economy* 5, No. 3: 365–83.

Wicksell, K. 1898; 1965. *Interest and Prices,* translated by R.F. Kahn (New York: A.M. Kelley).

Wray, L.R. 1992. "Alternative Approaches to Money and Interest Rates." *Journal of Economic Issues* 26, No. 4: 1–33.

4 Using the NAIRU as a Basis for Macroeconomic Policy: An Evaluation

MARK SETTERFIELD

In recent years, the policy focus of the Bank of Canada has been dominated by the rate of inflation. At a practical level, the most concrete reflection of this has been the bank's pursuit of restrictive monetary policy. At a theoretical level, the concern over inflation has been reflected by the primacy of the NAIRU (non-accelerating inflation rate of unemployment) in the bank's macroeconomic thought.

Succinctly defined, the NAIRU represents an equilibrium rate of unemployment defined in terms of supply-side variables at which the rate of inflation is unchanging over time.[1] According to NAIRU theory, this unique and stable unemployment rate is the only one at which wages and prices will not accelerate (or decelerate) without limit. There is no trade-off (at least in the long run) between inflation and unemployment: the Phillips curve is vertical in inflation/unemployment space. The policy implications of NAIRU analysis are quite straightforward: once-over increases or reductions in the level of demand can have no permanent effect on the level of unemployment. Monetary and fiscal policies, having no beneficial or adverse affects on the real economy in the long run, should therefore be oriented towards the reduction and/or stabilization of the rate of inflation.[2] It is this thinking that currently dominates Canadian macroeconomic policy.

Despite the technical sophistication of NAIRU theory, it is clear that the NAIRU is most profoundly a policy issue. The purpose of this chapter is to offer a critique of the NAIRU, designed to illustrate the weaknesses of this concept as a policy parameter. In the second section, the recent attitude of the Bank of Canada towards the NAIRU is examined. The following section discusses anomalies and flaws in the construction and behavioural postulates of NAIRU theory, and the phenomenon of hysteresis, which questions the very existence of a unique equilibrium rate of unemployment. In the fourth section, emphasis is placed on empirical issues in the context of the Canadian economy. These include difficulties associated with estimating the value of the NAIRU, and most importantly, evidence on the existence of the NAIRU and the relationship between long-run unemployment and aggregate demand. Finally, the last section offers some conclusions, the main one being that the NAIRU is unsuitable for use as a macroeconomic policy parameter in Canada.

THE NAIRU AND THE BANK OF CANADA

A representative example of the attitude of the Bank of Canada towards the NAIRU is found in Rose (1988). Rose argues that the accelerationist hypothesis associated with the vertical Phillips curve, which moved to prominence as a result of theoretical developments during the 1960s and the increasing concern with inflation as a policy issue during the 1970s, now represents a broad consensus amongst economists. Hence for Rose, the debate over fluctuations in the level of unemployment is bounded at either extreme by different interpretations of the relationship between the actual rate of unemployment and the NAIRU. New classical models claim that any change in the actual rate of unemployment (even in the short run) is explained by changes in the NAIRU in response to supply-side shocks. "Keynesian" models, meanwhile, allow for the possibility of short-run disequilibrium: the actual rate of unemployment may deviate from the NAIRU in the short run in response to fluctuations in aggregate demand. However, there is (apparently) no disagreement that in the long run, the rate of unemployment is determined on the supply side by the NAIRU.

In his assessment of the empirical literature, Rose points out that a range of point estimates of the NAIRU exists. An "element of judgment" is therefore necessary in order to determine the value of the NAIRU at any point in time. Rose vests sufficient faith in this process to claim at the time of writing that the NAIRU in Canada in the mid-1980s was approximately 8 percent.

Similar confidence in the concept of the NAIRU, and the ability of applied economists to measure it, is displayed by other staff members at the Bank of Canada. In their advocacy of the zero-inflation target, both Selody (1990) and Cozier and Wilkinson (1990) rely on the existence of and ability of the bank to know the NAIRU when insisting that the costs of deflationary monetary policies are of a strictly short-run nature.

The Bank of Canada combines a faith in NAIRU theory as a legitimate and broadly consensual approach to macroeconomic theorizing with a belief that econometric estimates of the NAIRU are sufficiently robust that, when combined with the correct "element of judgment," they will yield an estimate of the NAIRU that may be used to guide macroeconomic policy. These beliefs motivated the bank's commitment to a restrictive monetary policy in the late 1980s. High interest rates were employed to reduce the demand for money and rein in what were identified as demand-side inflationary pressures in an economy believed to be operating below its NAIRU.

TOWARDS A CRITIQUE OF THE NAIRU CONCEPT: THEORETICAL ISSUES

In spite of the claims made by Rose (1988), considerable scepticism has been expressed about the existence and/or stability of the NAIRU. A number of theoretical considerations question the propensity of the labour market to gravitate towards a long-run equilibrium level of unemployment determined by exogenously given supply-side variables.

The first problem for the NAIRU "consensus" concerns the determination of a long-run unemployment equilibrium in the context of the Phillips curve.[3] The NAIRU is conventionally calculated from a reduced-form price inflation Phillips curve of the form:

$$(1) \qquad \dot{p} = \alpha \dot{p}^e + \beta U + Z \gamma$$

where $\dot{p}$ is the rate of inflation, $\dot{p}^e$ is the expected rate of inflation, U is the rate of unemployment, and Z is a vector of other variables such as barriers to labour mobility, the rate of productivity growth, the level of trade union activity, etc., which affect wage-and-price setting behaviour. In the steady state, with $\dot{p} = \dot{p}^e$, and assuming that $\alpha = 1$, equation (1) can be solved to yield:

$$(2) \qquad \text{NAIRU} = U^* = \frac{-Z^* \gamma}{\beta}$$

where an asterisk (*) represents the steady-state value of a variable.[4] What equation (2) reveals, however, is that this solution process, which depends primarily on the assumption that $\alpha = 1$, is quite independent of the factors that ultimately influence the equilibrium level of unemployment (the components of the vector Z.) The NAIRU is thus exposed to the abuses of ad hoc theorizing; the vector of variables Z, and consequently the value of the NAIRU, can be arbitrarily adjusted without affecting the procedure for solving equation (1) outlined above. This has obvious empirical and policy ramifications. As long as plausible arguments can be made in favour of adding variables to or omitting variables from the vector Z, the estimated value of the NAIRU can always be reconciled with the current average actual rate of unemployment, in a manner that accommodates rather than tests prior theoretical and policy preferences concerning unemployment.

A second problem concerns a contradiction caused by the behavioural postulates of NAIRU theory. Unlike Friedman's natural rate of unemployment, the NAIRU need not be associated with labour-market clearing (see, for example, Layard, Nickell, and Jackman 1991, and endnote 1 above). Unemployment at the NAIRU may therefore be either voluntary or involuntary in nature, or some combination of the two.

However, most NAIRU models based on wage-and-price equations calculate the NAIRU by assuming that, in the long run, workers and firms do not confuse general and relative price changes.[5] The stability of the NAIRU in these models depends implicitly (the dynamics are seldom explicitly formalized) on the adjustment of expectations to satisfy the afore-mentioned criterion.[6] A once-over increase in aggregate demand may cause unemployment to fall below the NAIRU in the short run, if "price surprises" generate expectational error. But aggregate demand reduces unemployment only as long as workers are "fooled" into accepting lower real wages. This behaviour is consistent with the assumption that workers engage in "real wage bargaining," permanently adjusting the quantity of labour they supply only in response to changes in the real wage.

The difficulty this creates is that if involuntary unemployment exists at the NAIRU, workers whose labour supply is demand-constrained will be willing to increase the amount of labour they supply at or below the going real wage (Cornwall 1990). This is illustrated in Figure 1 below, which depicts a classical labour market exhibiting involuntary unemployment (N" − N') at the (externally determined) employment/real wage combination (N', w').

It is clear from the construction of Figure 1 that employment can be expanded up to the point N* at or below the going wage w', since the jobless will be willing to supply labour up to N* at wages in the interval between w" and w*. A once-over increase in demand will

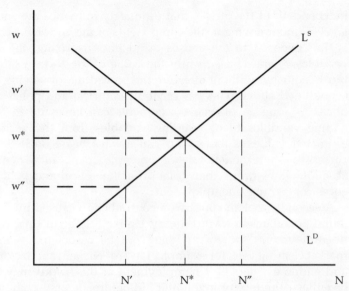

Figure 1
Involuntary Unemployment and the Willingness of the Unemployed
to Work

therefore permanently lower the rate of unemployment, even if the
going real wage falls in the process. Involuntary unemployment is
inconsistent with the notion of real wage bargaining, on which the
stability properties of many NAIRU models are implicitly based.

One of the most important recent criticisms of NAIRU theory arises
from the possibility that unemployment may be subject to hysteresis
effects. Hysteresis implies that the rate of unemployment at any given
point in time depends on previous levels of the actual unemployment
rate. This will occur when the determinants of the NAIRU are functionally related to past levels of the unemployment rate. Hence high
levels of unemployment may be associated with the scrapping of
physical capital, which can affect the quantity constraints on individual labour supply. High unemployment may also lead to the erosion
of human capital, especially where the latter comprises a significant
element of firm-specific skills. Furthermore, to the extent that rising
unemployment is associated with an increase in the duration of
unemployment spells, we may observe factors associated with negative duration dependence. The unemployed may become demoral-
ized, or lose valuable informal contacts within the labour market,
which may reduce the effectiveness of their search. In addition, long

spells of unemployment may act as negative credentials, which adversely affect workers' chances of finding new employment.

Hysteresis may also operate via structural features of the labour market. Blanchard and Summers (1987) argue that in an insider-outsider model, any increase in unemployment that changes the proportion of insiders to outsiders will result in a commensurate increase in the equilibrium rate of unemployment.

The implications of hysteresis for the NAIRU can be demonstrated by combining a formal characterization of this process with the accelerationist hypothesis.[7] Following Hargreaves Heap (1980), we can say that hysteresis exists when

$$(3) \quad U^*_{t+1} - U^*_t = -\delta(U^*_t - U_t) \, , \, \delta > 0 \, ,$$

i.e., when the change in the NAIRU in any period is inversely proportional to the excess of the NAIRU over the actual level of unemployment in the previous period. The accelerationist hypothesis, meanwhile, can be written as

$$(4) \quad \dot{p}_t - \dot{p}_{t-1} = \phi(U^*_t - U_t) \, , \, \phi > 0 \, .$$

This implies that inflation will be increasing (decreasing) when the level of unemployment is below (above) the NAIRU.

Suppose that in some initial period, the NAIRU, U^*, exceeds the actual rate of unemployment, U'. This will cause an acceleration of inflation (equation 4), but it will also lead to a subsequent fall in the NAIRU (equation 3). If in future periods, the NAIRU remains in excess of U', further increases in inflation and falls in the NAIRU will occur until the latter finally converges to the value U'.[8]

This relationship between the actual rate of unemployment, the NAIRU, and the rate of inflation is summarized by the reduced form of equations (3) and (4):

$$(5) \quad U^*_{t+1} - U^*_t = \frac{-\delta(\dot{p}_t - \dot{p}_{t-1})}{\phi} \, .$$

Equation 5 implies that an increase in the rate of inflation ($\dot{p}_t - \dot{p}_{t-1}$ > 0) will be associated with a subsequent decrease in the NAIRU – i.e., that a trade-off exists between the rates of unemployment and inflation. The reason for this is that when hysteresis exists, the NAIRU is indeterminate. No longer independent of past labour-market conditions, its value changes in response to variations in the actual rate of unemployment. In these circumstances, the concept of the NAIRU as a unique long-run equilibrium rate of unemployment ceases to have any useful meaning. The key determinants of the level of unemployment are the factors that affect the actual rate of unemployment in any period.

A CRITIQUE OF THE EMPIRICAL STATUS OF THE NAIRU IN CANADA

As intimated earlier, the survey by Rose (1988) acknowledges that a variety of point estimates of the NAIRU exist. Nevertheless, an "element of judgment" is all that is deemed necessary to overcome this problem, and to enable us to determine the value of the NAIRU in Canada. It is perhaps surprising, then, to find that the NAIRU estimates for the mid-1980s surveyed by Rose (1988: 42) vary from 6.2 percent to 11.5 percent – a range of over 5 percentage points.[9] In light of this formidable spread, Canadians excluded from the Bank of Canada's decision-making process might be forgiven for hoping that the bank's "element of judgment" is nothing short of divine.

The variability of the NAIRU estimates in Rose's ad hoc survey illustrates an important point about the empirical performance of NAIRU models. As demonstrated more rigorously by Setterfield, Gordon, and Osberg (1992), statistically satisfactory NAIRU models produce point estimates of the NAIRU that cover virtually the entire range of unemployment rates experienced by Canada during the postwar years.[10] This suggests that virtually any feasible unemployment rate could be interpreted as representing the NAIRU in Canada.

Even if the NAIRU exists, then, it is questionable whether it can be known with sufficient accuracy to make it a useful parameter in macroeconomic policy formation. A still more fundamental question, however, is whether the NAIRU does indeed exist: are quantity outcomes in the labour market dominated by a unique long-run equilibrium rate of unemployment determined on the supply side of the economy?

In order to pursue this question, it is useful to concentrate on the properties of a specific NAIRU model. The following reduced-form Phillips curve is analogous to the NAIRU estimating equation that Rose (1988) identifies with the Bank of Canada's RDXF model of the Canadian economy[11]:

$$(6) \qquad \dot{p}_t = v + \alpha \dot{p}_t^e + \beta U_t + Z_t \gamma$$

where for any period t, $\dot{p}$ denotes the rate of price inflation, $\dot{p}^e$ is the expected rate of inflation,[12] U is the unemployment rate and $Z_t =$

$[\dot{q}_t\ \dot{p}_{it}\ \theta]$ is a vector of variables comprising the rate of productivity growth $(\dot{q}_t)$, the rate of growth of the relative price of production to consumption $(\dot{p}_{it})$, and a wage/price controls dummy variable (θ). Setting $\alpha = 1$, and given that $\dot{p}_{it} = \theta = 0$ in the steady state, equation (6) can be solved for the NAIRU U^* as follows:

$$(7) \qquad U^* = \frac{-(v + \gamma_1 \dot{q}^*)}{\beta}$$

where an asterisk (*) denotes the steady-state value of a variable, and γ_1 is the first element in the column vector γ.

Estimating equation (6) using annual data from 1954 to 1987, we can calculate estimates of the prime-age male NAIRU from equation (7) for the period since the mid-1970s. The results of these estimates are reported in Table 1 below, where they are compared with the actual prime-age male unemployment rate in each year.

Looking at the annual statistics reported in Table 1, it is difficult to interpret the extent to which the estimated value of the NAIRU can be said to have varied with the actual rate of unemployment since the mid-1970s. The "change from previous period" in the NAIRU is of the same sign as the change in the actual rate of unemployment in five out of eleven cases. However, the period averages calculated at the bottom of Table 1 provide a clearer picture. Comparing 1982–87 with 1976–81, as the average value of the actual rate of unemployment increased over time, so too did the average value of the estimated NAIRU. What is less clear is which of these changes caused the other. Did the NAIRU increase during the 1980s in response to adverse supply-side conditions, pulling the actual rate of unemployment up behind it? In this scenario, the NAIRU can be seen as a "centre of gravity" towards which the economy is inevitably drawn, so that changes in the NAIRU explain changes in the actual rate of unemployment in the long run. Alternatively, was the estimated NAIRU simply tracking the actual rate of unemployment, which itself varied in response to changes in aggregate demand? In this scenario, the NAIRU is little more than a statistical artifact, whose numerical value responds passively to changes in actual macroeconomic conditions.

Following Jenkinson (1988), we approach these questions by eschewing the use of a structural model. Instead, we directly examine the equilibrium relationship implied by the RDXF NAIRU model in equation (7). The legitimacy of this equilibrium relationship is an issue of considerable importance. Recall that it is the determination of the NAIRU on the supply side that makes the long-run rate of unemployment invariant with respect to changes in aggregate

Table 1

NAIRU Estimates and Actual Prime-age Male Unemployment Rates (UM) in Canada, 1976–87

Date	NAIRU	Change from Previous Period	UM	Change from Previous Period
1987	6.5	+	7.0	−
1986	6.1	+	7.6	−
1985	5.9	+	8.3	−
1984	5.4	−	8.9	−
1983	5.6	−	9.3	+
1982	6.3	−	8.2	+
1981	6.4	+	4.9	+
1980	5.7	+	4.8	+
1979	5.1	+	4.6	−
1978	4.7	+	5.2	+
1977	3.9	+	4.9	+
1976	3.1	N/A	4.2	N/A
1976–81	4.8	N/A	4.2	N/A
1982–87	6.0	+	8.2	+

demand, and gives rise to the policy implications with which the Bank of Canada has been preoccupied in recent years.

By treating equilibrium as a statistical property of the time series in the RDXF NAIRU model, the equilibrium relationship in equation (7) can be statistically tested using cointegration techniques.[13] When two (or more) time series are cointegrated, their fluctuations in relation to one another occur around some constant long-run "factor(s) of proportionality." In the case of economic time series, this behaviour is frequently interpreted as evidence of an equilibrium relationship between the time series (see, for example, Granger 1986). Since cointegration is a necessary condition for the existence of any long-run relationship between two (or more) variables, it can be interpreted as a necessary condition for the existence of a long-run equilibrium relationship such as that postulated in equation (7).

In order to test for cointegration, we must first determine the order of integration of the time series in which we are interested. A series can be said to be integrated of order d (denoted as $I(d)$) if it becomes stationary – that is, displays constant mean and variance – after it has been differenced d times. It is only plausible to postulate cointegrating relationships between variables that are integrated of identical order. Tables 2 and 3 below report Cointegrating Regression Durbin-Watson (CRDW) and Dickey-Fuller (DF) tests of the hypotheses that the RDXF NAIRU variables are $I(0)$ and $I(1)$ respectively. UM denotes the unemployment rate of prime-age males, DTFP is the rate

Table 2
Testing Whether NAIRU Variables Are $I(0)$

Variable	CRDW	DF^a	Box-Pierce Q^b
UM	0.252^c	-1.33	14.06
DTFP	0.155^c	-1.37	21.03
YGAP	0.801^d	-2.37	18.26

Notes: a $DF \sim \tau$; $\tau_{0.05} = -2.97$ with $n = 25$.
b $Q \sim \chi^2$; $\chi^2_{0.10} = 32.01$ with 23 d.f.
c $CRDW \sim R$; $R_{0.05} = 0.770$ with $n = 31$.
d $R_{0.05} = 1.069$ with $n = 21$.

Table 3
Testing Whether NAIRU Variables Are $I(1)$

Variable	CRDW	DF^a	Box-Pierce
UM	1.68^b	-4.68	15.28^c
DTFP	1.82^b	-4.92	17.10^c
YGAP	1.96^d	-4.68	20.85^e

Notes: a $DF \sim \tau$; $\tau_{0.05} = -2.97$ with $n = 25$.
b $CRDW \sim R$; $R_{0.05} = 0.770$ with $n = 31$.
c $Q \sim \chi^2$; $\chi^2_{0.10} = 32.01$ with 23 d.f.
d $R_{0.05} = 1.069$ with $n = 21$.
e $\chi^2_{0.10} = 30.81$ with 22 d.f.

of growth of the Bank of Canada's index of total factor productivity, and YGAP is a proxy for aggregate demand, measured as the difference between actual and potential output in any given year.[14] The significance of this latter variable will become apparent shortly.

Both the CRDW and DF statistics test the null hypothesis of non-stationarity, with critical values given by Sargan and Bhargava (1983) and Dickey and Fuller (1981) respectively. Tables 2 and 3 reveal that, judging by these criteria, all of the variables under consideration are $I(1)$.[15] We may therefore seek cointegrating relationships between the time series as a means of testing the nature of any long-run relationships between them.

Table 4 below reports CRDW and DF tests of the hypothesis that the time series comprising the RDXF NAIRU are cointegrated.

The results in Table 4 exclude t-statistics, as these will be biased. Given the hypothesized relationship between productivity growth and the rate of unemployment, DTFP is of correct sign. However, both the CRDW and DF tests reveal that we cannot reject the hypothesis that an RDXF NAIRU-type relationship does *not* actually exist. This implies that the concept of the NAIRU as a unique equilibrium rate

Table 4
Testing for Cointegration in the RDXF NAIRU Model of Unemployment[a]

Variable	Parameter Estimate
DTFP	−0.541
Constant	5.647
CRDW[b]	0.354
DF[c]	−1.58
Box-Pierce Q[d]	17.22

Notes: a Cointegrating regression: $UM_t = \alpha_o + \alpha_1 DTFP_t + \varepsilon_{1t}$.
b $R_{0.05} = 0.770$ with $n = 31$.
c $\tau_{0.05} = -2.97$ with $n = 25$.
d $\chi^2_{0.10} = 32.01$ with 23 d.f.

of unemployment and its policy implications may be highly misleading. In so doing, it provides evidence against the hypothesis that the
increased average rate of unemployment in Canada since the 1970s
can be explained by an increase in some supply-side determined
equilibrium rate of unemployment, towards which the economy
inevitably converges in the long run.

Our second hypothesis is that the NAIRU is essentially a statistical
artifact, which conceals a true long-run relationship between unemployment and the level of aggregate demand. In Table 5 below, we
enter YGAP, a proxy for aggregate demand conditions, into the RDXF
NAIRU cointegrating regression. This enables us to test that hypothesis that there is a long-run relationship between demand and the
rate of unemployment.

In Table 5, both DTFP and YGAP are correctly signed. More importantly, the absolute value of both the CRDW and DF statistics has risen
considerably by comparison with Table 4. Both statistics now reject
the hypothesis that there is no long-run relationship between the
variables in Table 5. Since aggregate demand plays a role in this
relationship, the results suggest that a once-over reduction in aggregate demand will increase the long-run rate of unemployment. We
may therefore conclude that the concept of the NAIRU as a long-run
equilibrium rate of unemployment determined on the supply side is
a spurious statistical artefact, which has served only to conceal the
true long-run relationship between aggregate demand and unemployment in the Canadian economy. The average rate of unemployment in Canada has increased since the 1970s because the *actual* rate
of unemployment has increased in response to depressed aggregate
demand conditions. This result is in keeping with the theory of
hysteresis discussed in the second section, according to which the
NAIRU is a function of past and contemporary values of the actual

Table 5
Does Aggregate Demand Affect the Long Run Rate of Unemployment?[a]

Variable	Parameter estimate
DTFP	−0.701
YGAP	−0.625
Constant	6.009
CRDW[b]	1.695
DF[c]	−3.97
Box-Pierce Q[d]	19.53

Notes: a Cointegrating regression: $UM_t = \beta_0 + \beta_1 DTFP_t + \beta_2 YGAP_{t-1} + \varepsilon_{2t}$.
   b $R_{0.05} = 1.069$ with $n = 21$.
   c $\tau_{0.05} = -2.97$ with $n = 25$.
   d $\chi^2_{0.10} = 30.81$ with 22 d.f.

rate of unemployment. As demand conditions vary, so the actual and hence the long-run rates of unemployment vary, giving rise to a long-run unemployment-inflation relationship similar to the original (negatively sloped) Phillips curve.[16] These results and conclusions are in keeping with, amongst others, those of Jenkinson (1988) for the United Kingdom, and Fortin (1991, 1996) for Canada.

CONCLUSION

The analysis in this paper suggests that considerable uncertainty attaches to the concept of the NAIRU. NAIRU theory suggests that there exists a unique equilibrium rate of unemployment consistent with stable inflation, which is determined on the supply side of the economy. According to this theory, aggregate demand affects unemployment only in the short run. In the long run, the rate of unemployment will always be equal to the NAIRU, and variations in demand will be reflected solely in changes in the rate of inflation. Prudent monetary authorities can, therefore, engineer "long-run gain" from the "short-run pain" necessary to deflate the economy and achieve low rates of inflation.

   In the second section, it was pointed out that amongst the numerous theoretical shortcomings of the NAIRU construct, the theory of hysteresis suggests that no such unique equilibrium rate of unemployment exists: with hysteresis, long-run unemployment is sensitive to past and present short-run values of the unemployment rate, which are in turn influenced by general macroeconomic conditions, i.e., the state of aggregate demand. The evidence presented in the third section corroborates this latter view. Cointegration tests indicate that Canadian data do not display the equilibrium relationship between unemployment and supply side variables that is assumed by the Bank of Canada's RDXF NAIRU. However, the same tests suggest that we cannot reject the hypothesis of a long-run relationship between unemployment and a vector of variables that includes aggregate demand.

These results imply that the NAIRU is a spurious statistical artefact, which serves no greater purpose than to conceal the relationship between long-run unemployment and aggregate demand in Canada. The policy implications of this conclusion are considerable: government policies that affect the level of aggregate demand can alter the rate of unemployment, even in the long run. This in turn implies that Canadians would reap sustained benefits in terms of reduced joblessness from expansionary monetary and/or fiscal policies designed to stimulate demand.

In light of recent experience, few Canadians need reminding of the income loss, economic insecurity, and social distress that accompanies unemployment. By rejecting the NAIRU and reasserting the influence of demand on long-run unemployment, this paper suggests that changes in macroeconomic policy can and should be used to alleviate these ills. An unfortunate corollary of this conclusion is that macroeconomic policy has been mislead in its quest for "long-run gain" arising from "short-run pain" – that the high unemployment suffered by Canada in recent years has, as the title of this volume suggests, been "all for nought."[17] That policy-makers at the Bank of Canada continue to argue the contrary is a matter of the utmost concern.

ACKNOWLEDGMENTS

The author would like to thank, without implicating, Brian MacLean, John Cornwall, and John Smithin for their comments on an earlier version of this paper.

NOTES

1 Although it has been argued that the distinction between the NAIRU
and the natural rate of unemployment is now largely semantic (Jenkinson 1987; Cross 1991), the concepts have substantially different origins. Friedman (1968: 8) defined the natural rate of unemployment as "the level that would be ground out by the Walrasian system of general equilibrium equations," and clearly intended it to involve the coincidence of two distinct equilibria: one defined in the labour market (full employment) and the other defined in terms of stable price inflation.

The concept of the NAIRU, however, was originally developed on the basis of price-making behaviour. It was also intended to admit the possibility of involuntary unemployment, although long-run unemployment is still *classical* in NAIRU models, since it is invariant with respect to changes in aggregate demand (Cornwall 1990). The NAIRU therefore distinguishes between the two equilibria assumed coincidental in the natural rate hypothesis. In fact, the NAIRU is devoid of implications for equilibrium in the labour market: it is simply a level of unemployment at which the rate of inflation is stable. These considerations suggest that we must exercise care when discussing equilibrium unemployment concepts. For this reason, it is important to note that the primary concern of this paper is the NAIRU, as previously defined.

2 Note that stabilization of the rate of inflation is not the same as pursuing a zero-inflation goal. Indeed most variants of NAIRU theory emphasize real costs associated with the latter that would not arise (in the absence of shocks) in the case of the former.

3 The Phillips curve can be seen as representing a consensus technology for calculating the NAIRU. See Setterfield, Gordon, and Osberg (1992).

4 Note that $\beta < 0$ in equation (2) so that the value of the NAIRU in (2) is always positive.

5 This is equivalent to the assumption that $\alpha = 1$ in equation (1).

6 Important exceptions can be found in the work of Layard and Nickel (see, for example, Layard, Nickell, and Jackman 1991: 16) in which the stability of the NAIRU depends on an explicitly postulated real balance effect.

7 The following characterization is preferred to the more conventional unit-root characterization, as the latter constitutes a special case representation of hysteresis. See Cross (1991, 1993) and Setterfield (1993, 1996, chap. 2).

8 At this point, the rate of inflation will reach its terminal value, which will be given by

$$\dot{p} = \dot{p}' + \frac{\phi(U^* - U')}{\delta}$$

where $\dot{p}'$ represents the rate of inflation in the initial period. See Hargreaves Heap (1980: 618).

Note that this simplified illustration produces results identical to the "full hysteresis" case in unit-root representations of hysteresis, in so far as it predicts that the NAIRU will converge to U' in the absence of other shocks (see Setterfield 1993: 348–51). However, the dynamics of equations (3) and (4) as described above abstract from the NAIRU's stability mechanism, which will presumably also be operating in each of the periods for which $U_t \neq U_t^*$. Allowing for some increment in U_t over time owing to a real balance effect, for example, would result in long-run convergence to a NAIRU U^{**} where $U' < U^{**} < U^*$. This will likely imply a terminal rate of inflation that differs from that given above. Hence the characterization of hysteresis in equations (3) and (4) can, under plausible conditions, generate hysteretic outcomes that cannot be accounted for by unit root models.

9 It is difficult to escape noticing how close Rose's preferred value of the NAIRU at this time (8 percent) is to the simple mean of these extreme values.

10 Setterfield, Gordon, and Osberg study prime-age male unemployment. A model nesting alternative hypotheses about the precise form of the NAIRU estimating equation produces statistically satisfactory NAIRU estimates ranging from 4.42 percent to 9.88 percent. Using Fortin's (1989) link equation, this suggests a range of NAIRUS for the labour force as a whole varying between 4.74 percent and 10.59 percent.

11 The bank uses a wage-inflation equation to estimate the NAIRU. We use a price-inflation equation since price inflation is the issue of macroeconomic welfare significance. Indeed, it is questionable whether estimates of the equilibrium rate of unemployment based on wage equations can usefully be interpreted as NAIRUS (see, e.g., Grubb, Jackman, and Layard 1982).

12 Inflation expectations are modelled as an eight-quarter moving average of the actual rate of inflation. See Rose (1988).

13 A brief summary of the rationale behind cointegration is provided below. For a more detailed account, see Granger (1986).

14 Potential output is calculated by the Bank of Canada using a Cobb-Douglas aggregate production function.

15 The Box-Pierce Q statistics test the null hypothesis that the error structure of the Dickey-Fuller test regression is white noise. Rejection of the null hypothesis would mean that the DF statistic is biased.

16 This relationship is captured in equation 5 above.

17 Smithin (1996) supports this view when noting that, in practice, recovery from policy-induced recessions does not take place automatically, but comes about only when fiscal and monetary authorities reverse their contractionary policies, having decided that recession has proceeded far enough. The return of the original inflationary problem follows in swift succession.

REFERENCES

Blanchard, O.J., and L.H. Summers. 1986. "Hysteresis and the European Unemployment Problem." In S. Fischer, ed. NBER Macroeconomics Annual, 15–78. Cambridge, Mass.: MIT Press.

- 1987. "Fiscal Increasing Returns, Hysteresis, Real Wages and Unemployment." *European Economic Review* 31: 543–66.
Cornwall, J. 1990. *The Theory of Economic Breakdown*. Oxford: Basil Blackwell.
Cozier, B., and G. Wilkinson. 1990. "How Large are the Costs of Disinflation in Canada?" Bank of Canada Working Paper.
Cross, R. 1991. "The NAIRU: Not an Interesting Rate of Unemployment?" University of Strathclyde, Mimeo.
- 1993. "On the Foundations of Hysteresis in Economic Systems." *Economics and Philosophy* 9: 53–74.
Dickey, D.A., and W.A. Fuller. 1981. "The Likelihood Ratio Statistics for Time Series with a Unit Root." *Econometrica* 49: 1057–72.
Fortin, P. 1989. "How Natural is Canada's High Unemployment Rate?" *European Economic Review* 33: 89–110.
- 1991. "The Phillips Curve, Macroeconomic Policy and the Welfare of Canadians." *Canadian Journal of Economics* 24: 774–803.
- 1996. "The Unbearable Lightness of Zero-Inflation Optimism." This volume.
Friedman, M. 1968. "The Role of Monetary Policy." *American Economic Review* 43: 1–17.
Granger, C.W.J. 1986. "Development in the Study of Cointegrated Variables." *Oxford Bulletin of Economics and Statistics* 48: 213–28.
Grubb, D., R. Jackman, and R. Layard. 1982. "Causes of the Current Stagflation." *Review of Economic Studies* 49: 707–30.
Hargreaves Heap, S.P. 1980. "Choosing the Wrong 'Natural' Rate: Accelerating Inflation or Decelerating Employment and Growth?" *Economic Journal* 90: 611–20.
Jenkinson, T. 1987. "The Natural Rate of Unemployment: Does it Exist?" *Oxford Review of Economic Policy* 3, No. 3: 20–6.
Jenkinson, T.J. 1988. "The NAIRU: Statistical Fact or Theoretical Straitjacket?" In R. Cross, ed., *Unemployment, Hysteresis, and the Natural Rate Hypothesis*. Oxford: Blackwell.
Layard, R., S.J. Nickell, and R. Jackman. 1991. *Unemployment: Macroeconomic Performance and the Labour Market*. Oxford: Oxford University Press.
Rose, D.E. 1988. "The NAIRU in Canada: Concepts, Determinants and Estimates." Bank of Canada Technical Report No. 50.
Sargan, J.D., and A. Bhargava. 1983. "Testing Residuals from Least Squares Regressions for Being Generated by the Gaussian Random Walk." *Econometrica* 51: 153–74.
Selody, J. 1990. "The Goal of Price Stability: A Review of the Issues." Bank of Canada Technical Report No. 54.
Setterfield, M.A. 1993. "Towards a Long Run Theory of Effective Demand: Modelling Macroeconomic Systems With Hysteresis." *Journal of Post-Keynesian Economics* 15: 347–64.

- 1996. *Rapid Growth and Relative Decline: Modelling Macroeconomic Systems with Hysteresis.* London, Macmillan, forthcoming.

Setterfield, M.A., D.V. Gordon, and L. Osberg. 1992. "Searching for a Will o' the Wisp: An Empirical Study of the NAIRU in Canada." *European Economic Review* 36: 119–36.

Smithin, J. 1996. "Real Interest Rates, Inflation and Unemployment." This volume.

PART TWO

Unemployment Insurance: Culprit or Not?

5 Unemployment Insurance and Unemployment – Revisited

LARS OSBERG

In the ongoing debate on the connection between unemployment insurance and unemployment, there are three very different levels of evidence in use.

1 The discussion of individual observations is called "case-study analysis" by sociologists, but although samples of one are disparaged as "anecdotes" by economists, their constant reappearance in the dialogue testifies to their importance, in practice, in shaping attitudes on unemployment insurance.
2 The increasing availability of micro-data on individuals has spawned a huge econometric literature on unemployment incidence and duration, in which unemployment insurance variables often appear. The cross-sectional variation in unemployment insurance parameters among individuals and the impact over time of changes in unemployment insurance on panels of respondents have been used as sources of non-experimental evidence on the impacts of unemployment insurance.
3 Analysis of macroeconomic time-series data has often included measures of unemployment insurance "generosity" as explanatory predictors of aggregate unemployment.

Each of these research methodologies has its own problems. Small samples clearly purchase the virtues of vividness at the expense of statistical representativeness. Micro-data can provide very large, statistically representative samples, but they are usually drawn as a sample of households selected from a census of residences. Since household samples can only provide crude information on the characteristics of employers (e.g., industry), the explanatory variables available in most micro-econometric studies are limited to the supply-side characteristics of individuals, to the exclusion of any possible demand-side influences of unemployment insurance on firm behaviours. Although unemployment insurance can plausibly be argued to offer incentives to firms to change their behaviour, most available micro-data can only test hypotheses about the changed behaviour of workers.[1] Micro-data analysis also suffers from the problem that large cross-sectional samples have often only been analysed at a single point in the business cycle, and their results cannot necessarily be generalized to behaviour at other phases of the macroeconomic business cycle, when jobs are easier, or more difficult, to find.[2] On the other hand, the panels of micro-data that could be used to track the behaviour of individuals over the business cycle have typically been too small to offer statistical reliability in the estimation of labour-market behaviour (see Gordon, Lin, Osberg, and Phipps 1994).

Although micro-econometric work has typically been very unconvincing in its treatment of the demand side of labour markets, it does have the great virtue that micro-data can link measures of particular behaviours by individuals to the particular incentives of unemployment insurance that are relevant to them. There is also a clear way of aggregating the behaviour (if correctly modelled) of different individuals. These virtues are lost in macroeconomic time-series analysis. Although time-series models may be capable of modelling, in a simultaneous equations structure, both the demand and the supply side of labour markets, they must, of necessity, use aggregate variables such as "average unemployment insurance generosity." People may care about the generosity of the unemployment insurance system to themselves personally, but no real individual can be expected to care about "average" generosity. Measures of average generosity can change in perverse ways, for reasons unconnected to changes in unemployment insurance. There is no clear way to aggregate the presumed micro-behaviour of individuals into macroeconomic aggregates and there are many examples of how aggregation may be invalid. Hence, the connection between microeconomic theorizing and macroeconomic hypothesis testing is, at best, tenuous.

In some quarters, the adverse impacts of unemployment insurance on unemployment are taken as large and self-evident.[3] However, it is hard to imagine how a system as complex as Canadian unemployment insurance could spend as much as it did in the early 1990s (almost $20 billion in 1992) without affecting the economy. The very size and complexity of the unemployment insurance system ensures that it will have *many* impacts on the economy – some good, some bad, and some ambiguous.

The ambiguity of recent research results on the impacts of unemployment insurance stands, moreover, in distinct contrast to the certainty of much popular opinion. How can one explain, (1) the ambiguity of recent research results, and (2) the coexistence of firmly held popular beliefs with such ambiguity?

The plan of this chapter is to discuss the impacts of unemployment insurance on unemployment at each of the three levels of analysis – anecdotal, micro-econometric, and macro-econometric. The section that follows presents a case study in which repeat usage of unemployment insurance has no effect on behaviour, in contrast with the mathematical anecdote discussed in the fourth section. The third section discusses why micro-econometric evidence on the impacts of unemployment insurance may be incomplete. Section four assesses the meaning to be attached to the use of aggregate measures of unemployment insurance generosity in macro-econometric time-series analysis. The final section is a conclusion.

A CASE STUDY OF REPEAT UNEMPLOYMENT INSURANCE USAGE

In documentary films of the mass unemployment of the 1930s, one sometimes sees footage of the "shape-up," in which scores of unemployed workers arrived at plant gates in time for the start of the day's shift. The best of the lot were picked over for the day's work by the "boss"; those not selected were sent on their way. In the 1990s, casual labour and day-to-day employment insecurity still exist, but one does not see similar scenes. Telecommunications and the greater sophistication of market intermediaries have sanitized the visuals. Today, casual labour needs are filled by the personnel department placing an order by phone or fax with a temporary-help agency, which sends an appropriately screened worker to the proper location at the exact time requested.

As part of a larger series of case studies of Nova Scotia employers, I interviewed workers at a major temporary-help agency (a multinational agency with offices in Halifax). "Ron" is a "light industrial worker" in his early twenties who left school after "almost" completing Grade 12. Working as a labourer at the flour mill, or setting up and taking down trade displays, he earns between $5.80 and $6.00 an hour, but works alongside permanent unionized workers making over twice his hourly wage rate. Ron observes that many of these permanent workers were hired on after initially working as temporaries, and his main objective is to get hired on full time. He believes that if he can establish a good work reputation, employers will ask for him by name from the agency, and when a permanent vacancy becomes available, he may have some chance at the job. As things stand, he must make a remarkable effort to get to work, since he has no car and must often hitchhike to remote job sites, getting up very early in order to be there for a job start at 7:00 A.M.

In the labour market of the 1960s, Ron might have been able to go directly into a permanent job but in the 1990s that option is not available. His work in setting up and taking down trade exhibitions is inherently subject to short-run surges in activity, and one can understand the need for temporary workers. However his work at the flour mill was steady and predictable. For both employers the temporary-help agency is functioning as a waiting room for permanent employment. A process of "double screening" is going on, since the agency selects temporary workers from the general pool of applicants, and firms get a chance to look over workers at length, with no fuss about terminating an individual worker, and no presumption that employment rights are being established. Firms are also able to hire labour at substantially less than the hourly cost of their permanent employees. In a period of prolonged recession, firms are under increased pressure to reduce the number of high-cost permanent employees, and they can find a continual supply of low-wage workers on a "temporary" basis.

Given that he often does not know from one day to the next whether work will be available, Ron has also developed an interesting pattern of reliance on unemployment insurance. He has nothing in the bank to tide him over the two-week waiting period at the start of an unemployment insurance claim and often faces days when no work is available. Because of this, as soon as Ron establishes eligibility for unemployment insurance, he opens a claim with the Unemployment Insurance Commission (UIC), and then declares to the commission any days of work that may become available at the temporary-help agency. Although his earnings while on unemployment insurance claim are taxed at an extremely high rate (currently earnings in excess of 25 percent of the benefit rate are deducted, dollar for dollar from unemployment insurance payments), his earnings are also building up an entitlement to the *next* unemployment claim. Furthermore, at Ron's level of income, every dollar is worth having, and it is crucial for him to get immediate income replacement for the days when work is unavailable. Ron has weeks when he gets no work, and weeks when he gets one or two days of work. In those weeks, unemployment insurance puts a floor to his weekly income. During weeks when he gets three to five days of work, he derives no current benefit from being on unemployment insurance claim (but does establish entitlement for a future claim, which protects him against low-demand weeks in the future). The fundamental fact is that Ron is a quantity-constrained worker – at his level of income, his cash needs are such that he will always accept work, if it is available.

If this were the only case, the story might be dismissed as unique, but I also interviewed fish plant and hotel workers who follow the same pattern of use of unemployment insurance. The long-established custom in the fish-processing industry is that workers bear the cost of any fluctuations in the supply of fish, since they are sent home, or not called in, when no fish is available for processing. Any available work is allocated by seniority. Poor catches or the late arrival of trawlers therefore mean that low-seniority workers frequently face short-term lay-offs on a day-by-day basis. Chambermaids in hotels often work on a similar basis – they are called in (in order of seniority) to clean rooms *if* those rooms have been occupied the previous night.

However, both they and Ron have a long-term perspective – by accepting work whenever it is available, they hope to work their way into greater job security (in Ron's case, by acquiring a reputation that will get him a permanent job, and in the case of the fish plant or hotel workers, by moving up in seniority, and thereby avoiding future lay-offs). In the meantime, these workers are repeatedly dependent on the unemployment insurance system – but in a very real sense, the system is accomplishing what it was originally set up to do, that is, it is tiding over a low-income worker for short periods when no work is available.

Insecurity of employment is increasingly characteristic of the Canadian labour market. The Economic Council of Canada defined "non-standard employment" as consisting of work within the temporary-help industry, own-account self-employment, part-time, short-term, and temporary arrangements. The council estimated that 28 percent of all employment in 1989, and 44 percent of all employment growth in the 1980s, was in non-standard employment forms (1991: 81). The stories of Ron or the fish plant or hotel workers are therefore useful as more than simply "antidote anecdotes" that make the point that constraints on job availability and long-term returns to employment stability are characteristic of modern labour markets. These case studies are also useful in reminding us that unemployment insurance still does play its classic role of bridging financial need in a labour market characterized by short-term insecurity in labour demand.

Furthermore, interviews with low-wage workers are a useful way of reminding economic researchers that these can be quite "normal" people. The people I interviewed had relatively unattractive options to choose from, but they were not stupid. They could see clearly the long-run implications of short-run behaviour – in particular, they knew that casual work had poorer pay and fewer fringe benefits than a permanent job, and that an unstable work history would destroy their chances of ever getting a reasonably good job. They knew that a local reputation for dependability and effort, or the protection of seniority, were particularly important for people such as themselves who lacked educational credentials or specialized skills. And they had very normal aspirations for a better material standard of living – they *did not like* living in crummy apartments with little or nothing in the bank. They also knew, from direct experience, that a lifetime of that is what a cycle of casual work and transfer dependence implies.

MICRO-ECONOMETRIC EVIDENCE ON THE RELATIONSHIP BETWEEN UNEMPLOYMENT INSURANCE AND UNEMPLOYMENT

Unemployment insurance in Canada has become a very complex system, with a volume of detailed regulations, and a growing body of case law interpreted by a mini-industry of adjudicators and lawyers. The incentives, penalties and provisions of unemployment insurance also interact with the details of income tax legislation and the provisions of other social welfare programs, in ways that differ by jurisdiction and labour market across Canada. One of the underrated advantages of case-study analysis is the fact that it can reveal the importance of the details of unemployment insurance regulations in a manner that might otherwise not be apparent to academic analysts.[4]

It is easy, however, to drown in detail. Both academics and politicians would like to find simple answers to simplified questions, such as, "Does a more generous unemployment insurance system cause increased unemployment?"[5] To answer such questions, one needs a theoretical framework (in order, for example, to define more clearly unemployment insurance "generosity") and a data set that is representative of the broader population.

Micro-data on individuals can be derived from administrative records or from surveys of the population. Since administrative records usually contain, naturally enough, only the information needed for administrative purposes, such data may lack many of the variables (such as years of education) that are thought to be important as predictors of individual labour-market outcomes. Internal unemployment insurance administrative records have the advantage of a very large sample size, but are not easily accessible to outsiders.[6]

Economists have therefore tended to rely on public-use micro-data from cross-sectional samples such as the Current Population Survey (United States) or the Labour Force Survey (Canada), or on panel studies, such as the Panel Study of Income Dynamics. In these surveys, a sample of households is selected from a census of residences, and respondents are questioned about labour-market outcomes (e.g., wage rate, unemployment experience, job tenure, and search strategies used) and background social and demographic characteristics (e.g., education, age, number of dependents, and spouse's labour-force status). It is inherent in this methodology that one cannot obtain data that is beyond the knowledge of the individual respondent. Individual respondents cannot supply reliable data on the variability in their employers' sales or the capital intensity of their employers' production processes. In a random sample of households, there is no way to identify whether other respondents are employed by the same firm and, as a consequence, there is no way to isolate employer-specific effects on unemployment incidence or duration. Although a wealth of detail can be gathered on the characteristics of individual respondents and the households to which they belong that might influence the decisions of individual workers, there is virtually no information available on the factors that might influence the decisions of firms.

Econometric analysis of micro-data can, therefore, test hypotheses about the supply-side behaviour of individual workers, but most micro-data cannot test hypotheses about the demand-side behaviour of firms.[7] Observed outcomes in the labour market always depend on both demand and supply – after all, employment is the *joint event* where a firm makes a job offer, which an individual accepts. However, since demand-side hypotheses on firm behaviour cannot be tested with standard micro-data, economists have tended to emphasize models of individual supply-side behaviour, and to assume demand-side problems out of existence. In the literature on unemployment insurance, the two most influential approaches have been labour/leisure choice models and search models.

Labour/leisure Choice Models of Unemployment Insurance

The demand side of labour markets disappears entirely in labour/leisure models of the impact of unemployment insurance, of the sort

82   Lars Osberg

represented in Figure 1. In this framework, weeks of work are assumed to be available to individuals in whatever amount they desire, at a constant weekly wage. It is assumed that interruptions in work history have no consequences, either now or in the future, for wages or job availability. Individuals are presumed either to be myopic, looking only one year into the future, or (equivalently) to choose perpetually recurring annual cycles of labour and leisure. There are presumed to be no constraints on individual choice, other than the unchanging weekly wage rate and the parameters of the unemployment insurance system – enforcement of the job search and job acceptance requirements of unemployment insurance legislation are presumed not to exist. Individuals are assumed to derive utility from the consumption of material goods and from leisure – unemployment is presumed to be equivalent to leisure, with no stigma or disutility.

If one is willing to buy all this, the income/leisure alternatives open to an individual without unemployment insurance can be represented as line AF in Figure 1, while an unemployment insurance scheme similar to the Canadian system can be represented as the line ABCDEF. People who work less than the minimum period required to qualify for unemployment insurance are unaffected by unemployment insurance, and this situation can be represented by line segment AB. Once individuals become eligible for unemployment insurance, they can receive an amount equal to the benefit replacement rate (B/W) times the number of weeks worked (for workers who just qualify for unemployment insurance benefits, this can be represented as the vertical distance BC in Figure 1) – this creates an income effect on labour supply.

Substitution effects arise from the impact of unemployment insurance on the marginal return to a week of work. If individuals are acquiring additional weeks of unemployment insurance entitlement at the rate of one week of additional entitlement for each week of work (line segment CD), the marginal return is $[(1 + B/W) *$ weekly wage], and the substitution effect of unemployment insurance is positive. When individuals must give up a week of benefits for each week of additional work (because weeks worked + weeks of unemployment insurance entitlement > 52) the marginal return is $[(1 - B/W) *$ weekly wage], and the substitution effect is negative. A two-week waiting-period for benefits, plus the assumption of an annual decision-making horizon, implies that people who work more than fifty weeks per year are unaffected by the unemployment insurance system (line segment EF).

Since the whole point of this approach is that individuals respond to the incentives of the unemployment insurance system, it is

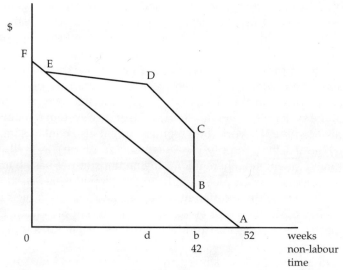

Figure 1

essential to model correctly those incentives. If wages or job availability in the future are put at risk by a history of unstable employment, clearly Figure 1 is not a good model of the incentives facing individuals. Figure 1 also represents a simplified model of the Canadian unemployment insurance system, and it is essential to represent accurately the actual incentives facing individuals. The work of Atkinson et al. (1984) remains a classic statement of the empirical importance of accurate representation of the unemployment insurance incentives facing individuals. As they conclude (25):

In the design of public policy, the use of empirical evidence on behavioral reactions is crucial – the alternative being reliance on anecdote and prejudice. However, it is essential that the empirical evidence be robust. "Robustness" does not mean that all estimates with different data must be identical, nor that simplifying assumptions are ruled out, nor that all sources of bias must be eliminated … In the present paper we have argued that the evidence about unemployment benefit and unemployment duration in Britain is far from robust. Despite the claims quoted at the beginning that the effect of benefits is "firmly established," the co-efficient turns out to be poorly determined – even within the framework of the earlier studies. There is considerable variation in the estimated elasticity when we consider alternative benefit variables, different specifications of the replacement rates, different time periods, and the inclusion/exclusion of family circumstances. With some combinations of assumptions, it is possible to reproduce the earlier finding of an elasticity around 0.6; with other – quite reasonable – formulations the estimated elasticity is not significantly different from zero. There is, therefore, substantial scope for the conclusions drawn to be influenced by prior beliefs.

The empirical importance of the incentives argument depends on accurate modelling of incentives, the magnitude of labour-supply elasticities, and the number of people affected by each characteristic of the system. The unemployment insurance system not only contains disincentives to work (line segment DE), it also contains incentives to *increased* labour supply (line segment AB or CD)[8] as well as regions (line segment EF) where unemployment insurance has no impact. The net impact of unemployment insurance depends on *how many* people are in each of these different situations and *how much* their behaviour changes. All the recent evidence on labour-supply elasticities argues that income and substitution elasticities of labour supply are very small.[9]

Phipps has demonstrated in a series of papers (see 1990a, 1990b, 1991a, 1991b, 1996) that utility-maximizing behaviour responds to incentives, but that such behaviour is also subject to constraints. She uses the framework of Figure 1 to ask whether better estimates of labour-supply behaviour can be obtained if one allows for the possibility that individuals may be constrained in the weeks of work that are available to them – the answer is unambiguously "yes." She also asks whether the supply-side incentives of the unemployment insurance system make much difference to individual behaviour, *given* that individuals may not be able to get all the weeks of work that they might desire at the going wage, and may not be able to increase labour supply when "incentives" increase – the answer is that unemployment insurance incentives have little impact on labour supply. Phipps and Osberg (1991) demonstrate that individuals respond in very different ways to the changed incentives created by unemployment insurance and by income taxation. More recently, Osberg and Phipps (1993) have reaffirmed the empirical importance of job availability as a constraint on the labour supply of Canadians.[10]

Search Models and the Impact of Unemployment Insurance on Unemployment

In search models of unemployment, an unemployed individual is represented as receiving job offers at some exogenous rate (λ) and as accepting those offers with some probability (P_a).

$$(1) \qquad P_a = 1 - F(w_r)$$

where F is the cumulative distribution function of the wage-offer distribution relevant to the individual and w_r is the reservation wage chosen by the individual. The probability of getting a job (P_{ue}) is then given by

$$(2) \quad P_{ue} = \lambda \cdot P_a .$$

In some respects, search theory is an elaborate expansion on the truism that the probability of an unemployed individual getting a job is equal to the probability that the individual will receive an offer times the probability that the individual will accept the offer – but it matters a good deal whether one emphasizes the determinants of the job-offer arrival rate (λ) or the job-offer acceptance probability (P_a).

In their encyclopaedic survey of the search literature, Devine and Kiefer (1991) note that most studies have taken the job-offer arrival rate as exogenous and have concentrated their attention on the determinants of the reservation wage. Again, the demand side of the labour market disappears. (Devine and Kiefer in fact argue that since the available empirical evidence indicates that most unemployed workers accept the first job offer that they receive, the emphasis on supply-side decision making has been unfortunate, and more effort in future research should be placed on an examination of the determinants of offer arrival rates).

Most analyses of the impact of unemployment insurance on the search process see a more generous unemployment insurance system as decreasing the relative cost of remaining unemployed and thereby increasing the reservation wage, which implies an increase in the probability of remaining unemployed, an increase in the average post-unemployment wage rate, and an increase in the average duration of an unemployment spell.[11] Devine and Kiefer (1991: 304), however, conclude as follows:

The difficult issue of the effect of unemployment benefits on unemployment durations is still unsettled. Estimates vary across samples and there is evidence that the benefit effect varies with labour market conditions (responsiveness declines with increases in local unemployment rates), elapsed duration, and age. Benefits also appear to have different effects on the behaviour of workers on temporary lay-off, relative to the effect on behaviour of workers on permanent lay-off. There is some empirical evidence that benefits affect search intensity and the choice of search method, on the supply side of the market. Estimates also vary with estimation techniques and this sensitivity suggests specification error in modelling the effect of benefits. In particular, the potential duration of benefits may be as important as the benefit level. Demand side analysis of benefit effects within the search frame-work has been rare, but limited evidence suggests that effects on firm behaviour are potentially more important.

To sum up, benefits appear to affect unemployment durations in a complicated way. There is probably no single number – a "benefit effect" – that applies to all workers and to each worker in all circumstances. Sharper modelling of the effects of benefit program parameters on the generation of offers (including lay- offs and recalls of workers by firms) would be a useful course for future research, especially in view of the finding that reservation wages are less important empirically than the arrival rate of offers.

Part of the reason for the ambiguity of research results may be the fact that most studies of the impact of unemployment insurance on unemployment have been done only once, at one particular point in the business cycle (but different studies have been done at different points in the cycle, with different results). However, one ought to expect that the influence of unemployment insurance would vary at different points in the business cycle. After all, one of the constraints that each individual job-seeker faces, in any point in time, is the state of the aggregate labour market – and economists normally expect that behaviour will change, when constraints change.[12] Using Labour Force Survey data from 1981, 1983, and 1986, Osberg (1993) examined the search strategies of jobless Canadians at a business-cycle peak, trough, and mid-point. He found significant changes in job-search strategies over the business cycle and, in related work, significant changes in inter-industry mobility patterns (Osberg 1991).[13]

Many years ago, Hamermesh (1977) noted that although more generous unemployment insurance payments may lead some individuals to decline job offers, the implications of this vary dramatically with the business cycle. When there are many jobs, but few job-seekers, a declined job offer means that the individual must search longer for an acceptable job, *and* the firm searches longer for an employee – hence more generous unemployment insurance causes an increase in the aggregate unemployment rate.

However, when there are many applicants for each available position, the job offer that is turned down by one individual is quickly snapped up by the next individual in the job queue. Periods of excess supply of labour therefore imply that the unemployment-insurance-induced increases in unemployment duration of some individuals produce *decreases* in the unemployment duration of those other individuals who receive offers they would not otherwise have got. In a cross-sectional comparison, the recipients of unemployment insurance may have longer durations of unemployment, relative to nonrecipients, but this may be largely a relative effect on the composition of the pool of the unemployed, and not an aggregate effect on the level of unemployment.

In labour economics, analysts are often interested in the determinants of the relative position of some individuals compared to others. Econometric analysis of a cross-section of micro-data on individuals at a particular point in time can provide such evidence, e.g., one can discover whether people with more education, or more unemployment insurance income, find jobs more or less quickly than do people with fewer years of education or less unemployment insurance income. However, micro-econometric cross-sectional analysis can explain only the *relative* outcomes of some individuals compared to others. If our interest is in the determinants of the average level of *all* outcomes (e.g., in explaining the absolute level of aggregate unemployment over time), the analysis of *cross-sectional* micro-data cannot do the job.[14]

In addition, Atkinson and Micklewright (1991) have recently surveyed international evidence on the connection between unemployment compensation and unemployment and have stressed the complexity of unemployment insurance systems and the inadequacy of a simple story of unemployment insurance disincentives. They argue that the cessation of search activity may be due to temporary withdrawal from the labour force, a return to school, or other training or a permanent retirement. A transition to employment from unemployment may represent the acceptance of a permanent job or short-duration, casual employment. These differing transitions have different causes, and different consequences – and are influenced to differing degrees by the provisions (both incentives and administrative) of unemployment insurance schemes. They conclude (1721):

Our review began with the effect of unemployment benefit levels, or replacement rates, on the probability of exit from (and entry to) unemployment. This has been the principle focus of much of the literature, but we concluded that the findings are far from robust. One has to look carefully to find significant replacement rate coefficients, and their size is typically small. There is evidence that benefits may influence temporary layoff in the us but with the effect coming from the demand side rather than the supply side.

Our principle argument in this paper has been that it is essential in the analysis of unemployment compensation to (a) distinguish different labour market states and (b) treat the institutional features of different forms of unemployment benefit...

Our review of the evidence leads us to conclude that there may be adverse effects on the incentive for the unemployed to leave unemployment but that these are typically found to be small, and there is little ground for believing that much voluntary quitting is induced by the unemployment insurance system. Moreover, the richer view of the relationship between unemployment compensation and the labour market that we have urged in this paper allows us to identify some of the ways in which it (unemployment compensation) may have a positive, rather than a negative, impact. This applies particularly to unemployment insurance, as opposed to unemployment assistance.

In general, Atkinson and Micklewright are highly sceptical that unemployment insurance can be blamed for the rising unemployment of the 1980s. Canada is not the only country where the increase in unemployment of the 1980s has coincided with a *decrease* in the generosity of unemployment compensation.

All these micro-econometric studies used standard micro-data tapes that, as noted previously, contain only information on the responses of individual workers. Osberg, Apostle, and Clairmont (1986) report the results of a study of unemployment incidence and duration where interviews were conducted with a stratified random sample of employers. Lists of workers from each were obtained and then a sample of the workers employed was interviewed. Since workers were interviewed in 1979 and re-interviewed in 1981, and since worker characteristics could be exactly matched to the characteristics of their 1979 employer, it was possible to nest models of the determination of unemployment incidence and duration that relied solely on the supply-side characteristics of workers within a more general model of unemployment that reflected both the supply-side characteristics of workers *and* the demand-side characteristics of firms. If one used only the information available from the worker interviews, "standard" econometric results on the impact of unemployment insurance generosity on unemployment incidence and duration over the period 1979 to 1981 could be obtained. However, if one allowed for the possible influence of firm level characteristics, such as sales variability or rigidity of job assignments, the adverse impacts of the benefit/wage ratio on unemployment incidence and duration disappeared. Although the sample is relatively small (119 employers, 1,563 employees), this study remains the only one that has attempted to use micro-data evidence on both the demand and the supply side of labour markets – and it appears that evidence from the demand side does make a difference to the presumed impact of unemployment insurance on individual unemployment.

In principle, micro-data and micro-econometric evidence have the potential to model the complex structure of unemployment insurance incentives and disincentives. However, theory has tended to ignore the potential role of demand-side variables, perhaps partly because available micro-data sets have generally not contained the variables that could convincingly test hypotheses about the influence of unemployment insurance on firm behaviours. As well, there is good reason to expect the influence of unemployment insurance on individual outcomes to vary over the business cycle and to be cautious about aggregating the impact of unemployment insurance on relative outcomes in cross-sectional evidence. Better data, and sharper modelling, are clearly called for.

MACROECONOMIC TIME-SERIES EVIDENCE

Simultaneous equations models of the macro-economy have the potential to model both the demand and the supply sides of labour markets. The original Grubel, Maki, and Sax (1975) model of the impact of unemployment insurance on Canadian unemployment rates followed such a simultaneous equations approach.[15] However, recent literature on the macroeconomic impacts of unemployment insurance has tended to use a reduced-form modelling strategy. Neither methodology gives a clear answer on the impacts of unemployment insurance on unemployment. In his contribution to this volume, Myatt (1996) surveys fourteen published studies that use macro time-series evidence to assess the impact of the 1971 unemployment insurance revisions on unemployment. Since seven found a significant positive effect, but five did not, and two found a significant effect in only three of ten provinces (not the same ones), he comments that "a more evenly divided result could not be imagined." Myatt's discussion emphasizes the collinearity of major data series, the surfeit of possible explanatory theories (and their associated causal variables), the dangers of specification search given a very limited number of observed data points, and the endogeneity of unemployment insurance instruments. In addition, three issues deserve close attention:

1 What does the estimated relationship mean?
2 How robust is the estimated relationship?
3 How does the aggregate macroeconomic variable used reflect the microeconomic incentives facing individual participants in the labour market?

The NAIRU and the Natural Rate

In thinking about the impact of unemployment insurance on unemployment, it is crucial to be clear about whether one is estimating a model of the impact of unemployment insurance on the NAIRU (the non-accelerating inflation rate of unemployment) or a model of the impact of unemployment insurance on the "natural" rate of unemployment (the rate of unemployment one would expect to observe, given the institutional and demographic structure of the labour market). The distinction is crucial, because the two concepts only coincide under *specific* assumptions about price-setting and wage-setting behaviour. As Osberg (1995) demonstrates, one can construct theoretical models of unemployment determination that have a "natural rate" of unemployment but which do *not* have the non-accelerating inflation property.

Since the welfare interpretation of the "natural rate" and the NAIRU are very different, the distinction between them goes to the heart of the policy debate on macroeconomics, but it is often not made.[16] In recent years, Fortin (1989) and Rose (1988) have estimated models of the NAIRU in Canada that included consideration of unemployment insurance generosity, while James (1991), Burns (1990, 1991), and Milbourne, Purvis, and Scoones (1991) have discussed the impact of unemployment insurance on the "natural" rate of unemployment.

In a NAIRU model, an explicit link is made between the rate of change of money wages, aggregate unemployment, and expected price inflation. Price inflation is derived as a mark-up from wage inflation, and the NAIRU equilibrium is defined as occurring when expected price inflation is equal to actual price inflation. An unemployment rate in excess of the NAIRU has clear implications for inflation, since excess unemployment implies a decline in the rate of inflation in wages and prices. Conversely, there is a clear (negative) welfare consequence of unemployment rates less than the NAIRU – wage-and-price inflation accelerates. Only at the NAIRU equilibrium can one expect a constant rate of wage-and-price inflation.[17]

Models of the "natural" rate of unemployment contain no explicit link between price inflation and unemployment. For example, James (1991) derives estimates of the natural rate of unemployment from an estimated employment rate, in which the quarterly employment rate 1971 to 1990 is regressed on a measure of unemployment insurance "generosity" (see discussion below), the average minimum-wage ratio, the difference between actual output and potential output, and the gap between current and trend real wages. Milbourne, Purvis, and Scoones (1991) got a hysteretic "natural rate" from a regression of the monthly unemployment rate on the previous month's unemployment rate, aggregate output, and a measure of maximum unemployment insurance benefits duration. In general terms, one has an estimated equation of the form of equation (3).

$$(3) \qquad U_t = \beta_0 + \beta_1\, UI_t + \beta_2 X_t + \varepsilon_t$$

where UI_t is some measure of unemployment insurance incentives, X_t is a vector of control variables, and ε_t is the stochastic error.

The "natural" rate of unemployment at time T is calculated as the conditional expectation of unemployment, given the parameters of the unemployment insurance system and the values of other control variables that existed at time T, as per equation (4).

$$(4) \qquad \begin{aligned} U_T^N &= E[U_T | UI_T, X_T] \\ &= \hat{\beta}_0 + \hat{\beta}_1\, UI_T + \hat{\beta}_2\, X_T \end{aligned}$$

The term "natural" has, in the English language, nice connotations. "Natural" is usually thought of as being both inevitable and, somehow, "good." However, it really would be more accurate to refer to equation (4) as a calculation of the *expected* rate of unemployment. After all, one could follow a similar methodology and regress the homicide rate on such variables as the average sentence for murder convictions, percentage of arrests in homicide cases, percentage of the population under thirty (and, perhaps, the unemployment rate). One could use the estimated coefficients from such a regression, and the current values of these variables, to calculate the expected homicide rate at any point in time, and one *could* also call this the "natural rate."

However, what are the policy implications of fewer homicides, or less unemployment, than the expected rate? What should policy-makers do if, in equation (3), $\varepsilon_t < 0$ – and actual unemployment is *less* than its expected level? Presumably, this is socially desirable, since lower unemployment typically means more employment, while fewer murders mean more living people. In "natural rate" models of aggregate unemployment, there is *no specified link* between unemployment and price inflation, or inflationary expectations. Hence, there are no adverse welfare implications to an actual rate of unemployment that is less than the expected (i.e., the so-called "natural") rate of unemployment.

The Robustness of Unemployment Insurance Impacts on the NAIRU

Because natural rate models of aggregate unemployment cannot validly be interpreted in terms of either accelerating or decelerating price inflation, the impact of unemployment insurance generosity on the NAIRU is the important issue for macroeconomic policy. However, estimates of the NAIRU in Canada are very imprecise, depending heavily on technical issues of estimation. Setterfield, Gordon, and Osberg (1992) examined the robustness of the NAIRU estimates of Rose (1988) and Fortin (1989) to alternative plausible specifications of the underlying variables. (See also Setterfield's contribution to this volume.) In addition to examining the impacts of alternative strategies of modelling unemployment insurance (whether one should model unemployment insurance as a composite index of generosity, or whether one should use a disaggregated measure of each component, either in rate of change or in levels), the implications of alternative specifications of the measurements of the rate of unionization, price expectations, and the impact of wage-and-price controls in Canada were examined. They conclude that one can find a NAIRU model with desirable econometric properties to recommend almost any feasible male unemployment rate as the NAIRU in Canada in the mid-1980s.

The Meaning of Aggregate Unemployment Insurance "Generosity"

The reason why unemployment insurance variables are entered in macroeconomic analyses of aggregate unemployment is that they are supposed to represent changes over time in the incentives that unemployment insurance offers to individuals to become or to remain unemployed. However, the incentives that actually face individuals are specified in legislation, which changes very infrequently. How is it that measured "unemployment insurance generosity" changes from year to year? How can one interpret a correlation between such measures of aggregate "unemployment insurance generosity" and total unemployment?

James (1991: 6) defines as a measure of aggregate unemployment insurance generosity "the ratio of average weekly unemployment insurance benefits to the average weekly wage in the business sector." (Rose (1988) and Fortin (1989) use a more complex composite index of unemployment insurance generosity, defined as the proportion of the labour force insured multiplied by the average replacement rate multiplied by the benefit duration ratio.) Table 1 presents some examples of the calculation of the James measure. To keep things simple, it assumes individuals are either employed or unemployed for all of the current year, ignores the issue of wage inflation over time, and calculates maximum insurable earnings, as in Canadian unemployment insurance legislation, as the simple average of the previous year's weekly earnings.[18] As in 1991 Canadian unemployment insurance

Table 1
Calculation of "Average" Unemployment Insurance Generosity

	Hours per Week	$ per Hour	$ Pay per Week	Unemployment Insurance Benefits Payable	Benefit/Wage Replacement Ratio
A	14	5	70	0	0
B	40	5	200	120	0.6
C	30	10	300	180	0.6
D	40	10	400	237	0.59
E	40	15	600	237	0.395
F	40	20	800	237	0.296

Note: Assume if hours per week are greater than fifteen, replacement rate = 0.6; maximum insurable earnings = $395.

1 If A and C lose their jobs, the average unemployment insurance benefits paid (to A and C) = $90. The average weekly wage of those remaining employed (B,D,E,F) = $500. Ratio = 0.18 = (90/500).

2 If B and C lose their jobs, the average unemployment insurance benefits paid (to B and C) = $150. The average weekly wage of those remaining employed (A,D,E,F) = $467.50. Ratio = 0.32 = (150/467.50).

3 If F and C lose their jobs, the average unemployment insurance benefits paid (to F and C) = $208.50. The average weekly wage of those remaining employed (A,B,D,E) = $317.50. Ratio = 0.66 = (208.50/317.50).

legislation, there is no unemployment insurance coverage if hours worked per week are less than fifteen, and the replacement rate is 60 percent of weekly earnings up to the maximum insurable earnings ceiling.

As one can see from Table 1, the James (1991) index of unemployment insurance generosity can vary considerably, depending on who it is that loses their jobs.[19] If employment loss is concentrated in the middle and low end of the earnings distribution, unemployment insurance "generosity" can be as low as 0.18. If job loss comes from the middle of the distribution of earnings, the generosity index is 0.32. If lay-offs come from the middle and high end of the earnings distribution, the denominator of the generosity index (average weekly wages) falls disproportionately. The numerator rises because highly paid workers are at maximum insurable earnings and receive maximum benefit. When the denominator falls and the numerator rises, a ratio (such as the unemployment insurance generosity index) must increase. In this example, the generosity index can be as high as 0.66, which is in fact higher than the legal replacement rate for anyone.[20]

All this, despite the fact that there is *absolutely no change* in the generosity of the unemployment insurance system to any particular individual. All the variation in the unemployment insurance generosity index is coming from changes in the composition of unemployment. Indeed, since the replacement rate is defined in legislation, and has changed only once (in 1977) over the period examined by James (1971 to 1990), essentially all the identifying variation in the ratio measure of unemployment insurance generosity *can only come* from changes in the composition of the populations of unemployed and employed individuals.

When the legislation that defines the benefit/wage replacement rate remains unchanged for many years (e.g., 1977 to 1992), it is clear that the replacement rate generosity of unemployment insurance to all individuals also remains unchanged. If all individuals face a constant degree of unemployment insurance generosity in benefit/ wage replacement, the *only way* in which such an index of unemployment insurance generosity can change over time is if changes in the composition of the populations of employed and unemployed individuals change the ratio of average unemployment insurance benefits received to average wages paid. As aggregate unemployment increases, joblessness penetrates further up the distribution of weekly earnings – average unemployment insurance benefits paid increase, and average weekly wages fall; hence their ratio rises. It is thus not surprising that, in time-series analysis, increased aggregate unemployment is positively correlated with an increase in the ratio of unemployment insurance benefits paid to weekly wages – *despite* the fact that there was no change at all in the replacement-rate generosity of unemployment insurance to *any* individual worker.[21] Higher unemployment *causes* a change in the composition of the employed and unemployed populations, which causes an increase in the ratio of average unemployment insurance benefits paid to average weekly wages – and which appears as a positive coefficient in time-series regressions.

Unemployment Insurance Benefit Duration and Aggregate Unemployment

What impact can one expect other aspects of unemployment insurance generosity to have on aggregate unemployment? Milbourne, Purvis, and Scoones (1991) have argued that by introducing regional unemployment rates into the calculation of extended-benefit-duration entitlement, the 1977 revisions to unemployment insurance increased the generosity of the unemployment insurance system and established incentives to individuals to decrease labour supply. They argue that the 1977 revisions were responsible for much of the increased unemployment of the Canadian economy during the 1980s, and the greater persistence of high unemployment following the 1981–82 recession.

In Milbourne, Purvis, and Scoones (1991) the focus is on the change that the 1977 revisions to unemployment insurance created for an "agent" who works the minimum weeks necessary to qualify for unemployment insurance, and who claims for the maximum weeks of entitlement. In a very real sense, this brings us back to the methodology of case studies, anecdotes, and stereotypes that this essay discussed in the second section. The mathematics that is used to derive the conclusion that those who are unemployed "will never choose to work more than the qualifying period n_q, nor collect benefits for less than the maximum number of weeks, n_b" (Milbourne, Purvis and Scoones 1991: 810) should not blind us to the fact that we are considering an "ideal" type of individual. There is no attempt whatsoever made to provide evidence that such an "agent" is representative of the population of Canadian unemployed persons. The persuasiveness of the argument depends entirely on the degree to which the reader feels the case is intuitively plausible.

Christofides and McKenna (1992: table 4.3) note that there is a "spike" in job duration at the ten weeks necessary to qualify for unemployment insurance. However, the spike is relatively small, since 1,281 of the 58,458 jobs observed in the 1986–87 Labour Market Activity Survey (LMAS) were of ten weeks' duration, compared to 636 that were of eleven weeks' duration. Ten-week jobs accounted for 2.19 percent of all jobs, which is quantitatively small, but the difference in number of jobs (1.1 percent) is statistically significant. With a large data set, such as the LMAS, one can be statistically fairly certain about empirically small differentials.

However, one must also be cautious about the interpretation of such differentials. Christofides and McKenna do not examine the sequence of jobs held by an individual, but some fraction of ten-week jobs were followed by a subsequent job, not by unemployment. It is also clear that some ten-week jobs are of that duration for demand-side reasons, because, for example, the tourist season, in many summer resort areas of Canada, stretches from the last week of June to the end of August (i.e., for ten weeks). A "spike" in job durations at ten weeks might also be partly due to the fact that high-school students who get summer jobs will work for ten weeks or less. In short, the impact of unemployment insurance – i.e., the *voluntary* ten-week unemployment insurance claimant – is *some fraction* of a fairly small percentage (2.2 percent).

Corak and Jones (1995) have noted that the vast majority (approximately three-quarters) of unemployment insurance claimants never reach the extended benefits phase. They calculate that "the exclusion of all regionally-extended benefit recipients above that prevailing during 1981 does not dramatically change the dynamics of the aggregate unemployment rate" (559). They note that the number of regionally extended beneficiaries is not unusually persistent over time and that the pre-1977 legislation would also have mandated increases in the extended benefit phase of unemployment insurance, in the wake of the recession of 1981–82. They conclude that "there is no evident direct mechanism for regional extended UI benefits, as generated by the 1977 legislative changes, that could account for the increased persistence of Canadian unemployment in the 1980s" (566).

Corak and Jones (1995) examined the evidence on the hypothesis of Milbourne, Purvis, and Scoones (1991) directly, by asking whether the data on regionally extended unemployment insurance beneficiaries could possibly account for the increased aggregate unemployment experienced in Canada during the 1980s. McGuire (1993) follows a more indirect route, arguing that if the hypothesis of Milbourne et al. is correct, one should observe, following the 1977 revisions, a greater increase in the unemployment rate for demographic groups with a more marginal attachment to the labour force.[22] Since the 1977 revisions clearly had very different impacts on Canada's economic regions, the persistence of unemployment that Milbourne, Purvis, and Scoones hypothesized to have been introduced by the 1977 revisions should also be greatest in high-unemployment provinces like Newfoundland and Nova Scotia.

As well, the hold-up by the Senate of Canada of Bill C-23 in 1990 produced a "natural experiment." When the Senate held up Bill C-23, the entrance qualification for unemployment insurance suddenly increased, between January and October of 1990, to fourteen weeks nationwide from the ten weeks previously required in many regions. It was then reduced again to ten weeks with the passage of Bill C-23. The model of Milbourne et al. should imply that persistence in aggregate unemployment would fall during this period, before rising again with the re-introduction of the amended variable entrance requirements across Canada – but that such a change in unemployment persistence should be entirely accounted for by the variable measuring maximum weeks' benefit duration (which turns out not to be true).

Milbourne, Purvis, and Scoones (1991) used data for the period 1966 to 1988, but extension of the estimating period to 1991 and examination of disaggregated demographic and regional trends in unemployment are not kind to their hypothesis. Using data to 1991, the introduction of maximum benefit entitlement into the regression does not imply that the coefficient on past unemployment reverts to its pre-1977 levels, contrary to their results. Although the hypothesis of Milbourne, Purvis, and Scoones argued that demographic groups with marginal labour-force attachment would show an increase in aggregate unemployment persistence, the youth unemployment rate showed a decrease in persistence after 1977. Persistence in aggregate unemployment in the 1980s appears to be strongest among males aged twenty-five to fifty-four (contrary to hypothesis) and it is clear that the relationship between the past unemployment rate and the current unemployment rate is not accounted for by the introduction of a variable measuring maximum benefit entitlement.

The results of Milbourne et al. (1991) can therefore be severely questioned, both on the basis of aggregate macroeconomic time-series evidence and on the basis of data on the frequency of the pattern of minimum weeks' unemployment insurance qualifiers drawing maximum weeks of regionally extended benefits. Yet the stereotype of the "10/40-week worker" has an impact on perceptions (and on policy) that is far greater than its actual empirical significance. If dressed up in mathematics, an anecdote about a utility-maximizing "agent" who works the minimum and draws the maximum can acquire a respectability in academic circles that real stories about real individuals do not possess, even if the mathematical anecdote is entirely hypothetical. As Corak and Jones (1995) state, "the empirical work of MPS [Milbourne, Purvis, and Scoones] makes essentially no use of the microeconomics" and there is no attempt made to show the stereotype to be statistically representative. Yet anecdotes and case studies have a vividness that transcends their empirical importance – particularly if they reinforce existing prejudices. Anecdotes shape perceptions, and they reappear constantly in the dialogue that surrounds the debate on unemployment insurance, even (perhaps especially) when the econometric evidence is complex and sometimes ambiguous.

To summarize, however:

1 In general, it is asking an enormous amount of a very limited number of observations to expect macroeconomic time-series data to reveal the influence of a system as complex as unemployment insurance.

2 Aggregate measures of unemployment insurance "generosity" hide the complexity of the actual system and do not correspond to any real person's incentive structure.
3 The empirically popular measures of unemployment insurance generosity used in Canadian macro time-series research are endogenous to measured unemployment, rather than causal.
4 The micro-theory that motivates macro-analysis depends heavily on mathematical anecdotes, of limited quantitative importance.

CONCLUSION

The reform of unemployment insurance in Canada in 1971 was a major public policy initiative. It has been argued that, with the subsequent failure of the 1973 Lalonde proposals for social assistance reform, the 1971 unemployment insurance reforms marked the end of the postwar expansion of Canadian welfare state programs. The steady, cumulative impact of a series of subsequent revisions, from 1975 to 1996, has decreased the generosity of Canadian unemployment insurance substantially since then, essentially erasing the increased generosity of the 1971 reforms, but unemployment insurance reform in 1971 was controversial at the time, and the size and the complexity of the program ensure that it will continue to be controversial for many years to come.

As a public policy initiative, however, unemployment insurance in Canada has attracted the attention of economists to an extent that is not fully explicable by its economic importance.[23] In part, unemployment insurance reform in Canada attracted economic analysis because it coincided with theoretical and empirical developments in economics that provided the conceptual framework and the empirical tools for its analysis. Micro-data on individuals and the low-cost computer hardware that made micro-data analysis possible did not exist before the early 1970s. The job-search approach to analysis of unemployment dates from the same period, and throughout the 1970s there was a new focus on analysis of the supply-side of labour markets. These influences combined to produce a series of studies of the impact on unemployment insurance (e.g., Jump and Rea 1975; Green and Cousineau 1976) that emphasized the adverse impact of unemployment insurance on aggregate unemployment, and the perspective of these early studies has continued to be extremely influential.

Since the early 1970s, the unemployment insurance system in Canada has changed considerably – the benefits/wage replacement rate has been cut in steps from 0.66 to 0.60 to 0.57 to 0.55; the minimum entrance requirement has been increased from eight weeks to between twelve and twenty weeks; penalties for those who quit or were discharged were first increased. More recently, those who quit or are discharged have lost entitlement to unemployment insurance benefits. The macroeconomic context of labour markets has also changed drastically, from an unemployment rate of 6.2 percent in 1972 to one of 10.3 percent in 1994. The institutional context of labour markets has also changed, with a rapid increase in part-time work, self-employment, and contractual arrangements, which are often not eligible for unemployment insurance protection.

One can reasonably expect that such changes would diminish the impact of unemployment insurance on aggregate unemployment. New theoretical work, new econometric techniques, and new data sources have also greatly increased the volume of research findings on the impacts of unemployment insurance. This article has quoted at length from several recent surveys in order to make the point that there is now a much more nuanced perspective on the impacts of unemployment insurance. In many academic circles, there is now greater awareness of the complexities of labour-market transitions, and of unemployment insurance, and much greater caution in assertions about the adverse impact of unemployment insurance. However, as Keynes said: "[I]n the field of economic and political philosophy there are not many who are influenced by new theories after they are twenty-five or thirty years of age, so that the ideas which civil servants and politicians and even agitators apply to current events are not likely to be the newest. But, soon or late, it is ideas, not vested interests, which are dangerous for good or evil" (1964: 383).

The models of the early 1970s had an easy-to-communicate simplicity, and represented the literature that was available in the early 1980s for the Macdonald Royal Commission, the Forget Commission of Inquiry, and the House Royal Commission to summarize.[24] Since it takes considerable time for new research to be published in academic journals, and much longer for it to be compiled as part of the literature review process of royal commissions, there can be long lags in the process by which new information filters into the public debate.

However, the objective of this article is to speed up the process a little. This article has not attempted to make a comprehensive review of unemployment insurance, job search, or labour supply, such as those written by Devine and Kiefer (1991), Atkinson and Micklewright (1991), or Pencavel (1986). It has focused on the different types of evidence, and their strengths and weaknesses, and it has concentrated its attention on a selection from the Canadian literature.

Much more needs to be known about the impacts of unemployment insurance on the Canadian economy. There is both great complexity in the Canadian unemployment insurance system and great incentive to improve it. However, the first step in learning is to recognize the limits of current knowledge. Hence, this article is aimed at encouraging an attitude of scepticism about current dogma on the magnitude of the causal role played by unemployment insurance in increasing unemployment.

ACKNOWLEDGMENTS

I would like to thank Miles Corak, Shelley Phipps, and Brian MacLean for their helpful comments – errors remaining are my own.

NOTES

1 One example of the incentives that unemployment insurance provides to firms to alter behaviour is the minimum-hours provision. Employers must pay an employer's contribution to unemployment insurance premiums (at 4.2 percent of wages) on all hours worked by an employee, *but only if weekly hours worked exceed fifteen*. This creates a "spike" in the marginal cost of labour, since the sixteenth hour worked costs the hourly wage plus unemployment insurance premiums on all sixteen hours worked (i.e., the marginal cost is 1.67 * wage). Employers can avoid this spike in labour cost by subdividing full-time jobs into part-time employment (e.g., offering two seven-hour "days" per week to each worker).
2 For exceptions, see Osberg, Apostle, and Clairmont (1986) and Osberg (1991, 1993), as discussed in the second section of this chapter.
3 For example, Milbourne, Purvis, and Scoones (1991) or the *Globe and Mail* editorial page (any issue).
4 In Ron's case, the crucial details are: (1) the two-week waiting-period of zero replacement of lost earnings; (2) the fact that one can establish eligibility for a future claim while working and on claim; and (3) the ceiling on earnings while on claim.
5 From a public policy perspective, the issue should be whether unemployment insurance causes an *excessive* increase in unemployment. One of the objectives of unemployment insurance is to improve the allocative functioning of labour markets by providing the liquidity to enable workers to search longer for the job that best matches their abilities. This necessarily implies an increase in aggregate unemployment, so the issue is whether the output foregone by increased unemployment-insurance-

induced unemployment exceeds the increment in output from better job/worker matching (usually proxied by the aggregate wage gain from increased search duration).

6 In the Canadian literature, Ham and Rea (1987) and Corak (1992) are exceptions. Due to the limitations of the administrative data, the Ham and Rea measure of unemployment insurance replacement rate generosity is relatively poor, but it is interesting to note that it was uncorrelated with unemployment duration. They did find a positive partial correlation between maximum benefit duration and unemployment duration. Corak (1992) did not find a benefit rate effect for males, but did for females. He emphasizes the role of aggregate demand as a determinant of spell duration for males.

7 An exception is the sample of workers selected from a sample of firms, reported in Osberg, Apostle, and Clairmont (1986).

8 Individuals who, prior to unemployment insurance, were working less than Ab weeks (Figure 1 below) face an unambiguous incentive to increase labour supply in order to gain access to benefits. This implies that the impact of unemployment insurance on measured unemployment may come partly from its impact on increased supply of labour, i.e., increases in labour force participation. Card and Riddell (1993: 185) argue that "the unemployment insurance system itself is not the cause of the high level of unemployment at the close of the 1980s" but they do note a relative increase in the percentage of people who just qualify for unemployment insurance. They argue that up to three-quarters of the growth in the 1980s in the unemployment gap between Canada and the United States is due to more Canadians looking for work, rather than being counted as not-in-labour force. They conjecture that unemployment insurance may entice some people into employment who would otherwise have withdrawn from the labour market. If so, the impact of unemployment insurance is to *increase* aggregate output. Individuals who were working less than d weeks face a positive substitution effect from EY, but a negative income effect (assuming leisure to be a normal good).

9 A recent Canadian study is Osberg and Phipps (1993). Surveys of the literature are contained in Killingsworth (1983), Osberg (1986), and Pencavel (1986). All agree that substitution and income elasticities are typically quite small (i.e., 0.1 or less).

10 See also Lin and Osberg (1992a and 1992b), or Ham (1982).

11 These predictions are not, however, unambiguous. Since jobs now come with an unemployment insurance entitlement attached, an increase in the generosity of the unemployment insurance system increases the total economic benefits attached to a short-duration job offer – thereby altering the wage-offer distribution facing individuals.

If the wage-offer distribution shifts, but the reservation wage increases, the net impact on probability of job acceptance is ambiguous, i.e., if F is the cumulative distribution function and $F(w^1) \neq F(w)$, the knowledge that $w_r^1 > w_r$ is consistent with $F^1(w_r^1) \gtreqless F(w_r)$.

12 If geographic identifiers are available, one can include the local unemployment rate, or other measure of local labour market conditions as a regressor in a regression using micro-data. While better than nothing, controlling for cross-sectional variation in labour-market conditions is *not* equivalent to controlling for time-series variation, since they will not have equivalent impacts on individual behaviour. For example, one can always migrate from a high-unemployment region to a low-unemployment area, but individuals cannot choose the phase of the business cycle they prefer.

13 In all three years, 1981, 1983, and 1986, unemployment insurance variables were usually statistically insignificant as determinants of job-finding probability, or entered with "wrong" sign, from the point of view of the "incentives" argument.

14 To put it in terms of an estimated regression model of unemployment, cross-sectional micro-data can test hypotheses about the sign and significance of the coefficients of particular variables, but cannot predict the magnitude of the constant term in the regression.

15 However, as Kaliski (1975) noted, Grubel, Maki, and Sax (1975) ignored the fact that unemployment insurance benefits became taxable in 1971. Re-estimation of their model including the taxation of unemployment insurance benefits considerably reduces the estimated impact of the 1971 revisions to unemployment insurance, from a 0.6 percent increase in the unemployment rate to 0.3 percent, or 0 percent, depending on the marginal tax rate assumption made.

16 Burns (1991: 157), for example, totally confuses the two issues.

17 For a formal derivation, see Setterfield, Gordon and Osberg (1992: 121–4).

18 Table 1 below also implicitly assumes employment last year, in order to calculate maximum insurable earnings as the average of all workers' weekly earnings. Complicating the example (e.g., by allowing for partial years of employment/ unemployment or the effect of unemployment last year on this year's maximum insurable earnings) would not materially affect the conclusions.

19 In the composite index of unemployment insurance generosity of Fortin (1989) or Rose (1988), variation in index generosity does not come through the replacement rate (which is fixed at its legal ratio) but instead comes through variation in the ratio of maximum weeks' unemployment insurance eligibility to minimum weeks needed to qualify. Since this ratio must (by legislation) increase as aggregate

unemployment increases, Myatt (1996) has argued that variations in index generosity necessarily *reflect* variations over time in the level of unemployment rather than playing a causal role.

20 And it should also be noted that the ratio measure of unemployment insurance generosity goes up as the actual average replacement rate to those unemployed goes down. When B and C are unemployed, the average replacement rate facing unemployed individuals is 0.6 but when F and C are unemployed, their average replacement rate is 0.45 (i.e., (0.6 + 0.296)/2). The ratio measure of James moves in a perverse direction because it is the ratio of the average unemployment insurance benefits of the unemployed to the average wages *of those who remain employed*.

21 Since James (1991) runs a regression with *employment* as the dependent variable, the "generosity"/employment correlation will be negative, as he found.

22 Milbourne, Purvis, and Scoones (1991: 809) refer to "students" or "those with working spouses" in the verbal discussion preceding their formal modelling.

23 Primary and secondary education in Canada absorb considerably more tax dollars than unemployment insurance (in 1987, $24.3 billion compared to $10.5 billion). Since most (94 percent) of the expenditures of the unemployment insurance system are transfers to individuals, while almost all the financial costs of primary and secondary education represent the consumptive use of goods and services, the economic use of resources by primary and secondary education is *far* greater than the use of resources by the unemployment insurance system. Arguably, the impact of primary and secondary education on the long-term productivity of the Canadian labour force is more important than the influence of unemployment insurance. Yet there is very little serious attention by Canadian economists to analysis of primary and secondary education – perhaps because it is hard to tell a simple story of utility maximization.

24 As someone who participated in all three, however, I think it is noteworthy that the House Royal Commission (Newfoundland) relied entirely on anecdotal evidence on the impacts of unemployment insurance, while the Macdonald Commission and the Forget Commission depended primarily on the published academic literature.

REFERENCES

Atkinson, A.B., and J. Micklewright. 1991. "Unemployment Compensation and Labour Market Transitions: A Critical Review." *Journal of Economic Literature* 29, No. 4: 1679–727.

Atkinson, A.B., J. Gomulka, J. Micklewright, and N. Rau. 1984. "Unemployment Benefit, Duration and Incentives in Britain: How Robust is the Evidence?" *Journal of Public Economics* 23: 3–26.

Burns, A.R. 1991. "The Natural Rate of Unemployment: Canada and the Provinces." In S. Gera, ed., *Canadian Unemployment: Lessons from the Eighties and Challenges for the Nineties*, 39–52. Ottawa: Economic Council of Canada.

Burns, A.R. 1990. "The Natural Rate of Unemployment: A Regionally Disaggregated Approach." Working Paper No. 2, Economic Council of Canada.

Card, D., and C. Riddell. 1993. "A Comparative Analysis of Unemployment in Canada and the United States." In D. Card and R. Freeman, eds., *Small Differences that Matter: Labor Markets and Income Maintenance in Canada and the United States*, 149–90. Chicago: University of Chicago Press.

Christofides, L.N., and C.J. McKenna. 1992. "Employment Tenure in Canada." Paper prepared for the Canadian Employment Research Forum Conference, Ottawa, March.

Corak, M. 1992. "The Duration of Unemployment Insurance Payments." Economic Council of Canada Working Paper No. 42.

Corak, M., and S. Jones. 1992. "The Persistence of Unemployment: How Important were Regionally Extended Unemployment Insurance Benefits?" *Canadian Journal of Economics* 28, No. 3 (August): 555–67.

Devine, T., and N. Kiefer. 1991. *Empirical Labour Economics: The Search Approach*. Oxford: Oxford University Press.

Economic Council of Canada. 1990. *Good Jobs, Bad Jobs: Employment in the Service Economy.* Ottawa: Economic Council of Canada.

– 1991. *Employment in the Service Economy.* Ottawa: Economic Council of Canada.

Follman, D.A., M.S. Goldberg, and L. May. 1990. "Personal Characteristics, Unemployment Insurance and the Duration of Unemployment." *Journal of Econometrics* 45: 351–66.

Fortin, P. 1989. "How 'Natural' is Canada's High Unemployment Rate?" *European Economic Review* 33 (January): 89–110.

Gordon, D., Z. Lin, L. Osberg, and S. Phipps. 1994a. "Predicting Probabilities: Inherent and Sampling Variability in the Estimation of Discrete-Choice Models." *Oxford Bulletin of Economics and Statistics* 56, No. 1 (February): 13–31.

Green, C., and J. Cousineau. 1976. *Unemployment in Canada: The Impacts of Unemployment Insurance*. Ottawa: Economic Council of Canada.

Green, D.A., and W.C. Riddell. 1992. "The Economic Effects of Unemployment Insurance in Canada: An Empirical Analysis of U.I. Disentitlement." Department of Economics, University of British Columbia, July.

Grubel, H.G., D. Maki, and S. Sax. 1975. "Real and Insurance-induced Unemployment in Canada." *Canadian Journal of Economics* 8: 174–91.

Ham, J.C. 1982. "Estimation of a Labour Supply Model with Censoring Due to Unemployment and Underemployment." *Review of Economic Studies* 49, No. 3: 335–54.

Ham, J.C., and S.A. Rea, Jr. 1987. "Unemployment Insurance and Male Unemployment Duration in Canada." *Journal of Labour Economics* 5, No. 3: 325–53.

Hamermesh, D.S. 1977. *Jobless Pay and the Economy.* Baltimore: Johns Hopkins University Press.

Hamermesh, D.S. 1990. "Data Difficulties in Labor Economics." In E.R. Berndt and J.E. Triplett, eds., *Fifty Years of Economic Measurement.* Chicago: University of Chicago Press.

James, S. 1991. "Hysteresis and the Natural Rate of Unemployment in Canada." Paper presented at the Canadian Economics Association Meetings, Kingston, Ontario, June.

Jump, G., and S. Rea. 1975. *The Impact of the 1971 Unemployment Insurance Act on Work Incentives and the Aggregate Labour Market.* Toronto: University of Toronto Institute for Policy Analysis.

Kaliski, S. 1975. "Real and Insurance-induced Unemployment in Canada: A Comment." *Canadian Journal of Economics* 8, No. 4: 600–3.

Kelvin, P., and J.E. Jarrett. 1985. *Unemployment: Its Social Psychological Effects.* Cambridge, U.K.: Cambridge University Press.

Keynes, J.M. 1936. *The General Theory of Employment Interest and Money.* London: MacMillan.

Killingsworth, M.R. 1983. *Labour Supply.* Cambridge, U.K.: Cambridge University Press.

Lin, Z. and L. Osberg. 1992a. "Intertemporal Substitution of Annual Hours in Canada." Dalhousie University Working Paper No. 92–06.

– 1992b. "Short-Run Intertemporal Substitution of Labour Supply in Canada." Dalhousie University Working Paper No. 92–07.

McGuire, T.C. 1993. *Unemployment Insurance: Induced Unemployment.* M.A. thesis submitted to Department of Economics, Dalhousie University, May.

Milbourne, R.D., D. Purvis, and D. Scoones. 1991. "Unemployment Insurance and Unemployment Dynamics." *Canadian Journal of Economics* 24, No. 4: 804–26.

Myatt, T. 1996. "Who Do We Know So Little About Unemployment Determination and Unemployment Insurance Effects?" This volume.

Osberg, L. 1979. "Unemployment Insurance in Canada: A Review of the Recent Amendments." *Canadian Public Policy* 5, No. 2: 223–35.

– 1986. "Behavioral Response in the Context of Socio-economic Microanalytic simulation." Statistics Canada Analytical Studies, Research paper No. 1, April.

– 1991. "Unemployment and Inter-industry Mobility of Labour in Canada in the 1980s." *Applied Economics* 23, No. 11: 1707–18.

- 1993. "Fishing in Different Pools: Job Search Strategies and Job-Finding Success in Canada in the Early 1980s." *Journal of Labour Economics* 11, No. 2: 348–86.
- 1995. "Concepts of Unemployment and the Structure of Employment." *Economie Appliquée* XLVIII, No. 1: 157–81.
Osberg, L., R. Apostle, and D. Clairmont. 1986. "The Incidence and Duration of Individual Unemployment: Supply Side or Demand Side?" *Cambridge Journal of Economics* 10: 13–33.
Osberg, L., D.V. Gordon, and Z. Lin. 1992. "Inter-Regional Migration and Inter-Industry Labour Mobility in Canada: A Simultaneous Approach." *Canadian Journal of Economics* 27, No. 1: 58–80.
Osberg, L., L. Mazany, R. Apostle, and D. Clairmont. 1986. "Job Mobility, Wage Determination and Market Segmentation in the Presence of Sample Selectivity Bias." *Canadian Journal of Economics* 19, No. 2: 319–46.
Osberg, L., and S. Phipps. 1993. "Labour Supply with Quantity Constraints: Estimates from a Large Sample of Canadian Workers." *Oxford Economic Papers* 45: 348–86.
Pencavel, J. 1986. "Labour Supply of Men: A Survey." In O. Ashenfelter and R. Layard, eds., *Handbook of Labour Economics*, Vol. 1, 3–102. Amsterdam: North-Holland.
Phipps, S. 1990a. "The Impact of the UI Reform of 1990 on Single Earners." *Canadian Public Policy* 16, No. 3: 252–61.
- 1990b. "Quantity-Constrained Household Responses to UI Reform." *Economic Journal* 100: 124–40.
- 1991a. "Equity and Efficiency Consequences of UI Reform in Canada: The Importance of Sensitivity Analyses." *Economica* 58, No. 230: 199–214.
- 1991b. "Behavioral Response to UI Reform in Constrained and Unconstrained Models of Labour Supply." *Canadian Journal of Economics* 14, No. 1: 34–54.
- 1996. "Does Unemployment Insurance Increase Unemployment?" This volume.
Phipps, S., and L. Osberg, 1991. "On Integrating Income Tax and Unemployment Insurance in Models of Labour Supply." Dalhousie University Working Paper No. 91–03.
Rose, D.E. 1988. *The NAIRU in Canada: Concepts, Determinants and Estimates.* Bank of Canada Technical Report No. 50.
Setterfield, M. 1996. "Using the NAIRU as a Basis for Macroeconomic Policy: An Evaluation." This volume.
Setterfield, M., D.V. Gordon, and L. Osberg. 1992. "Searching for a Will O'the Wisp: An Empirical Study of The NAIRU in Canada." *European Economic Review* 36 (January): 119–36.

6 Why Do We Know So Little about Unemployment Determination and the Effects of Unemployment Insurance?

TONY MYATT

Poverty, inequality, and regional imbalance are all connected with unemployment. The same is true for illness, crime, and domestic violence. In addition, unemployment may reflect inefficiencies and waste of productive resources. Hence, if the unemployment rate exhibits a long-term upward trend, there is cause for great concern.

Considering the very long-run trend of the unemployment rate, say from 1900 to the present, one could find reasons to be philosophical. The unemployment could be seen as possibly reverting to a low level of around 3 percent or 4 percent, despite quite long-lived excursions into the double-digit realm. However, if one considers only the recent period, say from 1966 on, a very different picture emerges – the unemployment rate seems to be cycling upwards. Each recession raises unemployment to new heights, and each boom involves successively higher minimum levels of unemployment. Moreover, this picture is not peculiar to Canada. Most European nations, including France and Germany, have been unable to get their unemployment rates down (see Gross 1996).

These facts continue to pose serious challenges to economists to provide convincing explanations and policy recommendations. Generally speaking, early explanations focused on demographic changes in the composition of the workforce, changes in minimum-wage rates, more liberal unemployment insurance, and changes in unionization rates. More recently, emphasis has been placed on structural changes, changes in the terms of trade, and the tax wedge between the real product wage and the real consumption wage. Despite this,

Table 1
A Selection of Previous Studies

Author/Date	Sample and Frequency	Approach[1]	Disaggregation	Measure of Unemployment Insurance[2]	Impact of 1971 Revisions[3]
Grubel et al. (1975a)	Annual/1963–72	RF/YGAP	None	RR	Yes
Grubel et al. (1975b)	Annual/1963–72	RF/YGAP	None	RR	No
Denton et al. (1975)	Qtrly/1956–73	RF/AD	None	Dummies	No
Maki (1975)	Annual/1962–74	RF/YGAP	Regional	RR	Yes
Lazar (1978)	Monthly/1966–75	Flow data	Demographic	Dummies	Yes–Significant (+) effect on ADS; (+) effect on turnover rate for females
Samson (1985)	Annual/1957–83	RF/AD	None	RR	No
McCallum (1987)	Annual/1954–85	RF/AD	Demographic	UICGEN	Yes
Miller (1987)	Annual/1966–83	RF/YGAP	Regional	RR	Yes
Landon (1987)	Qtrly/1967–83	RF/AD	None	RR	No
Fortin (1989)	Annual/1954–84	Phillips Curve	Demographic	UICGEN	Yes
Burns (1988a)	Qtrly/1963–87	RF/AD	None	UICGEN	No
Burns (1988b)	Qtrly/1966–87	RF/YGAP	Regional	UICGEN	No. (Only significant for PEI, NB and Sask.)
Keil/Symons (1990)	Qtrly/1966–86	Labour mkt. model	None	RR	Yes-significant effect on PR. Positive (insignificant) on W/P
Johnson/Kneebone (1991)	Annual/1961–86	RF/YGAP	Regional	UICGEN	No. (Only significant for Alb, Ont., and Sask.)

Notes:

1 RF means reduced-form approach to modelling unemployment rates. The effect of the business cycle is either captured by adding an output gap term (YGAP) or by explicitly incorporating aggregate demand shocks (AD).

2 The generosity of unemployment insurance is sometimes measured using the replacement rate (RR) and sometimes using Fortin's measure of unemployment insurance generosity (UICGEN).

3 ADS denotes the average duration of search.

no firm consensus has been built up as to the reasons for continuing high employment.

Consider, for example, the effect of the 1971 unemployment insurance reforms, which drastically liberalized access and benefits in Canada. Table 1 contains a summary of fourteen published studies bearing on this issue, all of which use macroeconomic time-series data. Of these studies, seven found a significant positive effect, five found no significant effect, and two found no significant effect in seven out of ten provinces.[1]

A more evenly divided result could not be imagined. Moreover, these differences do not seem to depend on the age of the study, the data period covered, the frequency of the data, the way the business cycle is measured, or the way that unemployment insurance "generosity" is measured. Considering the first eleven entries in Table 1, the presence of significant effects seems to be related to the use of either regionally or demographically disaggregated data – but even this generalization does not hold for the last three entries in the table. Moreover, Table 1 abstracts from the question of the magnitude of any effect. Thus, it seems that twenty-four years after the 1971 unemployment insurance reforms, we are still not sure of their impact, if any! The point here is not that the effect of the 1971 unemployment insurance revisions is particularly obscure. Rather, this merely serves to emphasize how little we know in general about the recent behaviour of unemployment.

The object of this paper it to discuss in general why we seem to know so little, and to speculate on which lines of research might seem to be the most fruitful, given the difficulties involved.

WHY DO WE KNOW SO LITTLE?

Probably the most important reason we know so little has been the paucity of the data. Until recently there has been an absence of good longitudinal micro-data sets (i.e., data sets that track the behaviour and attributes of specific individuals over time). To some extent this has been rectified with the Labour Market Activity Survey (LMAS) data sets, but these are only available from 1986, and as Jones and Riddell (1991) have pointed out, even this data is not without its problems. Analysts have had a choice – either use time-series data with all its aggregation problems, or use cross-section data from sources such as the census. Since the essence of the unemployment problem has been its tendency to increase over time, most analysts have used time series.

In addition to the data problem, and interacting with it, there is too much competing theory. (This means much the same thing as not enough theory, since we lack an encompassing theoretical framework.) There is literally a host of variables that have been suggested as affecting unemployment. Empirical economists, anxious to avoid omitted variable bias in any econometric estimation (i.e., anxious to begin with a fully specified model, a model that contains all the relevant variables) may start by including everything. They are then criticized by journal referees and conference discussants for engaging in "fishing expeditions." Moreover, the consensus on what constitutes a fully specified model is continually evolving over time.

To make things as concrete as possible, consider Table 2, which contains a list of the explanatory variables suggested in the literature as determinants of unemployment. This is a deadly combination – too much competing theory and not enough data.

At this point the sceptical reader might object that it is not clear that there is too much competing theory, nor that an encompassing theoretical framework cannot be derived. Furthermore, if a framework cannot be derived, then one should use non-nested hypothesis testing to determine which model is best. Yet, the practical problems are tremendous. Consider the varieties of wage-efficiency models in existence, or the number of possible ways to specify the "insider-outsider" hypothesis or a simple demand-and-supply model of the labour market – an equilibrium model, a short-side-dominates model, or an employment-equals-labour-demand model. We could introduce inter-temporal substitution in more than one way depending on our assumptions concerning expectations. The varieties of the labour-demand function boggle the mind, depending on assumptions about technology and costs of adjusting factors of production. And what factors of production are considered besides labour and capital? Perhaps energy, and raw materials. And do we allow for different skills of labour, and different vintages of capital? Finally, do we allow for different regions? And then do we not have to model migration simultaneously? There is no consensus on any of these questions.

The attempt to build an encompassing theoretical framework could be described as the "theoretical high road." It has its own pitfalls. Suffice to note that, in practice, as Table 1 makes abundantly clear, the vast majority of research has taken the "low road." In an attempt to short-circuit the difficult task of model building, by far the most popular approach has been to model unemployment directly via a reduced-form equation. Unfortunately, going this route, one comes up against too many competing variables and too little data, much of which is extremely multi-collinear. Let us consider this approach in more detail.

Table 2
Gone Fishing – Anyone for Lures?

Determinants of Unemployment Suggested in Literature

YGAP	Proportional output gap
ADSHK[j]	Shocks to aggregate demand – both fiscal and monetary
MINW	Minimum wages relative to average hourly earnings
WILF	The proportion of women in the labour force
YILF	The proportion of youth in the labour force
UIC	Either RR (the replacement ratio), or UICGEN (Fortin's (1984) measure), or DUMMIES
UNION	The proportion of the labour force unionized
REALR	The real interest rate (a determinant of search – Lucas and Rapping (1970))
SIG	Lilien's (1982) index of structural change
ERGAP	The gap between the exchange rate and its PPP (purchasing power parity) value
ENERGY	The real price of energy (Burns 1988a and 1988b)
ENSHK	The real energy price shock (Burns 1988a and 1988b)
TTSHK[j]	Other real commodity price shocks (Burns 1988a and 1988b)
WAGEGAP	Gap between current wage and the full employment wage (as suggested by Bruno and Sachs 1985)
DWEDGE	The change in the gap between real product wage and the real consumption wage (Keil and Symons 1990)
DFED	Real spending per capita on regional development (Myatt 1992)

Initially, the analyst must decide which procedure to use in order to select a final functional form (i.e., which subset of the variables from Table 2 truly explains the behaviour of the unemployment rate data). The so-called "kitchen sink" approach of including "everything" would *probably* find nothing significant initially, except the *lagged dependent variable* (i.e., it would uncover only that the level of the unemployment rate this year tends to depend upon its level last year). So, how to proceed? The process of eliminating insignificant variables is very sensitive to which variables are dropped first – the final functional form could be sensitive to seemingly innocuous choices. Moreover, it is often tempting to drop prematurely variables that are entering with awkward signs (e.g., variables that theory suggests should have a positive impact but that estimation finds have a negative impact).

Using an *algorithm* to choose the final functional form has the advantage of introducing hard-decision criteria, enhancing replication, and eliminating the subjective element of "data-mining." Unfortunately, there are many possible algorithms that could be employed.[2] Typically, when using aggregate data, different algorithms would produce different equations. In addition, since correctness of sign is not a criterion of choice, all three would be replete with more significant awkward signs than is ever seen in the journals.

AN EXERCISE IN NON-ROBUSTNESS

It is one thing to be told something; it is quite another to see it for oneself. As an exercise, let us unashamedly mine the data to see how the aggregative evidence can be made to fit almost any explanation for Canadian unemployment.

The following exercise uses annual data from 1966 to 1990. The variable definitions are those given in Table 2. The variables are YGAP (the proportional gap between acutal output and potential output), MINW (a minimum-wage indicator), WILF (proportion of women in the labour force), YILF (proportion of youth in the labour force), UICGEN (a measure of unemployment insurance generosity), REALR (a real interest rate indicator), SIG (an indicator of the dispersion of employment growth among nine sectors of the economy), ENERGY (a measure of real energy prices), ENSHK (a real energy price shock variable), and DWEDGE (a measure of the change in the gap between the real product wage and the real consumption wage). Precise definitions and data sources are given in the data appendix. The dependent variable is UR (the unemployment rate), and its lagged value is denoted UR(−1). Regression results are contained in Table 3.

Column (1) of Table 3 shows the result of applying the *backward elimination algorithm* (found in the "stepwise" procedure of the SAS statistical package) to a regression of the unemployment rate (UR) on all the independent variables. The real interest rate variable (REALR) was eliminated first, having the lowest partial-F score. Subsequently, the proportion of youth in the labour force (YILF), the measure of unemployment insurance generosity (UICGEN), and the measure of structural change (SIG) were eliminated. (Before elimination, UICGEN had the wrong sign.) All remaining variables are significant at the 10 percent level on a two-tailed test. All the remaining variables have their expected signs: the minimum-wage variable, the proportion of women in the labour force, and real energy prices all increase the unemployment rate. On the other hand, the rate of change of energy prices has a negative effect on UR. Figure 1 shows the implied long-run contributions of each structural variable to the change in UR since 1966 (where the long-run contributions are calculated by multiplying each variable by its short-run coefficient times $1/(1-L)$, where L denotes the coefficient of the lagged dependent variable).

From Figure 1 it is apparent that ENSHK (the energy shock variable) and DWEDGE (the wage-gap variable) are minor players. The domi-

Table 3
Aggregate Time-Series Equations Explaining the Unemployment Rate

	(1)	(2)	(3a)	(3b)	(4a)	(4b)
Constant	−11.52 (10.8)[1]	−12.42 (11.9)	−3.03 (1.2)	−4.94 (4.2)	2.08 (29.3)	2.13 (31.3)
YGAP	−34.75 (49.7)	−37.36 (52.7)	−29.72 (32.8)	−30.95 (36.3)	−27.58 (23.9)	−27.88 (23.9)
MINW	18.10 (13.8)	19.86 (16.7)	8.28 (2.9)	11.71 (7.6)	1st[2]	1st
WILF	23.57 (14.2)	17.47 (6.5)	OUT[3]	OUT	OUT	OUT
YILF	2nd	3rd	OUT	OUT	OUT	OUT
UICGEN	3rd (ws)[4]	2nd (ws)	0.34 (2.1)	4th	0.43 (3.5)	4th
REALR	1st	0.097 (7.7)	0.125 (10.8)	0.129 (13.6)	0.051 (1.4)	3rd
SIG	4th	63.89 (10.7)	57.72 (6.4)	69.53 (10.3)	OUT	OUT
ENERGY	0.0105 (17.9)	OUT	2nd	2nd	0.0055 (3.7)	0.0084 (14.9)
ENSHK	−1.38 (3.2)	1st	1st	1st	2nd	2nd
DWEDGE	3.48 (4.1)	3.37 (3.2)	1.79 (0.9)	3rd	2.38 (1.4)	5th
UR(−1)	0.37 (14.9)	0.87 (92.2)	0.84 (40.7)	0.98 (113.2)	0.48 (25.7)	0.49 (30.3)
R^2	0.9783	0.9750	0.9686	0.9635	0.9630	0.9526

Notes:
1 Numbers in parentheses indicate partial F-statistics.
2 If a variable was included in the initial regression, but was insignificant at the 10-percent significance level, it was dropped. "1st", "2nd", etc. indicate the order in which these variables were dropped.
3 "OUT" indicates that a variable was excluded from the initial regression.
4 The letters "ws" indicate that the variable had the "wrong" sign before it was eliminated from the regression.

nant roles are played by the remaining three variables. In particular, after increasing between 1966 and 1975, the minimum-wage variable (MINW) started on a downward trend. According to equation 1, by 1990 this variable was causing the unemployment rate to be 3 percentage points less than in 1966. On the other hand, real energy prices started their climb in 1973, and continued rising until 1985. At that point it had caused the unemployment rate to increase by 4.5 percentage points. But by 1990 this variable was only accounting for an extra 2 percentage points of unemployment relative to 1966. Finally, the really dominant variable appears to be the percentage of women in the work force. Its coefficient is large, and the upward trend is

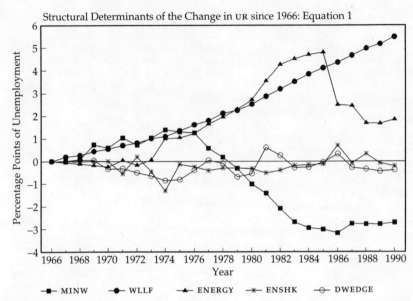

Figure 1
Determinants of UR According to Equation 1

relentless. According to equation 1, by 1990 this variable had caused the unemployment rate to be over 5 percentage points higher than in 1966.

Column (2) of Table 3 repeats the exercise but excludes the ENERGY variable. The reader is invited to imagine that we are not dropping this variable (which clearly would be illegitimate given its strong performance), but that it was never included to begin with. We can argue for its exclusion on *a priori* grounds that it makes no sense to think of changes in the real price of energy as causing permanent increases in unemployment. Certainly, such changes can affect the relative profitability of industries, and cause both structural changes and transitional unemployment. But, for the unemployment to remain permanently, there must be forces at work either hindering labour mobility, or preventing relative prices, factor proportions, and the output mix from adjusting – and it is those forces that should be included as explanatory variables in the UR equation. This could provide a sufficiently strong theoretical rationale for including only the *change* in real energy prices.

The effect of this exclusion is that the real interest rate variable (REALR) and the structural change variable (SIG) now enter significantly into the explanatory equation. In addition, the coefficient of the lagged dependent variable is substantially increased, which has the effect of dramatically enlarging the long-run coefficients. For

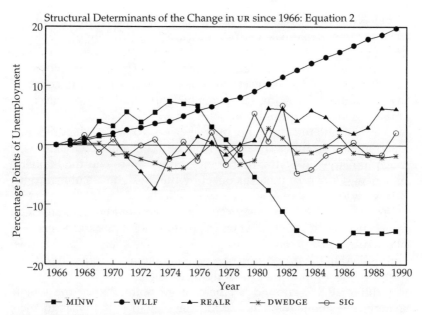

Figure 2
Determinants of UR According to Equation 2

example, the long-run coefficient on the variable for the percentage of women in the labour force (WILF) was 37.4 in equation 1, whereas this coefficient has increased to 134.4 in equation 2. Figure 2 shows the long-run contributions to the change in UR implied by equation 2.

The structural change variable, SIG, has no strong trend, though occasionally there are some quite large shocks. This does not seem to support the currently popular view that much of today's unemployment is due to "restructuring." (Prasad (1994) agrees with this negative evaluation of the restructuring view; see also de Broucker (1996).) On the other hand, the view that high real interest rates are aggravating the unemployment problem (see Smithin 1996) have some support. Indeed, equation 2 would suggest that in 1989 and 1990 they were responsible for 5 percentage points of added unemployment (compared to 1966). Unfortunately, the estimates of equation 2 lack credibility because of the enormously dominant role now assigned to the women in the labour force and minimum-wage variables. Apparently, the relentless upward trend of women in the labour force added 20 percentage points to the unemployment rate by 1990; happily, 15 percentage points of this was offset by the decrease in minimum wages!

Even if equation 2 passed a battery of diagnostic tests, its implications still would not be credible. The problem seems to be that WILF is behaving almost exactly like a trend variable, and since the unemployment rate has a strong upward trend ... bingo! Moreover, the importance attributed to this variable in both equations 1 and 2 does not reflect what we know about female/male unemployment rate differentials. Nevertheless, results like these are not uncommon in the literature. For example, a paper by Johnson and Kneebone (1991) employs two demographic variables – the proportion of youth in the labour force and the number of births per 1,000 of the adult population – and a cubic in time. The coefficients on the "youth" variable were much too large, implying that demography causes enormous unemployment. Of course this was offset by the mysterious cubic in time.

In view of the above, suppose we exclude demographic variables on *a priori* grounds. The justification for this could be that, although a consensus seems to be developing that demography must certainly play a role, it is unlikely that its quantitative size is large. For example, with regard to the proportion of women in the work force, Myatt and Murrell (1990) found that the long-run female/male unemployment rate differential is around 1.5 percentage points. Since the female share of the labour force increased from 0.27 in 1966 to 0.45 in 1990, the implied increase in the Canadian unemployment rate is less than 0.3 of a percentage point. With regard to youth, while the unemployment rate differential between that group and the rest is much higher, their share of the work force is much lower, so the same point holds.[3]

Columns (3a) and (3b) of Table 3 repeat the exercise excluding the two demographic variables, but readmitting the level of energy prices. In this case, however, neither ENSHK nor ENERGY are significant. Indeed, they are the first two variables to be dropped. Column (3a) reports the regression at this stage. Here we find evidence of significant unemployment insurance effects. The coefficient of UICGEN (the unemployment insurance generosity indicator) is positive and significant. Figure 3 plots the implied long-run contributions to the change in the unemployment rate since 1966.

The calculations suggest that the 1971 unemployment insurance reforms added about 5 percentage points to the Canadian unemployment rate. This amount seems to have fallen by nearly half as a result of subsequent tightening of the legislation in 1976–77. Finally, the recession of 1981–82 automatically led to more generous unemployment insurance, and this added a couple of percentage points to the structural unemployment rate for a good part of the decade. In relative terms, however, the effect of unemployment insurance was smaller than the effect of high real interest rates, which at their worst (in 1981, 1982, 1989 and 1990) were responsible for 6 percentage points of extra unemployment. This is the main message of equation 3a.

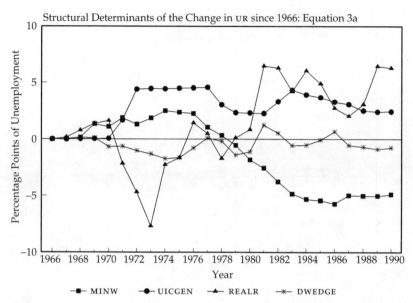

Figure 3
Determinants of UR According to Equation 3a

The problem with equation 3a is that it is little bit like a sieve. Notice the low partial F-statistic for DWEDGE (0.9). If this variable is dropped, the F-statistic for UICGEN falls to 1.6, and it too is subsequently dropped. Thus, column (3b) shows the final result of the backward elimination algorithm, and this contains only MINW, REALR, and SIG as structural variables.

If the foregoing has whetted the reader's appetite for more, consider columns (4a) and (4b). These estimations not only exclude WILF and YILF, but SIG as well. One could appeal to McCallum's (1987) argument that SIG is a "black box" approach, whereas what is needed are the actual determinants of the structural change – and these are captured by the level, and rate of change, in energy prices, and the wedge between the firm's real product wage and the post-tax real wage received by workers. In any event, column (4a) shows that it is possible to generate explanatory equations that contain both ENERGY and UICGEN at high levels of significance. In addition, it is our first example where the minimum wage performs badly, and is the first variable eliminated. The zealous reader may consult Figure 4 for the long-run contributions of UICGEN, REALR, ENERGY, and DWEDGE to the change in UR since 1966. I will not dwell on them here for the unfortunate fact that REALR is only significant at the 12 percent level (on a one-tailed test) and should be eliminated. Once

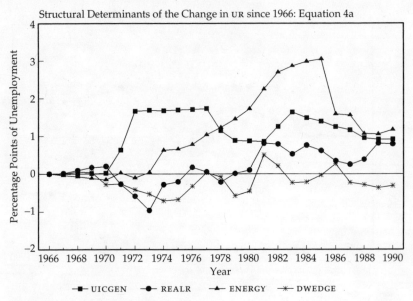

Figure 4
Determinants of UR According to Equation 4a

REALR is dropped, the significance of DWEDGE falls, and it too is dropped. This causes the significance of UICGEN to fall below the critical limit – leaving us only with YGAP, ENERGY, and UR(−1). Yet, as can be seen from equation 4b, we are still able to explain 95 percent of the annual variance in unemployment.

Of course, the root problem is the *multi-collinearity* between the explanatory variables (i.e., that in the sample data independent variables may be approximately linearly related). Table 4 shows the *simple correlation coefficients* between all the variables involved, highlighting correlation coefficients above 0.5. Nevertheless, even after studying this table, it is still hard to fathom why ENERGY, which has a simple correlation with the unemployment rate of 0.91, should become insignificant when WILF is no longer included in the regression. Or why MINW, which performed strongly in every other regression, should become insignificant when SIG is dropped.

To sum up, there are three points that need to be emphasized. First, single aggregate equations like this are not robust, and are consistent with almost any explanation for unemployment. Second, quite nice-looking equations may be derived that conceal absurd quantitative contributions of individual variables to unemployment. And finally, whether or not a variable is found to be significant depends in quite

Table 4
Simple Correlation Coefficients between All Variables

	YGAP	REALR	DWED	UIC	WMIN	ENER	DENER	SIG	WIL	UR
YGAP	–	–0.13	0.00	–0.33	0.14	–0.34	–0.03	0.00	–0.08	–0.53
REALR		–	0.54	–0.11	–0.77	0.67	- 0.19	0.00	0.68	0.57
DWED			–	–0.32	–0.37	0.29	- 0.30	0.21	0.16	0.21
UIC				–	–0.09	0.45	0.24	–0.31	0.34	0.59
WMIN					–	–0.73	0.41	0.07	–0.89	–0.71
ENER						–	0.04	–0.15	0.69	0.91
DENER							–	0.00	–0.27	–0.12
SIG								–	–0.17	–0.25
WILF									–	0.74
UR										–

Note: All simple correlation coefficients above 0.5 are written in bold type.

obscure and unpredictable ways on which other variables are also included in the regression. These factors alone are sufficient to explain why we know so little from the aggregate data. Add to the mix different data periods, frequencies, and ways of measuring variables, and we would predict a plethora of conflicting results – which is, in fact, exactly what we have. (The interested reader is referred to Setterfield et al. (1992) for an interesting demonstration concerning sensitivity to variable measurement differences.)

WHICH WAY FORWARD?

It seems clear that we must disaggregate as much as we can, while retaining the time-series dimension. The advantages of good-quality longitudinal micro-data are twofold: the complete elimination of aggregation problems (since we disaggregate all the way to the individual), and the multiplication of observations leading to a drastic increase in degrees of freedom. The hope is that the use of such data sets will reduce the incidence of non-robustness problems outlined above.

In my own research I have experimented with the use of provincially disaggregated data. In fact, provincial disaggregation has been relatively common, but analysts have either employed pooled estimations that constrain provincial coefficients to be the same across equations (see Miller 1987), or they impose no *cross-equation restrictions* at all. Constraining the provincial coefficients to be uniform across provinces does injury to reality since provinces do differ in their "sensitivity" to changes in the explanatory variables. Imposing no cross-equation restrictions just increases the number of coefficients to be estimated by the same order as the data set is increased, and so does not give us much extra leverage.

My own approach (borrowed from the earnings-disparity literature) has been to model provincial unemployment rate disparities directly, decomposing the dependent variable into a part due to different "endowments" and a part due to different "sensitivities." This has several advantages. First, such a system may be better equipped to deal with the hysteresis problem, which (in its strong form) abandons the notion of a unique natural rate of unemployment in favour of multiple equilibria. (An advantage is conferred providing equilibrium unemployment rate *disparities* exist.) Second, we now have ten equations to estimate *national* coefficients, without having to assume identical structure in each province. This should, and does, increase the robustness of the estimates.

Explaining the decomposition methodology is straightforward. Postulate a provincial UR reduced-form equation:

$$(1) \qquad UR^j = a^j + \sum_{i=1}^{n} b_i^j X_i + \sum_{i=1}^{m} c_i^j Y_i^j$$

where we have distinguished between national variables (X_i) that are common to all provinces (for example, the level of interest rates, or the change in real energy prices), and regionally specific variables (Y_i^j), whose values differ across provinces (for example, the level of the minimum wage, or unemployment insurance generosity). If equation (1) were applied to Canada as a whole we would have:

$$(2) \qquad UR = a + \sum_{i=1}^{n} b_i X_i + \sum_{i=1}^{m} c_i Y_i$$

where Y_i denotes the average Canadian values of the regionally specific variables Y_i^j. Subtracting (2) from (1) we obtain:

$$(3) \qquad UR^j - UR = (a^j - a) + \sum_{i=1}^{n} (b_i^j - b_i) X_i +$$

$$\sum_{i=1}^{m} c_i (Y_i^j - Y_i) + \sum_{i=1}^{m} (c_i^j - c_i) Y_i^j$$

The second term on the right-hand side of (3) reflects the influence of the national variables; this influence can only be exerted through different provincial "sensitivities" ($b_i^j - b_i$). The last two terms in equation (3) are obtained by adding and subtracting $\sum c_i Y_i^j$. This allows us to decompose the influence of the regionally specific variables into two parts: that part due to different "endowments" ($Y_i^j -$

Y_i), and that part due to different "sensitivities" ($c_i^j - c_i$). It is important to recognize that the coefficients of the endowment differences are the national coefficients, c_i.

I used this methodology on annual provincial data from 1966 to 1990. The system was estimated using Zellner's method of seemingly unrelated regressions (SUR), imposing the cross-equation restrictions. While the approach and the results are published in full elsewhere (Myatt 1992), it is worth reporting that intuitively plausible and highly significant effects were found for REALR, UICGEN, MINW, and SIG as structural variables.[4] However, for reasons outlined in the previous section, I excluded on *a priori* grounds both the demographic variables (WILF and YILF) and the level of real energy prices (ENERGY). In writing the present paper, I returned to the provincially disaggregated model and added these variables. The *t*-scores for the national coefficients of WILF and YILF were 0.7 and 0.3 respectively; in addition, the ENERGY variable was significant at the 10 percent level only in one province – Saskatchewan. Finally, the significance of the original variables was largely unchanged. UICGEN remained significant at the 1-percent level, while the significance of SIG and MINW was slightly reduced. Thus, it would seem as if this form of disaggregation also gives us the extra leverage we need, and allows more robust estimations to be made. I would encourage other researchers who use time-series data to disaggregate as much as possible, and to consider the decomposition methodology as a viable alternative.

Of course disaggregation is not a panacea. We still lack an encompassing theoretical framework; there is still the problem of multiple ways of defining variables designed to capture specific effects; there are still possible problems with endogeneity of the explanatory variables, and in particular, the unemployment insurance generosity variable.

Endogeneity of the unemployment insurance generosity variable occurs using either the replacement ratio, or Fortin's measure. The replacement ratio (the ratio of average weekly benefits to average weekly wages) will likely increase in a recession as the more remunerative but exposed jobs are laid off (for example, in manufacturing). However, this measure is rarely used today because it fails to capture changes in either the eligibility requirements or the duration of benefits. Fortin's measure encompasses these dimensions, but precisely because of this, it too has endogenous elements (see Osberg 1996).[5] In a recession the ratio of the maximum duration of benefits to the minimum-work requirement will increase. Furthermore, unemployment insurance is always more generous in the high-unemployment regions, again creating correlation between the measure of unemployment insurance generosity and the actual incidence of unemployment. This problem can be dealt with nominally by using lagged values of the explanatory variable as instruments. However, the frequency of *serial correlation* in the time-series data creates doubt as to whether this method really comes to grips with the problem. It is worth emphasizing that similar problems would crop up even in longitudinal (or micro-) data sets; individuals from high unemployment regions are more likely to be both unemployed and unemployed longer. Thus, these increased likelihoods will inevitably be correlated with more generous unemployment insurance, and perhaps inappropriately attributed to more generous unemployment insurance. Only slight mis-specifications of the explanatory equation could lead to this outcome. It would be especially important to specify correctly the regional dispersion of aggregate demand.

In other work (Myatt 1994), I have attempted to address the endemic problem of endogeneity of UICGEN. The crux of my approach is that unemployment insurance generosity increases in recessions (it moves *counter-cyclically*), whereas the weighted standard deviation of UR disparities across provinces (SDUR) decreases in recessions (it moves *pro-cyclically*). Therefore, when SDUR is the dependent variable, any residual endogeneity of the unemployment insurance generosity measure would tend to bias its coefficient in the *negative* direction. Thus, in this framework, it should be more difficult to show a positive relation between unemployment insurance and SDUR; but if we can show one, we should have more confidence in the result. In fact, a significant and positive relation between UICGEN and provincial unemployment rate disparities emerged in every single equation, despite extensive testing for non-robustness by using different variable-selection algorithms and different *a priori* exclusion of certain variables.[6]

CONCLUSION

This paper has argued that the fundamental reason why we know so little about the determinants of unemployment is because we have data that is insufficient and highly multi-collinear, interacting with too much competing theory. Several results follow from this. First, single aggregate equations are typically not robust. Second, quite promising equations can be derived that conceal absurd quantitative contributions of individual variables to unemployment. And finally, whether or not a variable is found to be significant depends on what other variables are also included in the regression. In such circumstances, a variety of conflicting findings is what we would predict to occur, and what does in fact occur.

Disaggregation is certainly the way future research should go. Good-quality longitudinal micro-data sets will help. However, I have argued that there may be more information that we can extract from the time-series data by using it in slightly novel ways.

Nevertheless, anyone attempting to point to unemployment insurance generosity as being an important determinant of higher Canadian unemployment rates has got some explaining to do. One immediate question a sceptic might ask is, "If Canada and Europe are so alike with respect to the unemployment problem, how can the 1971 unemployment insurance reforms be central to Canada's unemployment rate problem, when this is an event that happened in Canada alone?" A possible response might have two parts. First, the 1971 reforms brought Canada into line with the more generous unemployment insurance already existent in Europe; and second, the supply-side effects of any given unemployment insurance program may differ when unemployment is high compared to when it is low. Thus, subsequent to the reforms, interactions took place between shortfalls in aggregate demand and unemployment insurance generosity that produced similar outcomes in both places.[7]

In any event, why not assume for a moment that we know for certain that the 1971 unemployment insurance reforms increased measured unemployment by, let us say, 2 to 3 percentage points. What does this imply about its effect on employment, or its effect on output? And does this information help us in making policy recommendations to reduce the unemployment rate in Canada? Remarkably, the answers here are "nothing" and "very little."

Consider the implications for the employment rate. If more generous unemployment insurance attracts marginal workers into the labour force to establish eligibility for a claim, we would expect the employment rate to increase. There has been almost no work done on the effects of unemployment insurance on the employment rate. Or, consider next the implications on output. More generous unemployment insurance is predicted to increase search time that will lead to a better matching of workers with jobs. Clearly, this leads to efficiency and output gains. Thus, even if more generous unemployment insurance has increased the unemployment rate, it is not clear whether this is a better alternative because the more generous unemployment insurance is paying for itself indirectly.

However, we can go even further. Suppose that Card and Riddell (1993) are correct that the increase in Canadian unemployment, relative both to the previous decade and to the United States is not due to a change in employment, but is rather because Canadians are reclassifying themselves as unemployed rather than not in the labour force. Should we then recommend reducing the generosity of unemployment insurance? We must be careful because unemployment insurance also serves as an automatic stabilizer, and as a regional transfer.[8] Moreover, as emphasized by Osberg (1979), it forms an integral part of a larger social security framework whose instruments include job-creation programs, old-age pensions, and social security. Thus, when we do talk about changes to unemployment insurance, we must keep all these parameters in balance.

This having been said, what sort of reform to the unemployment insurance system would we recommend to a policy-maker? Does it help to know that unemployment insurance contributed 0.5 or 1, 2, or 3 percentage points to the unemployment rate? Again, the answer is "not a lot." We need to identify the primary mechanism that is generating the result. It could be, for example, that more generous unemployment insurance reduces the political pressure for full employment policies – that it actually operates on the demand side.[9] Or conversely, if it operates on the supply side, it may restrain out-migration. If so, it may be that unemployment insurance should be made *more* generous as a *condition* of out-migration. Since we already know that the long-term unemployed are an increasing proportion of the total, we need to know whether this is due to the stigma of unemployment itself, or to de-skilling. In the former case, the remedy might be providing work-experience programs, whereas in the latter it might involve linking unemployment insurance to retraining (see Hughes 1988).

On the other hand, what is clearly not recommended is ad hoc tinkering with the system. Disentitlement for quitting a job "without just cause," or for being fired for misconduct (introduced in 1992), is likely to reduce labour mobility even more, and shift the balance of power between worker and employer. It could lead to increased violations of occupational health and safety standards, and reduce the willingness of employees to speak out against sexual harassment. Perhaps it is time for economists to stop debating the question of how much unemployment is due to more generous unemployment insurance and to start considering how a more efficient and equitable system could be devised – one that encourages geographic mobility and the acquisition of skills.

DATA APPENDIX

YGAP   This denotes the proportional gap between actual output and potential output, where potential output is measured by regressing the logarithm of real Gross Domestic Product (GDP) on a constant, trend, a dummy equal to zero before 1974 and unity afterwards, and a dummy/trend interaction variable.

REALR   This denotes the real interest rate that is measured as the annual average nominal 91-day T-bill rate (Cansim B1401) minus the actual inflation that occurred over the course of that year. The inflation rate was calculated using the GDP deflator.

ENERGY   This is the level of real energy prices. The measure of energy prices used is that for petroleum and coal. This involved splicing the 1985 Cansim D544000 (from matrix 671) with the 1991 Cansim D693417. This nominal price index was then deflated by the GDP deflator, and expressed as a percentage change.

DENER   This is the rate of change of ENERGY.

UICGEN   This is Fortin's (1984) measure of the marginal cost of unemployment for a worker optimizing within the unemployment insurance regulations, averaged over all provinces, using labour-force shares as weights. It equals $[R * (D/M)* \text{tax} * \text{coverage}]$ where R is the replacement ratio calculated from unemployment insurance regulations, D is the maximum duration of benefits, and M is the minimum work requirement. Tax equals unity after 1971 and 1.25 prior to that date, to reflect the taxability of benefits since 1971. Coverage is the proportion of the labour force covered. Unemployment insurance was calculated using data found in the *Statistical Report on the Operation of the UI Act* (Statistics Canada 73-001). An accurate and simple method of calculating both D and M is outlined in Coe (1989).

MINW   This is the ratio of the minimum hourly wage rate and average hourly earnings, averaged over all provinces, using labour-force shares as weights. The minimum hourly wage was obtained from Employment and Immigration Canada. Average hourly earnings in manufacturing (in nominal dollars per hour) was obtained from "Employment Earnings and Hours" (Statistics Canada Catalogue #72-002).

SIG   This is Lilien's (1982) dispersion index. Employment by sector is published in the labour-force survey post 1976. Pre-1976 data was purchased from Statistics Canada. It uses a nine-sector breakdown. The sectors are agriculture; other primary; manufacturing; construction; transportation; trade; finance, insurance, and real estate; services; and public sector.

DWEDGE   The wedge is described in the data appendix to Keil/Symons (1990). It measures the wedge driven between the firm's real labour costs and the post-tax real wage received by labour suppliers.

126   Tony Myatt

NOTES

1 It is worth noting that these latter studies disagree on which three provinces have the significant positive effect, though they both include Saskatchewan – a province that still has one of the lowest unemployment rates in Canada!

2 For example, the "backward elimination technique" includes every variable initially, and then sequentially drops the least significant variable, until only variables above a predetermined significance level remain. In this version, once a variable has been dropped, it stays out. An alternative, the "forward selection procedure," begins by adding variables sequentially on the basis of best marginal increment to R^2. In this version, once a variable has gained "admittance" to the equation, it stays in. A third algorithm – the maximum R^2 procedure – allows freedom of entry *and* exit as we increase the number of variables in the equation.

3 For example, suppose the unemployment rate for youth is 20 percent, and for the rest it is 10 percent, and the proportion of youth doubles from 0.1 to 0.2. This implies an increase in average UR of only 1 percentage point.

4 The results suggest that the 1971 revisions increased the national UR by about 3.5 percentage points. In Newfoundland, regionally extended benefits (unemployment insurance is at its most generous in this province) and the province's extra "sensitivity" combine to produce the highest UR response – a 9-percentage-point increase in UR in Newfoundland as a result of the 1971 revisions. The effect of the unemployment insurance revisions is least in Ontario, where both "sensitivity" and benefits were least, producing an increase of 1.8 percentage points. Thus, the 1971 revisions opened up a 7-percentage-point differential between Newfoundland and Ontario. This is close to Riddell's (1980: 98) estimate of a 5- to 6-percentage-point differential. However, between 1977 (when the aggregate unemployment insurance generosity index was at its most generous) and 1990 the UIC generosity index decreased by 45 percent. The attributable unemployment decreased correspondingly.

5 Fortin's measure is equal to $[R * (D/M) * tax * coverage]$ where R is the replacement ratio calculated from unemployment insurance regulations, D is the maximum duration of benefits, and M is the minimum-work requirement. Tax equals unity after 1971 and 1.25 prior to that date, to reflect the taxability of benefits since 1971. Coverage is the proportion of the labour force covered.

6 In fact UICGEN emerged as the single most important structural determinant of increased provincial UR disparities.

7 It seems significant that the Phillips curve undergoes a structural break

in 1971 (Fortin 1991), the year of dramatic unemployment insurance reform.

8 To give an idea of the magnitudes involved, in 1977 the three Maritime provinces received $452.8 million in unemployment insurance premiums, whereas premiums collected were only $145.7 million. This dwarfed DREE expenditure of $97.8 million.

9 This is Pierre Fortin's insight, shared in conversation.

REFERENCES

Bruno and J.D. Sachs. 1985. *Economics of Worldwide Stagflation*. Cambridge, Mass.: Harvard University Press.

Burns, A. 1988a. "Unemployment in Canada: Frictional Structural and Cyclical Aspects." Unpublished manuscript, Economic Council of Canada.

– 1988b. "The Natural Rate of Unemployment: A Regionally Disaggregated Approach." Unpublished manuscript, Economic Council of Canada.

Card, D., and W.C. Riddell. 1993. "A Comparative Analysis of Unemployment in Canada and the United States." In D. Card and R. Freeman, eds., *Small Differences that Matter: Labor Markets and Income Maintenance in Canada and the United States*, 149–90. Chicago: University of Chicago Press.

Coe, D.T. 1989. "Structural Determinants of the Natural Rate of Unemployment in Canada." IMF working paper No. 89/31.

de Broucker, P. 1996. "Low Unemployment in Japan: The Product of Socioeconomic Coherence." This volume.

Denton, F.T., C.H. Feaver, and A.L. Robb. 1975. "Patterns of Unemployment Behaviour in Canada." Economic Council of Canada Discussion Paper No. 36.

Fortin, P. 1984. "Unemployment Insurance Meets the Classical Labour Supply Model." *Economics Letters* 14: 275–81.

– 1989. "How 'Natural' is Canada's High Unemployment Rate?" *European Economic Review* 33, No. 1: 89–110.

Gross, D. 1996. "Unemployment Persistence in France and Germany." This volume.

Grubel, H.G., D. Maki, and S. Sax. 1975a. "Real and Insurance-Induced Unemployment in Canada." *Canadian Journal of Economics* 8: 174–91.

– 1975b. "Real and Insurance-Induced Unemployment in Canada: A Reply." *Canadian Journal of Economics* 8: 603–5.

Hughes, P.R. 1988. "Is Unemployment Reversible." *Applied Economics* 20: 31–42.

Johnson, James A., and Ronald D. Kneebone. 1991. "Deriving Natural Rates of Unemployment for Sub-National Regions: the case of Canadian Provinces." *Applied Economics* 23: 1–10.

Jones, S.R.G., and W.C. Riddell. 1991. "The Measurement of Labour Force Dynamics with the Labour Market Activity Survey: The LMAS Filter." UBC Department of Economics Discussion Paper No. 91–17.

Keil, M.W., and J.S.V. Symons. 1990. "An Analysis of Canadian Unemployment." *Canadian Public Policy* 16: 1–16.

Landon, S. 1987. "Unanticipated Policy Shocks, Regime Changes, and Unemployment in Canada, 1976–83." *Applied Economics* 19: 1065–81.

Lazar, F. 1978. "The Impact of the 1971 Revisions on Unemployment Rates: Another Look." *Canadian Journal of Economics* 11: 559–69.

Lilien, D.M. 1982. "Sectoral Shifts and Cyclical Unemployment." *Journal of Political Economy* 90: 777–93.

Lucas, Robert E., and Leonard A. Rapping. 1970. "Real Wages, Employment and Inflation." In Edumudn S. Phelps, ed., *Microeconomic Foundations of Employment an Inflation Theory.* New York: W.W. Norton and Co.

McCallum, J. 1987. "Unemployment in Canada and the United States." *Canadian Journal of Economics* 20: 802–22.

Maki, D.R. 1975. "Regional Differences in Insurance-Induced Unemployment in Canada." *Economic Enquiry* 13: 389–400.

Miller, F. 1987. "The Natural Rate of Unemployment: Regional Estimates and Policy Implications." *Canadian Journal of Regional Science* 10: 63–76.

Myatt, A. 1992. "Provincial Unemployment Rate Disparities: A Case of No Concern?" *Canadian Journal of Regional Science* 15, No. 1: 101–19.

– 1994. "Provincial Unemployment Rate Disparities Revisited." University of New Brunswick Working Paper No. 94-7.

Myatt, A., and D. Murrell. 1990. "The Female/Male Unemployment Rate Differential." *Canadian Journal of Economics* 23: 312–22.

Osberg, L. 1979. "Unemployment Insurance in Canada: A Review of the Recent Amendments." *Canadian Public Policy* 5:223–35.

– 1996. "Unemployment Insurance and Unemployment – Revisited." This volume.

Prasad, E. 1994. "Labour Market Aspects of Industrial Restructuring." *Canadian Business Economics* 2, No. 1: 28–35.

Riddell, W. 1980. *Unanticipated Inflation and Unemployment in Canada, Ontario and Newfoundland.* Economic Council of Canada Discussion Paper No. 182.

Samson, L. 1985. "A Study of the Impact of Sectoral Shifts on Aggregate Unemployment in Canada." *Canadian Journal of Economics* 18: 518–30.

Setterfield, M., D. Gordon, and L. Osberg. 1992. "Searching for a Will o'the Wisp: An Empirical Study of the NAIRU in Canada." *European Economic Review* 36: 119–36.

Smithin, J. 1996. "Real Interest Rates, Inflation and Unemployment." This volume.

7 Does Unemployment Insurance Increase Unemployment?

SHELLEY PHIPPS

For years, people have argued that Canadian unemployment insurance increases unemployment excessively.[1] In 1985 the Macdonald Royal Commission recommended changes to minimize the adverse incentive consequences of the program; in 1987 the Forget Commission advocated an alternative set of changes with a similar goal; in 1990 the minimum conditions for qualification were increased and the maximum duration of benefits was decreased in lower-unemployment regions (see Phipps 1990a) in an effort to "reduce the work disincentives in the unemployment insurance programme" (Employment and Immigration Canada 1989: 5). In 1993, the federal government amended unemployment insurance to disqualify anyone who quits "without just cause" in an effort to minimize labour-market disincentives.[2]

Is this attention to the negative work incentives of unemployment insurance warranted? It is certainly true that the very simple neoclassical model of labour-supply behaviour found in any undergraduate labour economics text predicts that unemployment insurance will increase unemployment for some individuals (see Gunderson and Riddell (1988) or Ehrenberg and Smith (1991) for an explicit treatment of the incentive effects of unemployment insurance from the perspective of the neoclassical labour/leisure-choice model). Thus, anyone who has taken a basic labour economics course will have a theoretical apparatus with which to predict that if we reduce the "cost" of being unemployed, individuals will "choose" more unemployment. And, almost everyone has a story of some individual who has quit his or her job in order to collect unemployment insurance and go skiing (or sailing or ...). Thus, for many people it is easy to believe that unemployment insurance increases unemployment. But, does recent research in labour economics indicate that there is any empirical credibility for this claim?

This chapter will examine the evidence generated over the past fifteen years of research in labour economics in an attempt to assess the credibility of the textbook predictions, based on a very simple neoclassical model of labour supply, that unemployment insurance will increase unemployment. The following section of the chapter surveys Canadian estimates of the wage elasticity of labour supply to answer the question: "How big are the labour-supply responses we should expect from changes in unemployment insurance?" The third section surveys the literature on labour-supply quantity constraints (Canadian and foreign, principally those in the United States) to address the question: "Are workers able to adjust their hours of work in response to incentives from unemployment insurance?" The fourth section asks whether workers respond to a dollar of unemployment insurance in the same way as they respond to a dollar of wage income. The final section concludes.

CANADIAN ESTIMATES OF THE WAGE ELASTICITY OF LABOUR SUPPLY

A simple textbook model of labour-supply behaviour, incorporating the incentive consequences of the Canadian unemployment insurance program (see, for example, Gunderson and Riddell 1988) assumes that individuals make annual labour-supply plans, taking as given their individual wage rates as well as the availability of unemployment insurance.[3] Unemployment insurance alters the options that would otherwise be available to workers. Some individuals are predicted to *choose* additional weeks of paid employment since, for a period of time, additional weeks increase unemployment insurance entitlement – unemployment insurance effectively generates a "wage subsidy" as workers receive both their wages and weeks of unemployment insurance entitlement as compensation for weeks of employment.[4] However, if individuals are making annual plans, then it is possible for them to earn sufficient weeks of unemployment insurance to allow them to quit and collect benefits for the rest of the year. For such people (and given this framework), working additional weeks means giving up weeks of potential unemployment insurance. Thus, unemployment insurance effectively generates a "tax" on wages – the worker nets only his or her wage less the foregone unemployment insurance benefits. The textbook model thus predicts that individuals facing this "implicit tax" will *choose* more unemployment.[5]

Notice that a critical assumption of the framework outlined above is that individuals are free to *choose* any amount of employment they desire. There is no mention of the possibility of demand-side restrictions on worker choices through involuntary unemployment. The third section of this paper investigates empirical evidence that questions the validity of this assumption. However, even in the absence of any constraints on worker choices, we need to know the magnitude of labour-supply elasticities in order to make any predictions about the likely magnitude of response to an "unemployment insurance tax." This section of the chapter surveys Canadian estimates of the own-wage elasticity of labour supply.[6]

There have been remarkably few studies of the labour-supply behaviour of Canadian men using micro-data. I could find only five papers cited in the *Journal of Economic Literature* EconLit database. The results of these studies are reported in the first section of Table 1. Estimates of the gross own-wage elasticity of labour supply ranged from a high of +0.64 to a low of −0.58. However, both extreme values are taken from the same paper (Baffoe-Bonnie 1989), which uses potentially unreliably small samples of micro-data[7] – only 360 and 170 observations. If the Baffoe-Bonnie elasticities are eliminated, then

Table 1
Survey of Estimated Own-Wage Labour-Supply Elasticities
for Canadian Men and Women

	Men		
Survey	Single	Married	Single/Married Together
Osberg and Phipps (1993) 1986 LMAS	–	–	0.05 → 0.028 (15,292 observations)
Phipps (1991) 1982 SCF	0.10 (1796 single men)	–	–
Phipps (1990b) 1982 SCF	–	0.07 → 0.13 (2,000 married men)	–
Baffoe-Bonnie (1989) 1979 GSS	–	−0.58 (360 married men in "primary labour" markets of NS, NB, PEI) 0.64 (170 married men in "secondary" labour market of NS, NB, PEI)	–
Ham/Hsiao (1984) 1971 Canadian Census	–	–	0.46 (2,516 observations)

Table 1 (cont'd)

Survey	Women		Single/Married Together
	Single	Married	
Osberg and Phipps (1993) 1986 LMAS	–	–	−0.005 → 0.073 (12,716 observations)
Phipps (1991) 1982 SCF	0.06 (2297 single women)	–	–
Phipps (1990b) 1982 SCF	–	0.15 → 0.18 (2,000 married women)	–
Baffoe-Bonnie (1989) 1979 GSS	–	−0.90 (47 married women in "primary" labour market of NS, NB, PEI)	–
		2.32 (183 married women in "secondary" labour market of NS, NB, PEI)	
Smith and Stelcner (1988) 1981 Canadian Census	–	0.028 → 0.149 (2,851 married women)	–
Prescott, Swidinsky, and Wilton (1986) 1974 MBAIS	0.74 (182 low-income single women)	0.0 (430 low-income married women)	–
Stelcner and Breslaw (1985) 1979 SCF	–	0.40 (2,439 observations; married Quebec residents)	–
Robinson and Tomes (1985) 1979 QLS	–	–	−0.85 → 0.19 (195 and 324 observations)
Nakamura and Nakamura (1983) 1971 Canadian Census	–	−0.197 → 0.036 (533 to 1,994 married women)	–
Nakamura, Nakamura, and Cullen (1979) 1971 Canadian Census	–	−0.320 → −0.299 (607 to 4,762 married women)	–

Abbreviations:
GSS: General Segmentation Survey
LMAS: Labour Market Activities Survey
MBAIS: Manitoba Basic Annual Income Survey
NB: New Brunswick
NS: Nova Scotia
QLS: Quality of Life Survey
SCF: Survey of Consumer Finance

the range of estimates for the own-wage elasticity of labour supply for Canadian men is −0.05 to +0.46. These results are comparable with the range of −0.38 to +0.14 reported in the comprehensive Killingsworth (1983) survey (of studies primarily from the United States). Thus, it seems safe to conclude that the labour-supply behaviour of Canadian men is inelastic – highly inelastic if we use the most recent estimates that have the advantage of much better data.[8]

There have been many more studies of the labour-supply behaviour of Canadian women than of Canadian men – presumably because earlier evidence had indicated that the labour supply of men is very inelastic, but that women are responsive to wage changes. (For women, Killingsworth (1983) reports a range of gross own-wage labour-supply elasticities from −0.89 to +15.24.) The results of Canadian studies of women's labour supply are summarized in the second section of Table 1. Both the high and low estimates are again provided by the Baffoe-Bonnie study, which uses even smaller samples for women than for men (47 and 183 observations) and hence may be rather unreliable, given the results of Gordon, Osberg, and Phipps (1991). If these are eliminated, the range of estimated own-wage labour-supply elasticities for Canadian women is −0.85 to +0.74. Further, the representativeness of the estimate of +0.74 might also be questioned as it was derived using a sample of only 182 low-income women who participated in the 1974 Manitoba Basic Annual Income Survey (Prescott et al. 1986). If this estimate is also disregarded, then the range of reported elasticity estimates is from −0.85 to +0.40.

Thus, the range of estimated elasticities for Canadian women is very similar to that reported for Canadian men (−0.05 to +0.46), though there appears to be more evidence of backward-bending labour-supply curves for women. This, of course, conflicts with the conventional wisdom that female labour supply is highly elastic (see, for example, Killingsworth 1983). Why are these Canadian estimates so low? The reason is that all of the Canadian estimates are what Killingsworth would label "second-generation studies." For example, they employ micro-data; they make adjustments for the sample selectivity bias that can arise from excluding non-participants when estimating labour-supply functions; and in many cases they take account of the effects of taxes on labour supply. The Killingsworth survey includes many older studies of women's labour supply that were much less sophisticated. Other more recent studies such as Pencavel (1986) and Killingsworth and Heckman (1986) also conclude that labour supply of both men and women is inelastic. In a highly influential study of women's labour supply, Mroz (1987: 795) concludes:

The range of labor supply estimates that we fail to reject suggests that the labor supply behavior of working married women matches the estimated behavior of prime-aged males. Such a conclusion conflicts with most commonly held beliefs about female labor supply... In this study, we are able to obtain large estimates of the income and wage coefficients. Our statistical tests, however, emphatically reject the economic and statistical assumptions needed to obtain these large wage and income effects.

Finally, Hum and Simpson (1993) survey experimental evidence from both Canada and the United States and again argue that labour supply is inelastic for both men and women.

Thus, the Canadian evidence is not unusual. Modern empirical labour economics concludes that the labour-supply behaviour of men *and* women is inelastic – highly inelastic if we focus on the most recent estimates using the best available data.

What are the implications of these findings for predictions about the extent to which unemployment insurance increases unemployment? Consider the following example of the likely labour-supply consequences of the current proposal to reduce the benefit-replacement ratio from 60 percent to 57 percent. From the perspective of the simple model of labour supply outlined above, this reduction in the benefit-reduction rate will reduce the implicit unemployment insurance tax from 60 percent to 57 percent, an increase in the "net wage" of 7.5 percent.[9] Neoclassical theory predicts that this change will increase incentives to paid employment for anyone affected by the unemployment insurance tax. But, how big should we expect such responses to be? Using estimated elasticities for men and women taken from Osberg and Phipps (1993) – −0.05 for men and +0.018 for women, I calculate that an average unemployed woman will increase hours of paid employment by 0.94 hours *annually*, while an average unemployed man will *reduce* hours of paid employment by 3.68 hours *annually*.[10] Thus, while the predicted impact of the policy change for women is in the anticipated direction, the magnitude of the response is tiny – about the equivalent of two coffee breaks. For men, the predicted response is very slightly larger, but in the direction opposite to that anticipated, given the backward-bending labour-supply function for men.[11]

QUANTITY CONSTRAINTS AND LABOUR SUPPLY

There is by now a substantial empirical literature that points out that to understand observed labour supply, we need to recognize the importance of quantity constraints generated on the demand side of the labour market. Table 2 summarizes the finding of twelve papers on this topic published during the past ten years. Some of these papers focus on the problem of involuntary unemployment; others focus on potential underemployment (or overemployment) that can occur when workers are offered only fixed packages of wages and hours that may not correspond with their desired labour supply. In either case, these papers point out how inappropriate are labour/leisure-choice models that assume that workers can continuously vary their hours of work in response to changes in wage rates or transfer programs. The general consensus of this literature is that constraints *do* matter. Ignoring them will lead to upward biases in estimates of labour-supply elasticities, and perhaps even more importantly for the topic addressed in this paper, ignoring the possibility that some workers *do not have the choice* of increasing hours of paid employment may lead us to incorrect policy conclusions about the likely consequences of, for example, reducing unemployment insurance benefits.

Consider, first, the descriptive evidence on the prevalence of quantity constraints presented in these papers. Osberg and Phipps (1993), using the Canadian Labour Market Activities Survey (LMAS), report that 13.4 percent of men (aged twenty-five to fifty-four) wanted additional *weeks* of work in 1986; 12.9 percent of women wanted additional weeks.[12] Further, 67.8 percent of men (60.1 percent of women) who experienced some unemployment in 1986 wanted additional weeks of work. Finally, using estimated "desired" labour-supply functions, Osberg and Phipps calculate that underemployed men would like, but are unable, to increase annual employment by 244 hours(approximately 31 eight-hour days); underemployed women would like, but are unable, to increase annual employment by 115 hours (14 eight-hour days).

Lin and Osberg (1992), also using the LMAS, report that 14.1 percent of men (aged twenty-five to fifty-four) who had some paid employment in *both* 1988 and 1989 wanted additional weeks in 1988; 14.9 percent wanted additional weeks in 1989; 6.3 percent wanted additional weeks in *both* 1988 and 1989. Thus, a significant number of Canadian men experienced labour-market constraints in two consecutive years. For women, the prevalence of constraints in 1988–89 was even higher. From the sample of women who had some paid employment in both 1988 and 1989, 16.3 wanted additional weeks in 1988; 15.2 wanted additional weeks in 1989; 7.6 percent wanted additional weeks in both years. Again, there appears to be persistence in the experience of constraints.

Table 2
Survey of Evidence on Quantity Constraints

	Data with Self-reporting
Osberg, Phipps (1993) (1986) LMAS (Canada)	13.4% of men (25–54) with some paid employment wanted additional *weeks* (15,292 observations). 12.9% of women (25–54) with some paid employment wanted additional *weeks* (12,716 observations). Ignoring quantity constraints yields biased estimates of the parameters of the labour-supply function.
Altonji, Paxon (1992) 1968–83 (United States)	The effect of changes in the demographic structure of the family (e.g., birth of a child) is larger for wives who change jobs than for those who do not, a finding consistent with the view that constraints on hours of work imposed by firms limit the labour-supply responsiveness of workers.
Kahn, Lang (1992) 1981–82 PSID (United States) March 1985 CPS (United States)	41% of wage and salaried male heads of household (25–54) desired more work (hours or weeks not specified) (759 observations). 35% of wage and salaried male heads of household (25–54) desired additional hours at the *same* rate of pay. Neither the agency model nor the firm-specific capital model is able to explain the observed pattern of constraints.
Lin, Osberg (1992) 1988–89 LMAS (Canada)	14.1% of men (25–54) with some paid employment in *both* 1988 and 1989 wanted additional weeks in 1988; 14.9% wanted additional weeks in 1989; 6.3% wanted additional weeks in both years (10,710 observations). 16.3% of women (25–54) with some paid employment in *both* 1988 and 1989 wanted additional weeks in 1988; 15.2% wanted additional weeks in 1989; 7.6% wanted additional weeks in both years (9,470 observations). Results reject the real business-cycle view that unemployment represents voluntary consumption of leisure.
Kahn, Lang (1991) 1985 SWR, Supplement to June 1985 LFS (Canada)	40.6% of non-union private non-agricultural male workers (25–64) wanted more hours than they were observed to work (2,230 observations). 33.0% of male unionized employees (25–64) wanted more hours (1,266 observations). 32.0% of female private non-agricultural employees (25–64) wanted more hours (2,792 observations). Information on *desired* hours suggests that the use of observed hours in estimation of labour-supply elasticities yields a small upward bias.
Altonji, Paxon (1988) 1968–83 PSID (United States)	61% reported themselves *unable* to increase hours of work; 27% reported that they would like additional hours (13,118 observations). Some support is found for the hypothesis that workers must be compensated for taking jobs that do not provide desired hours.

Table 2 (cont'd)

	Data with Self-reporting
Maloney (1987) 1976 PSID (United States)	7.8% of husbands wanted additional hours; 11.0% of wives wanted additional hours (1,585 married couples who had remained together over the period 1974–76, were both aged 29–64 and neither was self-employed, retired, disabled or a student). Results indicate that wives' desired labour supply is positively associated with husbands' underemployment, though constraints faced by the wife may limit observed labour-supply responses.
Ham (1982) 1971 PSID (United States)	Ignoring quantity constraints leads to biased estimates of labour-supply functions (835 men aged 25–50).

	Data without Self-reporting
Dickens, Lundberg (1993) 1972 DIME (United States)	Desired hours are estimated to exceed observed hours by, on average, thirteen hours per week for a low-income sample of married men, aged 18–59 (555 observations). Estimated labour-supply elasticities are larger when constraints are ignored.
Phipps (1991) 1982 SCF (Canada)	An estimated 82.7% of single women who experience unemploy-ment would prefer additional weeks of work; an estimated 79.4% of single unemployed men would prefer additional weeks of work (1,796 single men and 2,297 single women with positive earnings and < 65 years). Estimated labour-supply elasticities are larger when constraints are ignored.
Tummers, Woitticz (1991) 1985 LMS (The Netherlands)	The incorporation of hours restrictions in the estimation of labour-supply equations yields a much better approximation of the actual hours distribution than estimates that ignore constraints.
Phipps (1990) 1982 SCF (Canada)	An estimated 81.4% of couples where the husband experienced unemployment but the wife did not prefer additional weeks of employment; 68.7% of couples where the wife experienced unemployment preferred additional employment; 97.5% of cou-ples where both experienced unemployment preferred additional weeks (2,000 married-couple households, both with positive earnings and both < 65 years). Estimated labour-supply elasticities are larger when constraints are ignored.

Abbreviations:
CPS: Current Population Survey
DIME: Denver Income Maintenance Experiment
LMAS: Labour Market Activities Survey
LFS: Labour Force Survey
LMS: Labour Mobility Survey
PSID: Panel Study on Income Dynamics
SCF: Survey of Consumer Finance
SWR: Survey of Work Reduction

Kahn and Lang (1991) also make use of a Canadian data source that contains self-reported information on the experience of labour-market constraints. A supplement to the Labour Force Survey (LFS) in June 1985 asked workers about desired *hours* of work. Of non-union male workers aged twenty-five to sixty-four, 40.6 percent reported that they wanted additional hours; 33.0 percent of unionized male workers wanted additional hours; 32.0 percent of female workers (union and non-union combined) wanted additional hours of paid employment. These numbers appear much higher than those obtained using the LMAS, but recall that the definition of constraint differs between the two surveys. The LMAS asks about constraints in terms of *weeks* of work; the LFS supplement asks about constraints in terms of *hours*. Many workers, even with fifty-two weeks of employment, may be underemployed in terms of hours. By either estimate, however, a substantial number of Canadian workers face quantity constraints that will limit possible increases in their hours/weeks of paid work.

In the United States, the principal source of information on the existence of quantity constraints is the Panel Study on Income Dynamics (PSID). Kahn and Lang (1992) use the 1981–82 PSID to calculate that 41 percent of male heads of household (aged twenty-five to fifty-four) who work for wages and salaries wanted more work (hours or weeks was not specified). An alternative source of information used by Kahn and Lang is the March 1985 Current Population Survey (CPS), which reports that 35 percent of a similarly defined sample of men wanted additional hours of work at the *same* rate of pay. Further, Altonji and Paxson (1988) use the PSID (1968–83) to calculate that 61 percent of workers feel that they would be unable to increase their hours of employment, whether or not they actually had any desire to do so. Of these people, 27 percent reported that they would like to increase hours of employment. These numbers are thus not substantially different from those obtained for Canada. On the basis of this evidence we can conclude that at least *one third* of paid employees in either country want to work more but are unable to do so.

Despite this rather overwhelming evidence for the existence of quantity constraints on labour supply, some readers may argue that respondents to a national survey who are presently unemployed and perhaps collecting unemployment insurance may be reluctant to admit that they do not actually want more work for fear of penalty. For such sceptics, there is also evidence on the importance of quantity constraints that does not rely on self-reporting (though the authors of these studies themselves argue that surveys that provide such information are preferable). Dickens and Lundberg (1993) estimate (without using self-reports on quantity constraints) that desired hours exceed observed hours for low-income married men (aged eighteen to fifty-nine) in the United States by an average of thirteen hours per week. Phipps (1991) estimates (again without using self-reports) that 83 percent of single women who experience some unemployment would prefer additional weeks of work; 79 percent of single unemployed men would prefer additional weeks. Phipps (1990a) estimates that 81 percent of couples in which the husband experiences some unemployment but the wife does not would prefer additional weeks; 68 percent of couples where the wife experiences unemployment would prefer additional weeks of work; and 98 percent of couples where both are unemployed would prefer additional weeks of employment. Notice that these estimates of the probability of constraint among unemployed workers are higher than the self-reports documented in Osberg and Phipps (1993) (indicating that 68 percent of unemployed men and 60 percent of women with some unemployment in 1986 reported that they wanted additional weeks).

What are the determinants of quantity constraints? Three papers use probit techniques in an effort to assess which characteristics are associated with a higher probability of facing quantity constraints. For the United States, Kahn and Lang (1992) find that being white, well-educated, and having substantial work experience reduces the probability of being constrained. On the other hand, additional children are associated with a higher probability of constraint. Altonji and Paxson (1988) confirm that being white, well-educated, and having substantial work experience reduces the probability of being constrained. They also find that having additional hours of work per week is associated with a lower probability of being constrained, while being married increases the probability of being constrained. For Canada, Osberg and Phipps (1993) find that higher hours (per month) are associated with a lower probability of constraint in terms of weeks of work. A higher hourly wage rate and unionization both reduce the probability of being weeks constrained. Receipt of unemployment insurance, social assistance, and/or worker's compensation is positively associated with the probability of being constrained. But, the most important reason for being constrained is having a "shortage of jobs in the area." In summary, evidence indicates that constraints are generated on the demand side of the labour market and that less-advantaged workers (e.g., those with lower hourly wage rates or lower levels of education) are most likely to face quantity constraints.

What are the consequences of quantity constraints for the estimation of labour supply? One major conclusion common to many of these studies (Osberg and Phipps 1993; Ham 1982; Kahn and Lang 1991; Dickens and Lundberg 1993; Phipps 1990a; and Phipps 1991) is that if quantity constraints are ignored and it is assumed that observed hours/weeks of employment are equal to desired hours/weeks of employment in the estimation of labour-supply functions, then biased estimates will be obtained. Moreover, ignoring quantity constraints will yield upwardly biased estimates of labour-supply elasticities.

Given this conclusion, it is important to note that of all the labour-supply elasticities reported in the second section of this chapter, only the Phipps (1990a; 1991) and Osberg and Phipps (1993) estimates were obtained using procedures that take account of quantity constraints and, from this perspective at least, may be considered unbiased.

Thus, research indicates that the existence of quantity constraints will affect estimated models of labour supply. But, another important implication of this work is that individuals who face quantity constraints will be unable to adjust their hours of work, regardless of the elasticity of their desired labour-supply functions. Dickens and Lundberg (1993: 189) make the following point: "Traditional labor supply models, which ignore hours constraints, are likely to overestimate tax responses. This overestimation results from biased utility parameters due to misspecification *and* from ignoring the direct effect of restricted hours." Kahn and Lang (1991: 609–10) argue:

The divergence between actual and desired hours and the distribution of both actual and desired hours have additional implications about both the estimation of labor supply elasticities and about their applicability to policy analysis. The most obvious implication derives from the very existence of hours constraints. If workers cannot work their chosen number of hours, policies designed to encourage additional labor supply will be ineffectual.[13]

Consider again the likely behavioural consequences of the proposal to reduce the benefit-replacement rate from 60 percent to 57 percent. In the absence of any quantity constraints on labour supply, estimated elasticities (Osberg and Phipps 1993) led to the prediction that the average unemployed woman would increase work effort by 0.94 hours per year; the average unemployed man would reduce work effort by 3.68 hours per year. However, evidence from the 1986 LMAS indicates that 60.1 percent of unemployed women were unable to obtain as many weeks of work as desired. Thus, the already small predicted behavioural response must be qualified by the fact that a majority of the unemployed will be unable to increase hours of work. If the average unemployed woman has a 60 percent chance of being *unable* to work additional weeks, then the expected value of her increased labour supply would be only 0.60 * 0.94 = 0.56 hours per year. (Reducing hours is presumably easier than increasing hours in the face of quantity constraints so it may not be necessary to modify the predicted reduction in male labour supply as a result of the reduction in the benefit-replacement rate.)

For simplicity, this paper has thus far focussed exclusively on changes in the unemployment insurance benefit-replacement rate. However, it is important to remember that unemployment insurance is a complicated program with many parameters that may have behavioural consequences (see Atkinson and Micklewright 1991). Phipps (1990b; 1991) simulates the behavioural responses to the Macdonald Royal Commission proposals for the reform of unemployment insurance, to the Forget proposals (1990b, 1991) and to the 1990 reform of unemployment insurance (1990a) using labour-supply elasticities estimated using a methodology that recognized the possibility of demand-side constraints *and* recognizing the direct impact of demand constraints in limiting behavioural responses, regardless of desired changes in labour supply. Results indicate that the behavioural changes to be expected even from very major changes in the structure of the unemployment insurance program are minimal. For example, in 1985 the Macdonald Royal Commission proposed (1) decreasing the benefit-replacement rate from 60 to 50 percent; (2) eliminating regionally extended benefits; (3) increasing the minimum eligibility requirement to fifteen weeks from a variable requirement of ten to fourteen weeks; and (4) requiring two weeks rather than one week of employment for one week of unemployment insurance benefits. Phipps (1990b) predicts that this entire package of changes would have reduced average weeks of unemployment from 4.13 to 3.98 weeks for married men; from 10.98 to 10.60 weeks for married women (in 1981).[14] These small changes in behaviour are due to small estimated labour-supply elasticities (though not so small as more recent estimates using better data would suggest are appropriate) and to quantity constraints that limit the ability of many workers to make any response at all.

The evidence surveyed in this paper has all been microeconomic. However, the conclusions reached – that the disincentives to individual labour supply generated by the Canadian unemployment insurance system are likely to be extremely small – have implications for macroeconomic discussions of the impact of unemployment insurance on the non-accelerating inflation rate of unemployment (the NAIRU).[15] Presumably, if at the micro-level individuals are not responsive to unemployment insurance, then it cannot follow that at the macro-level unemployment insurance takes significant responsibility for increasing the NAIRU. A more detailed development of this point may be found in Osberg (1996) or Setterfield, Gordon, and Osberg (1992).

CAN THE INCENTIVE CONSEQUENCES OF UNEMPLOYMENT INSURANCE BE MODELLED AS A "TAX" ON WAGES?

The discussion thus far has accepted that it may be appropriate to model the incentive consequences of unemployment insurance using a simple labour-supply framework, but has questioned the magnitude of labour-supply elasticities and has pointed out the important role played by quantity constraints in limiting worker options. This section questions the appropriateness of the framework.

First, should we treat time spent unemployed as utility-enhancing "leisure time"? This assumption may not appear offensive if we assume that all unemployment is voluntary (the "ski bum" story), but is surely inappropriate for individuals who are involuntarily unemployed – a large majority of cases, according to the LMAS. Kelvin and Jarrett (1985) report how unemployment is viewed as a process of psychological deterioration. An individual will first react to unemployment with shock. Then, he or she will optimistically begin active job search. If no job is located, anxiety and pessimism will follow. Eventually, the unemployed individual will become apathetic and resigned to his or her new situation. Social psychological evidence (see Kelvin and Jarrett) suggests that most unemployed individuals eventually pass through all of these stages. Differences of personality or circumstance (e.g., alternative sources of income) will affect only the speed of transition. From this perspective, unemployment is not the outcome of individual choice. It is something that happens *to* an individual with negative consequences for perception of self and for relationships with other people (see also Osberg 1986). Unemployment is not simply "leisure time."

Second, the simple labour-supply model suggests that any rational individual confronted with the "unemployment insurance tax" should respond. Yet, evidence reported by Glenday and Alam (1982) suggests that a large number of eligible unemployed workers do *not* establish claims. Using administrative data from the unemployment insurance commission, they report that over half (52.8 percent) of the spells during which Canadian workers were not in paid employment from 1974–79 did *not* result in claims being established. Of these spells outside paid employment, 88.4 percent were preceded by enough employment to establish eligibility. Glenday and Alam (45) thus concluded that for the overwhelming majority of non-claimants, "it was a voluntary decision not to establish a claim upon losing or leaving their jobs."

Why would eligible individuals *not* establish unemployment insurance claims? This does not make sense in terms of the simple, static model of labour supply outlined above. But, if we move outside this framework, there are explanations for this behaviour. For example, it is possible that there is "stigma" associated with the collection of unemployment insurance. Research in the United States on the incentive consequences of Aid for Families with Dependant Children (AFDC – similar to our social assistance) indicates that estimates may be biased if they overlook the possibility that some individuals do not claim available benefits as a result of perceived stigma. According to Moffit (1983: 1024): "Individuals are not indifferent as to the composition of their income, preferring a larger mix of private income than welfare income. Hence, it is not true that 'income is income,' from whatever source it is derived."[16]

It also seems likely that individuals have longer time horizons than would be suggested by the static labour-supply model. If so, then it should be obvious that another week of paid employment yields positive benefits in addition to the money wages paid. Continuity of employment yields long-run benefits such as accumulated experience, a reputation for reliability and (in some jobs) access to promotion. Another week of unemployment has exactly the opposite implications. "Human capital" may deteriorate, the individual will lose seniority and possible chances for advancement. Taking account of such longer-term considerations is surely sensible behaviour on the part of utility-maximizing agents.

Finally, there is evidence that Canadian workers do *not* treat a dollar of unemployment insurance (net of tax) and a dollar of wages (net of tax) as equivalent. Phipps and Osberg (1991) present simple econometric evidence that these two forms of income do not elicit the same behavioural responses, questioning the appropriateness of simply incorporating unemployment insurance in a simple, static model of labour-supply behaviour.

CONCLUSION

Does unemployment insurance increase unemployment? Textbook presentations of a simple, static model of labour supply predict that unemployment insurance will encourage workers to choose more unemployment and imply that this is entirely undesirable. However, if unemployment insurance gives unemployed workers the opportunity to search for jobs that are appropriate for their skills and experience, then some increase in unemployment is a positive thing. Moreover, a survey of empirical research in labour economics suggests that the textbook arguments about the likely incentive consequences of unemployment insurance are misleading.

First, recent estimates of the wage elasticity of labour supply are extremely small, for both men and women. Thus, even if unemployment insurance does create implicit taxes or subsidies, changes in labour supply in response to these incentives will be negligible.

Second, a burgeoning literature on quantity constraints on labour supply indicates that many workers, particularly unemployed workers, may be unable to modify their work hours or weeks in response to changes in the incentives they face. A worker who is already unable to obtain as much work as desired will not suddenly be able to increase labour supply if, for example, we cut the unemployment insurance benefit-replacement rate. Notice that small wage elasticities of labour supply and the existence of quantity constraints on hours or weeks of work mean that behavioural responses to changes in labour-market policies other than unemployment insurance (e.g., social assistance) are also likely to be minimal.

Finally, textbook models of labour supply use a very simple, static framework. Such models do not take account of the fact that by "choosing" a spell of unemployment, workers will be choosing to lose seniority and (possibly) promotion opportunities, for example, which many rational agents may regard as important. If workers take a longer-term perspective in making their work choices, then the prediction that unemployment insurance will increase unemployment derived from a simple, static model of labour supply is unlikely to be accurate.

Overall, this survey of the micro-econometric labour-supply literature concludes that unemployment insurance does not increase unemployment by an amount sufficient to warrant the extreme concern exhibited in recent policy debates. Moreover, mounting evidence about the importance of quantity constraints on individual labour supply suggests that we should focus on the lack of jobs rather than on the lack of incentives to take paid work when we seek to understand continuing high rates of unemployment in Canada.

ACKNOWLEDGMENTS

I would like to thank Peter Burton, Miles Corak, Lars Osberg, and an anonymous reviewer for helpful comments, and the Social Sciences and

Humanities Research Council of Canada for financial support. This paper incorporates a few minor corrections to the version published in *Canadian Business Economics* 1, No. 3 (Spring 1993): 37–50.

NOTES

1 Unemployment insurance was *designed* to increase unemployment a little as it helps people while they search for jobs appropriate to their skills and experience.

2 Currently, those who quit "without just cause" must wait from seven to twelve weeks beyond the normal two-week waiting-period.

3 This *model* of labour-supply behaviour has also been used to study the incentive consequences of other programs such as social assistance or child benefits (see Gunderson and Riddell 1988, chap. 4). Analytically, the treatment is no different than the treatment of unemployment insurance discussed in this paper. Thus, most of the arguments made here in the context of unemployment insurance are also relevant for analyses of other labour-market programs. The assumption of an *annual planning horizon* has often been made by empirical researchers to accommodate data that are only available on an annual basis.

It is also popular to model the incentive consequences of unemployment insurance using a *search framework*. See Ham and Rea (1987) or Corak (1992) for Canadian examples of research of this type. Ham and Rea find significant though very small increases in the duration of unemployment as a result of increases in unemployment insurance entitlement. They are unable to establish a benefit-replacement rate effect. Corak finds no benefit-replacement rate effect for men, but a significant effect for women. In a recent survey of the international evidence on the effects of unemployment insurance benefit levels on the probability of exit from (or entry to) unemployment, Atkinson and Micklewright (1991: 1721) conclude that "the findings are far from robust. One has to look carefully to find significant replacement rate coefficients, and their size is typically small."

4 This prediction assumes individuals will increase hours of paid employment as wage rates increase. However, this is not true if at at some point individuals respond to a wage increase with a reduction in hours of paid employment because, with higher incomes resulting from higher wage rates, they eventually prefer to have more time off than more income. In this case labour-supply functions are said to be backward-bending.

5 Again, this prediction assumes labour supply is not backward-bending. Note that this model also assumes that individuals quit their jobs and collect unemployment insurance while enjoying leisure time. However, since it is a crime to establish a fraudulent unemployment insurance

claim (e.g., to falsely report that you are looking for work while you are actually sitting on the beach), this may serve as a deterrent to many – either because they are morally averse to law breaking or because they are afraid of being caught. (Considerable effort and resources are devoted to prosecuting individuals making illegal use of unemployment insurance.)

6 Elasticities of labour-supply measure the responsiveness of labour supply to changes in the wage rate (such as are generated through the unemployment insurance "tax" and "subsidy" effects discussed above). The "own-wage elasticity of labour supply" measures the percentage change in labour supply resulting from a 1-percent change in wage rate. Thus, for example, an own-wage elasticity of +0.5 percent indicates that a 1-percent increase in wage rate will result in a 0.5-percent increase in labour supply. If the own-wage elasticity is less than 1.0, labour supply is said to be "inelastic" – i.e., very unresponsive to changes in wage rates. If the elasticity is greater than 1.0, then labour supply is "elastic" – i.e., very responsive to changes in wage rates.

7 By estimating identical specifications of models of labour supply on sub-samples drawn from the same large sample of micro-data, Gordon, Osberg, and Phipps (1991) demonstrate the empirical importance of sampling variability in the estimation of individual labour-supply functions. The paper concludes that samples of at least 5,000 observations are required for reasonable certainty regarding the wage elasticity of male labour supply.

8 For readers unfamiliar with the data sources referenced in Table 1, it is important to note that earlier micro-data sets were rather inadequate for the purposes of estimating labour-supply functions. (This presumably helps to explain the small number of earlier studies.) For example, Ham and Hsiao (1984), who used the 1971 census, were severely constrained by the fact that these data report hours of work per week and weeks of work per year *by intervals* only. Their paper is thus a very clever, very complicated attempt to surmount this data limitation. The Survey of Consumer Finance, used in the two Phipps studies (1990a; 1991), reports weeks of work per year, but not hours of work. Another limitation is that no "wage rate" variable is recorded, necessitating the calculation of a "wage" as annual earnings divided by weeks of work, a technique that can lead to biased estimates. The newer Labour Market Activities Survey (LMAS) used by Osberg and Phipps (1993) thus has many advantages over earlier Canadian micro-data sets insofar as both annual hours and hourly wages are recorded. In addition, other important labour-market information such as union status and satisfaction with weeks of work is collected.

9 At the same time, this will, of course, reduce the implicit unemployment insurance subsidy.

10 Men (aged 25–54) with at least one week of unemployment in 1986
had, on average, 982 hours of paid employment (LMAS 1986). Women
with at least one week of unemployment in 1986 had, on average,
693 hours of paid employment. For men, a 1-percent increase in wage
rate will *reduce* hours of employment by –0.05 percent; a 7.5-percent
increase in wage rate will thus reduce hours by –0.0005 * 7.5 * 982 =
–3.68 hours. For women, a 1-percent increase in wage rate will
increase hours of employment by 0.018 percent; a 7.5-percent increase
will thus increase annual hours by 0.00018 * 7.5 * 693 = 0.94 hours.

11 Using the largest reasonable estimate of the gross own-wage elasticity
of labour supply for women (0.40 from Stelcner and Breslaw (1985)),
the proposed reduction in the benefit-replacement rate would increase
annual hours of paid employment by 20.8 hours, for the average
woman with some unemployment. Using the smallest reasonable estimate of the gross own-wage elasticity of labour supply for women
(–0.85 from Robinson and Tomes (1985)), the reduction in the benefit-
replacement rate would *reduce* paid employment by 44.18 hours annually. For men, the largest estimated elasticity (0.46 from Ham and
Hsiao (1984)) yields a predicted increase of 33.88 hours per year and
the smallest estimated elasticity (–0.05 from Osberg and Phipps (1993))
yields a predicted reduction of 3.68 hours per year.

12 The skip structure of the LMAS questionnaire makes calculating the
number of workers who wanted more weeks of work somewhat difficult since not all respondents are asked directly whether they wanted
additional weeks of paid employment. To find all quantity-constrained
workers, three groups of respondents must be included: (1) workers
who responded affirmatively to the question "Did you want additional
weeks of employment?"; (2) workers with some paid employment
during 1986 who ended the year unemployed and searching for work;
and (3) workers without any paid employment during 1986 but who
searched for work. Individuals in groups (2) and (3) were not *asked*
whether they wanted additional weeks of work, but since they spent
time unemployed and searching, we can determine that they did want
more weeks of employment.

13 Thus, Kahn and Lang argue that quantity constraints can limit behavioural responses to *any* policy change intended to increase labour supply. Thus, this point is relevant not only to unemployment insurance,
but to policies such as social assistance or child benefits.

14 Phipps (1990b) reports the behavioural consequences of each of the
program changes individually.

15 The idea of a unique equilibrium rate of unemployment consistent
with a stable rate of inflation is often termed the NAIRU. The idea is
that we can only reduce unemployment below this rate if we are prepared to accept the penalty of accelerating inflation.

16 Essentially, Moffitt assumes that utility depends both on income and
    on "stigma." Thus, it is possible that collection of benefits is not utility-
    maximizing even when it is income-maximizing. This may help to
    explain observations such as those recorded by Glenday and Alam
    (1982). Moffitt (1983) estimates the probability of program participation
    and hours of labour supply simultaneously, using maximum-likeli-
    hood techniques. He concludes that accounting for "stigma" is impor-
    tant if we are to understand the incentive consequences of tax and
    transfer programs. Moffit (1033) concludes, for example, that "manipu-
    lation of the tax rate appears to be a poor policy instrument for alter-
    ing work incentives, contrary to the conventional wisdom."

REFERENCES

Altonji, J.G., and C.H. Paxson. 1988. "Labor Supply Preferences, Hours Constraints, and Hours-Wage Trade-offs." *Journal of Labor Economics* 6, No. 2:
254–76.
– 1992. "Labor Supply, Hours Constraints, and Job Mobility." *Journal of
Human Resources* 27, No. 2: 256–78.
Atkinson, A.B., and J. Micklewright. 1991. "Unemployment Compensation
and Labor Market Transitions: A Critical Review." *Journal of Economic
Literature* 29: 1679–727.
Baffoe-Bonnie, J. 1989. "Family Labour Supply and Labour Market Segmen-
tation." *Applied Economics* 21: 69–83.
Corak, M. 1992. "The Duration of Unemployment Insurance Payments."
Economic Council of Canada. Research Paper No. 42.
Dickens, W.T., and S.J. Lundberg. 1993. "Hours Restrictions and Labor Sup-
ply." *International Economic Review* 34, No. 1: 169–92.
Ehrenberg, R.G., and R. Smith. 1991. *Modern Labor Economics: Theory and Pubic
Policy.* 4th ed. New York: Harper Collins.
Employment and Immigration Canada. 1989. "Success in the Works: A Policy
Paper." Ottawa: Employment and Immigration Canada.
Glenday, G., and J. Alam. 1982. *The Effects of Unemployment Insurance Benefits
on the Structure of Employment in Seasonally and Cyclically Sensitive Sectors.*
Ottawa: Employment and Immigration Canada.
Gordon, D., L. Osberg, and S. Phipps. 1991. "How Big is Big Enough? The
Problem of Adequate Sample Size in Empirical Studies of Labour Supply."
Dalhousie University Working Paper No. 91-03.
Gunderson, M., and W.C. Riddell. 1988. *Labour Market Economics: Theory,
Evidence and Policy in Canada.* Toronto: McGraw-Hill Ryerson.
Ham, J. 1982. "Estimation of a Labour Supply Model with Censoring Due to
Unemployment and Underemployment." *Review of Economic Studies* 49,
No. 3: 335–54.

Ham, J., and C. Hsiao. 1984. "Two-Stage Estimation of Structural Labor Supply Parameters using Interval Data from the 1971 Canadian Census." *Journal of Econometrics* 24: 133–58.

Ham, C., and S.A. Rea, Jr. 1987. "Unemployment Insurance and Male Unemployment Duration in Canada." *Journal of Labor Economics* 5, No. 3: 325–53.

Hum, Derek, and Simpson, Wayne. 1993. "Economic Response to a Guaranteed Annual Income: Experience from Canada and the United States." *Journal of Labor Economics* 11, No.1 (part 2): S263–S297.

Kahn, S., and K. Lang. 1991. "The Effect of Hours Constraints on Labor Supply Estimates." *Review of Economics and Statistics* 93: 605–11.

– 1992. "Constraints on the Choice of Work Hours: Agency versus Specific Capital," *Journal of Human Resources* 27, No. 4: 661–78.

Kelvin, P., and J.E. Jarrett. 1985. *Unemployment: Its Social Psychological Effects.* Cambridge: Cambridge University Press.

Killingsworth, M.R. 1983. *Labor Supply.* Cambridge, U.K.: Cambridge University Press.

Killingsworth, M.R., and J.J. Heckman. 1986. "Female Labor Supply: A Survey." In O. Ashenfelter and R. Layard, eds., *Handbook of Labor Economics,* vol. 1. Amsterdam: North Holland.

Lin, Z., and L. Osberg. 1992. "Intertemporal Substitution of Annual Hours in Canada." Dalhousie University Working Paper No. 92-06.

Maloney, T. 1987. "Employment Constraints and the Labor Supply of Married Women: A Reexamination of the Added Worker Effect." *Journal of Human Resources* 22, No. 1: 51–61.

Moffitt, R. 1983. "An Economic Model of Welfare Stigma." *American Economic Review* 73: 1023–35.

Mroz, T.A. 1987. "The Sensitivity of an Empirical Model of Married Women's Hours of Work to Economic and Statistical Assumptions." *Econometrica* 55, No. 4: 765–99.

Nakamura, A., and M. Nakamura. 1983. "Part-time and Full-time Work Behaviour of Married Women: A Model with a Doubly Truncated Dependent Variable." *Canadian Journal of Economics* 16, No. 2: 229–57.

Nakamura, M., A. Nakamura, and D. Cullen. 1979. "Job Opportunities, the Offered Wage, and the Labor Supply of Married Women." *American Economic Review* 69: 787–805.

Osberg, L. 1986. Economic Theory and Unemployment: An Essay on Constraints, Choices and Blind Spots. Report to the Commission of Inquiry on Unemployment Insurance. Also published as "The Ratchet Effect of Economic Theory on Unemployment: Constraints, Choices and Blind Spots." Dalhousie University, Department of Economics. Working Paper No. 87-01.

– 1996. "Unemployment Insurance and Unemployment – Revisited." This volume.

Osberg, L., and S. Phipps. 1993. "Labour Supply with Quantity Constraints: Estimates From a Large Sample of Canadian Workers." *Oxford Economic Papers* 5, No. 2: 269–91.

Pencavel, J. 1986. "Labor Supply of Men: A Survey." In O. Ashenfelter and R. Layard, eds., *Handbook of Labor Economics*, vol. 1, 3–102. Amsterdam: North Holland.

Phipps, S. 1990a. "The Impact of the UI Reform of 1990 on Single Earners." *Canadian Public Policy* 16, No. 3: 252–61.

– 1990b. "Quantity-Constrained Household Responses to UI Reform." *Economic Journal* 100: 124–40.

– 1991. "Behavioral Response to UI Reform in Constrained and Unconstrained Models of Labour Supply." *Canadian Journal of Economics* 14, No. 1: 34–54.

Phipps, S., and L. Osberg. 1991. "On Integrating Income Taxes and Unemployment Insurance in Models of Labour Supply." Dalhousie University Working Paper No. 91-03.

Prescott, D., R. Swidinsky, and D. Wilton. 1986. "Labour-supply Estimates for Low-income Female Heads of Household Using Mincome Data." *Canadian Journal of Economics* 19, No. 1: 134–41.

Robinson, C., and N. Tomes. 1985. "More on the Labour Supply of Canadian Women." *The Canadian Journal of Economics* 18, No. 1: 156–63.

Setterfield, M.A., D.V. Gordon, and L. Osberg. 1992. "Searching for a Will o' the Wisp: An Empirical Study of the NAIRU in Canada." *European Economic Review* 36: 119–36.

Smith, J.B., and M. Stelcner. 1988. "Labour Supply of Married Women in Canada, 1980." *Canadian Journal of Economics* 21, No. 4: 857–70.

Stelcner, M., and J. Breslaw. 1985. "Income Taxes and the Labor Supply of Married Women in Quebec." *Southern Economic Journal* 51, No. 4: 1053–72.

Statistics Canada. 1986. *Labour Market Activities Survey, 1986.*

Tummers, M., and I. Woittiez. 1991. "A Simultaneous Wage and Labor Supply Model with Hours Restrictions." *Journal of Human Resources* 26, No. 3: 393–423.

PART THREE

Unemployment in Comparative Perspective

8 The Rise of Unemployment in Ontario

ANDREW SHARPE

Ontario experienced an unprecedented rise in unemployment beginning in 1989, with the unemployment rate more than doubling from 5 percent in 1989 to 10.8 percent in 1992. Indeed, the province went from a virtual full employment economy to a situation of mass unemployment. The unemployment crisis in Ontario – the rate in 1995 is still well above the 1989 rate – has had extremely important ramifications in a number of areas, including the fiscal positions of both the federal and provincial governments.

The objective of this chapter is to provide a comprehensive overview of the period during which the unemployment rate in Ontario more than doubled. Section two, which follows, provides the historical context of the Ontario labour market up to 1989, pointing out that Ontario almost always outperformed the national average. The third section gives a detailed analysis of the deterioration of the Ontario labour market between 1989 and 1992, looking at trends in employment, unemployment, and other labour-market variables. The fourth section, the longest in the chapter, examines the nature of the rise in unemployment in Ontario, identifying the groups and sectors that have been particularly hard hit. Section five analyses the factors behind the rise in unemployment in this province and the final section briefly comments on the short- to medium-term prospects for the unemployment rate.

The outline of the chapter is as follows. After enjoying boom conditions in the 1980s, with the unemployment rate falling to extremely low levels, Ontario experienced a severe economic contraction in the early 1990s. Indeed, Ontario accounted for a very large share of the overall Canadian fall in output and employment, and the rise in unemployment. Within Ontario, the Metropolitan Toronto area in turn accounted for a disproportional part of the rise in unemployment.

The decline in employment was concentrated in two sectors – construction and manufacturing. Consequently blue-collar men who had attained low levels of formal education experienced the largest increases in unemployment. An explanation of developments in construction and manufacturing is the key to an understanding of the rise in unemployment. As both these sectors are interest rate sensitive, the rise in interest rates in the late 1980s and early 1990s provides part of the story. The manufacturing sector was also hit hard by a large loss of international cost-competitiveness, particularly in the American market, due to an overvalued Canadian dollar and very weak productivity growth. The massive overbuilding in the commercial real estate and housing sectors in the late 1980s also sowed the seeds for a future contraction in the construction industry.

THE ONTARIO LABOUR MARKET TO 1989[1]

The Ontario labour market, like the Ontario economy in general, has historically performed better than the national average. Since 1946, the first year for which data from the Labour Force Survey are available, the unemployment rate in Ontario has been below the national average ever year (Figure 1). Over the 1946–89 period, the Ontario rate averaged 77.9 percent of the national rate, and was never higher than 91.3 percent (in 1975). It hit an all-time relative low in 1988 when it fell to 64.1 percent of the national rate.[2]

Ontario's aggregate labour-force participation rate has also always been above the national average. Between 1953 and 1989, it averaged 4.6 percent above the national average, never dipping below 4 percent or rising above 6.4 percent. Reflecting the influence of both the below-average unemployment rate and the above-average participation rate, Ontario's employment/population ratio has also always been above the national average.

Over the 1966–89 period, Ontario experienced slightly faster growth in the key labour-market variables than did the rest of Canada. Working-age or source population advanced at a 2.1-percent average annual rate (Table 1), compared to 1.8 percent in the rest of Canada, labour force, 2.8 percent versus 2.5 percent; and employment 2.6 percent versus 2.3 percent. Participation rate growth was the same (0.7 percent). Ontario's faster population growth reflected

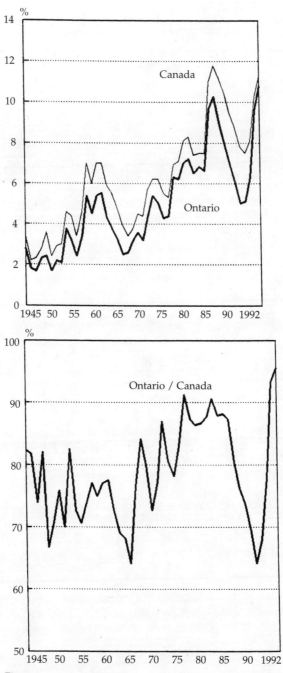

Figure 1
The Unemployment Rate in Ontario and Canada

Table 1
The Ontario Labour Market, 1966–92

	Working-age Population	Labour Force	Employment	Unemployment	Participation Rate (%)	Unemployment Rate (%)	Employment/ Population Ratio (%)
				(000s)			
1966	4,660	2,787	2,714	72	59.8	2.6	58.2
1973	5,658	3,532	3,380	152	62.4	4.3	59.7
1981	6,601	4,463	4,171	292	67.6	6.6	63.2
1989	7,469	5,214	4,949	264	69.8	5.1	66.3
1990	7,591	5,268	4,937	331	69.4	6.3	65.0
1991	7,723	5,276	4,770	506	68.3	9.6	61.8
1992	7,857	5,286	4,714	572	67.3	10.8	60.0
AVERAGE ANNUAL RATE OF CHANGE							
1966–73	2.8	3.4	3.2	–	0.6	–	0.4
1973–81	1.9	3.0	2.7	–	1.0	–	0.7
1981–89	1.6	2.0	2.2	–	0.4	–	0.6
1966–89	2.1	2.8	2.6	–	0.7	–	0.6
1989–92	1.7	0.5	-1.6	–	-1.2	–	-3.3
ANNUAL AVERAGE RATE OF CHANGE							
1990	1.6	1.0	-0.2	–	-0.6	–	-2.0
1991	1.7	0.2	-3.4	–	-1.6	–	-4.9
1992	1.7	0.2	-1.2	–	-1.5	–	-2.9

Source: Historical Labour Force Statistics, cat. 71-201, February 1993, Statistics Canada.

net interprovincial migration to Ontario from the other provinces over the 1966–89 period and the province's ability to attract a disproportional share of immigrants to Canada. The more rapid population growth explains the faster labour-force and employment growth.

The 1966–89 period can be divided into three sub-periods using the business-cycle peak years of 1973 and 1981. Ontario enjoyed faster source population, labour-force, and employment growth than the rest of Canada in the 1966–73 and 1981–89 sub-periods, but not in the 1973–81 sub-period.

Of the three sub-periods, Ontario's relative labour-market performance was by far the best in the 1980s, due to the province's very strong growth performance. Between 1981 and 1989, source population advanced at a 1.6-percent average annual rate in Ontario, compared to 0.9 percent in the rest of Canada. Labour-force growth was 2 percent per year in Ontario versus 1.4 percent in the rest of Canada and employment growth 2.2 percent per year versus 1.2 percent.

Since employment growth exceeded labour-force growth in Ontario in the 1980s, the unemployment rate declined from 6.6 percent in 1981 to 5.1 percent in 1989, the lowest rate since 1974 (except for the 5-percent figure recorded in 1988). In contrast, labour-force growth exceeded employment growth in the rest of the country, raising the unemployment rate from 8.1 percent in 1981 to 9.1 percent in 1989.

The Ontario economy tends to exhibit greater cyclical variation in economic activity than the rest of the country because of the greater relative importance of the cyclically sensitive manufacturing sector, particularly durable goods, in this province. For example, in 1989 manufacturing accounted for 20.8 percent of total employment in Ontario, compared to 14.5 percent in the rest of the country. Consequently, labour-market trends also tend to be more cyclical. This can be seen in the movement of the unemployment rate. In recessions, the gap between the Ontario unemployment rate and that in the rest of Canada closes. During expansions, it widens (see Figure 1).

DETERIORATION OF THE ONTARIO LABOUR MARKET SINCE 1989

Since the 1989 peak, labour-market conditions in Ontario have deteriorated both in absolute terms and relative to those in the rest of the country. This section provides an overview of developments in output, employment, productivity, unemployment, and other labour-market variables in the early 1990s.

Table 2
Trends in Real Output, Employment, and Output per Worker since 1989
(Percentage Change)

	Ontario	Canada	Rest of Canada
GDP AT MARKET PRICE (1986 DOLLARS)			
1990	−3.0	−0.2	1.7
1991	−2.9	−1.8	−1.2
1992	0.5	0.6	0.7
1989–92	−5.5	1.5	1.1
EMPLOYMENT			
1990	−0.2	0.7	1.3
1991	−3.4	−1.8	−0.9
1992	−1.2	−0.8	−0.6
1989–92	−4.7	−1.9	−0.1
OUTPUT PER WORKER			
1990	−2.8	−0.9	0.4
1991	0.5	0.0	−0.3
1992	1.7	1.4	1.3
1989–92	−0.5	0.5	1.3

Sources: Output data for Ontario from Ontario Economic Outlook, Ontario Ministry of Finance, November 1994; output data for Canada from National Income and Expenditure Accounts, cat. 13-001, August 1994, Statistics Canada; rest of Canada derived residually; employment data from Historical Labour Force Statistics, cat. 71-201, February 1993, Statistics Canada; output per worker derived residually.

Real Output

The growth performance of the Ontario economy since 1989 has been disastrous. According to estimates prepared by the Ontario Ministry of Finance (1994), real Gross Domestic Product (GDP) fell 3 percent in 1990 and a further 2.9 percent in 1991 (Table 2). In 1992 real GDP rose only 0.5 percent. Consequently, over the 1989–92 period (1989 base), real GDP fell 5.5 percent, or at a 1.8-percent average annual rate.[3] This was by far the worst performance for any three-year period in Ontario's economic history since the 1930s. For example, in the early 1980s, Ontario experienced only one year of negative growth, a 4-percent decline in output in 1982.

This performance was by far the worst of any region of Canada. Indeed, between 1989 and 1992, real output in the rest of Canada was up 1.1 percent, compared to the 5.5-percent fall in Ontario. In other words, Ontario was responsible for all the national output decline of 1.5 percent over the period.

Ontario's slump in output in the early 1990s lies in marked contrast to its robust output performance in the 1980s. Between 1981 and 1989, real output advanced at a very strong 4.3-percent average annual rate in this province. Output growth was much slower in the rest of the country, at 2.5 percent per year.

Employment

Employment in Ontario fell only 0.2 percent in 1990, the first year of the recession, as employers did not adjust their workforce size in response to the fall in output. Starting in 1991, these adjustments were made, with employment falling 3.4 percent that year and a further 1.2 percent in 1992. Between 1989 and 1992 employment fell a total of 4.7 percent, a decline of 235,000 jobs. Over the same period, employment declined only marginally in the rest of Canada (it rose 1.3 percent in 1990 and fell a cumulative 1.5 percent in 1991 and 1992), making Ontario's job loss equal to virtually all the net national job loss. Of course, employment levels were not unchanged in each region, as employment losses in Quebec and Atlantic Canada were offset by gains in Western Canada, primarily in British Columbia.

Productivity

Productivity trends since 1989 have been very closely linked to cyclical developments and have reflected the lagged response of hiring and lay-off decisions to changes in output.[4] Output per worker fell sharply (2.8 percent) in 1990 because employers had insufficient time to adjust their employment levels to the new macroeconomic climate of declining output. By 1991, a greater degree of adjustment in actual employment levels to desired levels had been made and productivity rose 0.5 percent.

By 1992, firms had had adequate opportunity to respond to the deteriorating economic situation and the low levels of corporate profitability, and had "downsized" their workforces. This factor, combined with the recovery in output, albeit weak, resulted in a 1.7-percent rise in output per worker.

It should be noted that the strength of productivity gains in 1992 was not particularly surprising given the stage in the cycle. It certainly does not herald a fundamental upward shift in productivity growth due to economic restructuring, as some analysts claim.[5]

Output per worker was down 0.5 percent in Ontario between 1989 and 1992, compared to a 1.3-percent increase in the rest of Canada.

Ontario's poorer performance may be associated with the province's much larger output decline. The negative cyclical impact of the downturn on productivity may not yet have been offset by the positive impact of the recovery, given its weakness. It should be noted that if productivity growth had been as strong in Ontario as in the rest of Canada over the period, employment would have declined even more, and unemployment would have been higher. The poor productivity performance cushioned or dampened the impact of falling output on employment.[6]

Source Population

Source population growth is determined by demographic trends, in particular the number of persons reaching the working age of fifteen, and the number of deaths in the fifteen-and-over population, and to a lesser extent, by net migration. The first of these factors is not sensitive to the business cycle, at least in the short- to medium-term, while the second factor does respond to changes in economic conditions, although in the case of immigration targets, with a lag.

Overall, source population growth in Ontario in the early 1990s does not appear to have been affected by the recession. Between 1989 and 1992, source population grew at an average annual rate of 1.7 percent, slightly faster than the 1.6 percent rate of increase recorded in the 1980s.

Labour-force Participation

The aggregate labour-force participation rate in Ontario reached an all-time high of 69.8 percent in 1989. Since then, reflecting the fall in employment opportunities, it has fallen precipitously, decreasing 0.6 percent in 1990, 1.6 percent in 1991, and 1.5 percent in 1992. The decline over the 1989–92 period was more than twice as great in Ontario as in the rest of Canada: −1.2 percent per year versus −0.5 percent. Consequently, the Ontario participation rate fell from 104.2 percent of the national average in 1989 to 102.7 percent in 1992, its lowest relative level in nearly forty years.

Labour Force

Labour-force growth is determined by source population and participation rate growth. Consequently, falling labour-force participation in Ontario since 1989 has resulted in very weak labour-force growth, with the labour force advancing 1 percent in 1990 and only

0.2 percent in both 1991 and 1992. Over the 1989–92 period, the average annual rate of increase of the labour force in Ontario was 0.5 percent. This was about one-half that in the rest of Canada (0.9 percent), due to the smaller decline in the participation rate in the other provinces.

Unemployment Rate

Reflecting the drop in employment, the unemployment rate has risen dramatically in Ontario in the early 1990s. In 1989, following the boom years of the late 1980s, the unemployment rate was 5.1 percent, virtually the lowest it had been since 1974 (it was slightly lower at 5 percent in 1988). It was also very low relative to the national average – 68 percent.

The unemployment rate then rose to 6.3 percent in 1990, 9.6 percent in 1991, and 10.8 percent in 1992, a total jump of 5.7 percentage points over the 1989–92 period. This rise in unemployment was much greater in Ontario than in the rest of Canada, where the unemployment rate rose only 2.5 points from 9.1 percent to 11.6 percent between 1989 and 1992. The Ontario rate consequently rose from 68 percent of the national average in 1989 to 95.6 percent in 1992, its highest relative level ever recorded.

The deterioration of labour-market conditions, as reflected by trends in the unemployment rate, was also more serious in the early 1990s than in the early 1980s. The unemployment rate in 1992 of 10.8 percent was higher than it was in 1983, when the rate peaked at 10.3 percent. Equally, the 5.7 percentage-point rise in the unemployment rate between 1989 and 1992 was greater than the 3.7-point increase between 1981 and 1983.

The number of unemployed in Ontario more than doubled from 264,000 in 1989 to 572,000 in 1992 (Table 3). In the rest of the country the number of unemployed only rose 31 percent over the same period. Ontario, which accounted for one-quarter of the total number of unemployed in Canada in 1989, was responsible for 57.2 percent of the increase in the number of unemployed between 1989 and 1992.

The rise in unemployment in Ontario has led to large increases in the welfare rolls, as those who exhaust unemployment insurance benefits are forced to turn to public assistance. In June 1992, 17 percent of those sixty and under in the province were receiving some form of provincial or municipal welfare, up from 4 percent in 1981 and 8 percent in the late 1980s (Shephard 1993). Ontario has become the province with the largest share of welfare recipients in its population.

Table 3
Trends in Labour-market Variables in Ontario, Canada, and Rest of Canada, excluding Ontario

	Ontario Share of National Total		1989–92			
	1989	1992	Ontario %Δ	Canada %Δ	Rest of Canada %Δ	Ontario Contribution to National Change
Real GDP (86 $)	40.9	39.5	−5.2	−1.1	1.7	185.9
Labour force	38.6	38.3	1.4	2.2	2.7	–
Source population	37.1	37.3	5.2	4.6	4.2	–
Employment	39.6	38.5	−4.7	−2.0	−0.1	95.9
Unemployment	25.9	36.8	116.7	52.8	30.5	57.2
LFS discouraged workers	11.8	28.8	375.0	94.1	56.7	46.9
Job losers	22.4	36.4	189.7	78.4	46.2	54.3
Voluntary part-time employment	24.8	35.6	128.8	59.3	36.4	53.8
Manufacturing employment	48.4	47.1	−18.3	−15.9	−13.7	55.6
Construction employment	42.8	37.3	−22.3	−10.9	2.3	88.0

Sources: Historical Labour Force Statistics, cat. 71-201, February 1993, Statistics Canada; The Labour Force, December 1989, cat. 71-001, January 1990, Statistics Canada and Labour Force Annual Averages 1992, cat. 71-220, March 1993, Statistics Canada.

Employment/population Ratio

Reflecting the combined impact of developments in the participation rate and the unemployment rate, the employment/population ratio in Ontario fell from a record 66.3 percent in 1989 to 60 percent in 1992 (−2.0 percent in 1990, −4.9 percent in 1991, and −2.9 percent in 1992). The fall was less than half as severe in the rest of Canada: −1.4 percent per year over the 1989–92 period versus −3.3 percent in Ontario. These trends resulted in the decline of Ontario's employment/population ratio, as a proportion of the national average, from a record 106.9 percent in 1989 to 103.3 percent in 1992, the lowest ever recorded.

A Comparative Perspective on Ontario's Labour-market Performance

By all criteria, Ontario experienced the greatest deterioration in labour-market performance of all five major regions in Canada over the 1989–92 period. Ontario suffered the largest run-up in the unemployment rate, and the greatest fall in employment and in the labour-force participation rate. These labour-market developments were driven by output developments, as the economic downturn in Ontario was much more severe than in other regions.

Despite the massive deterioration of the labour-market situation in Ontario, the average Ontario unemployment rate over the 1990–92 period was, in absolute terms, lower than that in Atlantic Canada, Quebec, and British Columbia. Only the Prairie provinces enjoyed a lower rate. The very low unemployment rate in Ontario in 1989 (5.1 percent) meant that despite the run-up in the rate during the downturn, the average rate remained low compared to other regions.

THE NATURE OF THE RISE OF UNEMPLOYMENT IN ONTARIO

This section provides a detailed discussion of the nature of the rise in unemployment in Ontario since 1989. Topics covered include trends, employment and unemployment by industry, unemployment by occupation, unemployment by gender, unemployment by age group, unemployment by educational attainment, unemployment by metropolitan area, duration of unemployment, and the temporary/permanent nature of job loss.

There are at least three ways to assess the current unemployment situation for different groups and sectors. *First*, absolute unemployment rates can be examined. A *second* approach is to look at absolute changes in the unemployment rate since the last cyclical peak in 1989. A *third* approach is to focus on the relative percentage increase in the unemployment rate. It should be noted that the groups with the largest percentage increase in their unemployment rates are not necessarily those with the largest absolute increases, due to difference in the base rates. All three perspectives will be used in this section.

Employment and Unemployment by Industry

It has been the goods-producing industries that have borne the brunt of the employment losses since 1989. Over the 1989–92 period, employment in Ontario fell 17.4 percent in the goods sector, while advancing 1.3 percent in the service sector (Table 4). Within the goods sector, primary industries excluding agriculture experienced the largest percentage drop in employment (−22.6 percent), followed closely by construction (−22.3 percent), and manufacturing (−18.3 percent).

Construction and manufacturing, because of their greater importance, accounted for the bulk of the job loss. In construction, employment was down 73,000 between 1989 and 1992, 30.9 percent of the

Table 4
Employment by Industry in Ontario

	1981	1989 (thousands)	1992	Δ	1989–92 %Δ	% of total Δ
TOTAL	4,171	4,950	4,714	−236	−4.8	100.0
GOODS PRODUCING	1,510	1,590	1,314	−276	−17.4	116.9
Agriculture	143	118	114	−4	−3.4	1.7
Other primary	62	53	41	−12	−22.6	5.1
Manufacturing	1,037	1,030	841	−189	−18.3	80.1
Construction	216	327	254	−73	−22.3	30.9
SERVICE PRODUCING	2,661	3,359	3,401	42	1.3	−17.8
Transportation and communication	247	304	330	26	8.6	−11.0
Trade	674	822	802	−20	−2.4	8.5
Finance, insurance, and real estate	248	318	333	15	4.7	−6.4
Community, business, and personal services	1,221	1,612	1,687	75	4.7	−31.8
Public administration	272	303	314	11	3.6	−4.7

Source: Historical Labour Force Statistics, cat. 71-201, February 1993, Statistics Canada.

overall decline in employment. In manufacturing, employment fell by 189,000 (80.1 percent of the total fall). Together these two industries alone, which in 1989 employed only 27.4 percent of the workforce, accounted for 111 percent of the net job loss.

The decline in employment in the construction sector was much worse in Ontario in the early 1990s than in the rest of Canada during the same period and than in Ontario in the early 1980s. In the rest of Canada construction sector employment only fell 2.3 percent between 1989 and 1992 (Table 4). Ontario thus accounted for 88 percent of the national decline in employment in this sector. Between 1981 and 1983 (i.e., during the recession of the early 1980s) construction sector employment only fell 6.5 percent in Ontario.

The fall in manufacturing employment in Ontario in the early 1990s was also greater than in the rest of Canada, and than that experienced in Ontario in the early 1980s, although the differences were considerably less than in the construction sector. This suggests that the factors affecting manufacturing were national in scope, while those affecting construction were unique to Ontario. Manufacturing employment decreased 13.7 percent in the rest of Canada between 1989 and 1992, compared to 18.3 percent in Ontario. But because Ontario has nearly one-half of the country's manufacturing employment (48.4 percent in

1989) due to the greater relative importance of manufacturing in the province, it was responsible for 55.6 percent of the national decline in employment in the sector. Between 1981 and 1983 manufacturing employment in Ontario fell 9.8 percent, about one-half the decline experienced in the early 1990s.

All two-digit Standard Industrial Classification manufacturing industries experienced employment losses between 1989 and 1992, with the exception of chemicals (Table 5). Moreover, all industries except food and beverage (and chemicals) had job losses of 10 percent or more. The largest declines were in leather (−41.7 percent), clothing (−40.5 percent), and furniture (−39.3 percent). The crisis in Ontario manufacturing was therefore a widespread phenomenon and not concentrated in a small number of industries. Indeed, the industry responsible for the greatest number of job losses (primary metals) accounted for only 12 percent of the total employment decline.

Not surprisingly given the employment trends discussed above, the unemployment rate increased the most for workers who had been employed in goods industries. The unemployment rate for the overall goods sector increased 8.1 points from 5.6 percent in 1989 to 13.7 percent in 1992. In the service sector, the rate rose only 4.3 points from 4.4 percent to 8.7 percent. Within the goods sector, the unemployment rate increased 8.8 points in construction (to 22.7 percent, by far the highest industry level), 7.5 points in primary industries excluding agriculture, and 6.9 points in manufacturing. Within the service sector, the unemployment rate rose only 1.3 points in public administration and 2.2 points in finance, insurance, and real estate.

Unemployment by Occupation

Following from trends in employment, it has been blue-collar workers who have been hardest hit by the recession, with their unemployment rate rising more in both absolute and relative terms. Between 1989 and 1992, the unemployment rate in Ontario for blue-collar occupations (defined as primary occupations; processing, machining, and fabricating; construction; transport-equipment operating; and materials handling and other crafts) rose 9 percentage points or 145 percent from 6.2 percent to 15.2 percent. In contrast, the unemployment rate for white-collar occupations (defined as managerial and professional, clerical, sales, and service occupations) increased only 4.4 points or 105 percent from 4.2 percent to 8.6 percent.

The highest unemployment rate by occupation in 1992 in Ontario was in construction trades (22.1 percent), followed by processing

Table 5
Employment in Manufacturing in Ontario

	1981	1983	1989	1992		1989–92	% of
		(thousands)			Δ	%Δ	total Δ
TOTAL MANUFACTURING	1,037	934	1,030	841	−189	−18.3	100.0
NON-DURABLES	459	438	458	377	−81	−17.7	42.9
Food and beverage	99	92	95	89	−6	−6.3	3.2
Rubber and plastics	41	41	49	35	−14	−28.6	7.4
Leather	19	17	12	7	−5	−41.7	2.6
Textiles	27	30	27	18	−9	−33.3	4.8
Clothing	41	36	37	22	−15	−40.5	7.9
Paper	53	43	48	35	−13	−27.1	6.9
Printing and publishing	63	71	89	72	−17	−19.1	9.0
Petroleum and wood	10	12	7	5	−2	−28.6	1.1
Chemicals	57	51	52	53	1	1.9	−0.5
Miscellaneous manufacturing	48	43	41	37	−4	−9.8	2.1
DURABLES	577	497	572	464	−108	−18.9	57.1
Wood	27	26	29	24	−5	−17.2	2.6
Furniture	33	32	28	17	−11	−39.3	5.8
Primary metal	88	65	77	54	−23	−29.9	12.2
Metal fabricating	101	80	90	72	−18	−20.0	9.5
Machinery	63	47	43	32	−11	−25.6	5.8
Transportation and equipment	129	115	179	159	−20	−11.2	10.6
Electrical and electronic	111	108	100	86	−14	−14.0	7.4
Non-metal mineral products	26	25	27	21	−7	−22.2	3.7

Source: Unpublished Labour Force Survey data supplied by Statistics Canada.

occupations (14.2 percent), and materials-handling occupations (13.2 percent). The largest absolute increase in unemployment by occupation between 1989 and 1992 was in construction trades (up 14.0 points), followed by processing (8.9 points), transport-equipment operating (7.0 points), and materials handling (6.6 points).

All white-collar occupations except services in 1992 had unemployment rates below the provincial average and also experienced below-average absolute increases in unemployment rates between 1989 and 1992. Workers in managerial and professional occupations enjoyed the lowest unemployment rate in 1992 (5.4 percent) and experienced the smallest increase in unemployment between 1989 and 1992 (2.7 points). As in past recessions, white-collar workers were not as hard hit by the rise in unemployment in the early 1990s as blue-collar workers.

Unemployment by Gender

Historically, the female unemployment rate has been higher than the male rate in Ontario, with the differential varying with the cycle. In recessions, the gap between the two rates fell as the male rate rose more than the female due to the greater proportion of men in cyclically sensitive sectors. In booms, the opposite occurred.

In 1989 the male unemployment rate in Ontario was below the female rate: 4.7 percent versus 5.6 percent. Between that year and 1992, the male rate rose 7.2 percentage points to 11.9 percent, while the female rate increased only 4.1 points to 9.6 percent. The recession had a much greater negative impact on men and resulted in an unprecedented deterioration of the male rate relative to the female rate. In 1992, the female rate was 19.3 percent below the male rate, by far the largest gap ever recorded. This situation is largely explained by the unprecedented decline of employment in the male-dominated construction and manufacturing sectors.

Unemployment by Age Group

Absolute increases after 1989 in the unemployment rate by age group fall as one moves from the younger age groups to the older groups. Between 1989 and 1992, the unemployment rate increased 10.2 points for those aged fifteen to twenty-four, 5.3 points for those twenty-five to forty-four, and 4.1 percent for those forty-five to sixty-four. However, percentage increases in the unemployment rate for the three age groups showed much less variation, although youth still experienced a slightly larger increase: 127.5 percent compared to 110.4 percent for those aged twenty-five to forty-four and 117.1 percent for those forty-five to sixty-four. This smaller variation reflects the much higher unemployment rate for youth.

A different story emerges when the unemployment rate for the three age groups is broken down by gender. The unemployment rate of the two older male age groups increased more than for youth. On the other hand, the unemployment rates of the two older female age groups increased less than that for youth. It has been the male labour force aged twenty-five and over that has experienced the largest relative increase in unemployment.

Unemployment by Educational Attainment

In absolute terms, the unemployment rate in Ontario increased the most between 1990 and 1992 for those will low educational attainment, in particular those with only some secondary education.7 The unemployment rate for this group increased 7.4 percentage points. All other educational attainment groups had absolute increases in their unemployment rates near the overall average (4.5 points), except those with a university degree. Those with a university degree experienced only a 2.5 percentage-point increase, although in relative terms it was the largest increase because of this group's very low unemployment rate in 1990 (2.7 percent).

The rise in the unemployment rate of the "poorly educated" in Ontario in the early 1990s, both in absolute and relative terms, was much greater than it was in the rest of Canada during that period and in Ontario in the early 1980s. The large declines in employment in manufacturing and construction, which have traditionally offered significant employment opportunities to these workers, may explain this development.

Unemployment by Metropolitan Area

The rise in unemployment in Ontario has been particularly concentrated in and around the Metropolitan Toronto area. In 1989 this area had enjoyed a situation of virtual full employment, with an unemployment rate of 4 percent (Table 6). By 1992, the rate had nearly tripled to 11.5 percent, a rate higher than the Ontario and national average. The 7.5-percentage-point increase in the unemployment rate in Toronto was well above the 4.7-point increase in the rate in Ontario excluding Toronto. Indeed, in this three-year period, Toronto experienced one of the most drastic turnarounds in labour-market conditions ever experienced by any major metropolitan area in Canada since the Great Depression, going from extremely low unemployment to mass unemployment.

The number of unemployed in Toronto increased by 149,000 from 81,000 to 230,000 between 1989 and 1992. This one city alone accounted for nearly one-half (48.4 percent) of the total increase in the number of unemployed in Ontario between 1989 and 1992, although in 1989 it had only 30.7 percent of the unemployed in the province. From a national perspective, Toronto was responsible for 27.7 percent of the total increase in unemployment between 1989 and 1992, even though in 1989 the city had only 8 percent of unemployed in Canada.

The massive rise of unemployment in Toronto was due to a very large fall in employment. Between 1989 and 1992, employment in Toronto decreased 8.5 percent (or by 165,000) compared to only 2.4 percent in the rest of the province. While Toronto accounted for 39.2 percent of total provincial employment in 1989, it was respon-

Table 6
Labour-market Trends in Ontario Metropolitan Centres

	Employment (000s)		Unemployment (000s)		Unemployment rate (%)	
	1989	1992	1989	1992	1989	1992
Ottawa-Hull	445	440	28	43	6.0	8.9
Sudbury	61	61	5	8	7.9	11.8
Oshawa	99	104	4	14	4.1	12.2
Toronto	1,940	1,775	81	230	4.0	11.5
Hamilton	312	290	17	34	5.1	10.6
St. Catharines-Niagara	140	162	11	20	7.2	12.6
London	165	164	7	15	4.2	8.6
Windsor	127	115	11	17	8.1	12.8
Kitchener-Waterloo	182	186	9	20	4.9	9.6
Thunder Bay	61	58	3	6	4.7	10.0
Ten metropolitan areas	3,532	3,335	176	407	4.7	10.9
Ontario	4,950	4,714	264	572	5.1	10.8

Sources: The Labour Force, December 1989, cat. 71-001, January 1990, Statistics Canada; Labour
Force Annual Averages 1992, cat. 71–220, March 1993, Statistics Canada.

sible for 69.9 percent of the provincial decline in employment
between 1989 and 1992. At the national level between 1989 and 1992,
this one metropolitan area accounted for 67.1 percent of job losses.

The metropolitan areas in the Golden Horseshoe around Toronto
also experienced large increases in unemployment. The unemployment rate rose 8.1 points between 1989 and 1992 in Oshawa, 5.5 points
in Hamilton, 5.4 points in St. Catharines, and 5 points in Kitchener-
Waterloo. The further from Toronto, the smaller the increase in
unemployment. The unemployment rate rose "only" 2.9 points in
Ottawa-Hull and 3.9 points in Sudbury.

Duration of Unemployment

Reflecting the below-average unemployment rate, the duration of
unemployment spells in Ontario has traditionally been below the
national average. This situation changed dramatically in the early
1990s, with the average duration of unemployment in Ontario rising
above the national average. Between 1989 and 1992, the average
duration of uncompleted spells of unemployment rose 9.9 weeks in
Ontario from 13.5 weeks to 23.4 weeks, the longest duration ever
recorded in the province. At the national level, average duration
increased 4.7 weeks from 17.9 weeks to 22.6 weeks. When Ontario is
excluded from the national total, average duration increased only
around two weeks. Thus Ontario workers have been hit much harder

than workers in other provinces in terms of the increased duration of unemployment.[8]

Temporary/permanent Nature of Job Loss

There has been much speculation that the nature of job loss in Ontario in the early 1990s is different from that experienced during previous downturns. More specifically, many believe that a much greater proportion of the jobs lost in manufacturing than in the past are gone forever, due to the forces restructuring the economy such as the Canada-United States Free Trade Agreement, the introduction of new technologies, and globalization.

Probably the most widely cited evidence to support this view are the data collected by the Ontario Ministry of Labour on the reasons for major plant lay-offs. These data show that, compared to the 1980s, a much greater percentage of lay-offs in the early 1990s were due to complete and partial plant closures (as opposed to temporarily reduced operations). Questions have been raised concerning the quality of these data, so this evidence is by no means conclusive.

A second source of information on whether a greater proportion of job loss is now permanent is the Labour Force Survey, which provides data on the number of workers on temporary lay-off. These data do not support the view that there has been a structural change in the nature of job loss. Over the 1989–92 period inclusive, 17.7 percent of workers who lost their job were on temporary lay-off. This is virtually identical with the percentage in the 1981–84 period (17.5 percent). This implies that the relative importance of permanent lay-offs has not increased at the economy-wide level.

It is too early to offer a definitive answer to this issue. Of course, past employment levels in certain, mature, uncompetitive goods industries may never be regained. However, if the past is any guide, new employment opportunities in emerging sectors, even within manufacturing, will likely more than offset these job losses, particularly if a macroeconomic climate favourable to growth can be established, and will lead to higher aggregate employment levels.

FACTORS BEHIND THE RISE OF UNEMPLOYMENT IN ONTARIO

A Basic Lack of Jobs

The rise in unemployment in Ontario is a demand-side phenomenon, reflecting the collapse of labour demand due to the recession. The current unemployment situation reflects a basic lack of jobs. One measure of the relative importance of inadequate aggregate demand unemployment versus labour-market mismatch unemployment due to frictional/structural factors is the Canadian Labour Market and Productivity Centre job vacancy rate, which is based on trends in Statistics Canada's Help Wanted Index. Unfortunately, data for the job vacancy rate are only available at the national level, but since the Ontario unemployment rate was very close to the national rate in 1992, national trends are probably very close to those in Ontario.

In 1992 the national job vacancy rate was 2 percent, compared to the national unemployment rate of 11.3 percent. The number of persons unemployed due to labour-market mismatch is defined as equal to the number of job vacancies (which includes both easy-to-fill and hard-to-fill openings), as there would be no mismatch if all vacancies were filled. Inadequate demand unemployment is defined as the difference between total unemployment and mismatch unemployment. Thus last year a basic lack of jobs was responsible for 82 percent of national unemployment, while labour-market mismatch was responsible for 18 percent.

This situation represents a radical reversal from that prevailing at the 1989 cyclical peak. In that year, the job vacancy rate was 4.8 percent, and the unemployment rate 7.5 percent. Sixty-four percent of unemployment was then due to labour-market mismatch and 36 percent due to a basic lack of jobs. The rise in the number of unemployed between 1989 and 1992 can be completely explained by the rise of inadequate demand unemployment. To explain the rise in unemployment, one must therefore explain the fall in demand.

Three factors can be identified as being particularly important elements in the explanation of the collapse of the Ontario economy in 1990 and 1991 and the very weak recovery in 1992: high interest rates, decreased international cost-competitiveness, and overbuilding in the construction sector in the late 1980s. These factors account for the output and employment declines in construction and manufacturing, which, as has been seen, were the two sectors responsible for all the net job loss.

High Interest Rates

Because of fear of inflation, the Bank of Canada raised interest rates substantially in 1989 and 1990. The ninety-day commercial paper rate peaked at 13 percent in 1990. Interest rates increased more in Canada than in the United States, as evidenced by the rise in the nominal Canada-United States interest rate differential for commercial paper to an average of 3.43 percentage points over the 1989–92 period inclusive, compared to 1.59 points in the 1981–88 period and 0.75 points in the 1971–80 period.

High interest rates reduce expenditure on interest-sensitive categories, such as consumer durables, housing, and business investment. Since domestic production of both investment goods and consumer durables is concentrated in Ontario, this province's manufacturing sector was particularly hard hit by the decision to raise interest rates, with real output falling 12 percent between 1989 and 1992 (Statistics Canada 1993).

Loss of International Cost-competitiveness

Since the Ontario manufacturing sector is very dependent on the American market, deterioration of Ontario's cost-competitiveness vis-à-vis the United States can be very detrimental to sales south of the border. In the second half of the 1980s, Canadian manufacturing experienced a very large deterioration of its cost-competitiveness in the American market.[9] (Unfortunately, data are not available on Ontario cost trends, but they undoubtedly closely resemble national trends, since Ontario accounts for such a large share of Canadian manufacturing).

Between 1985 and 1991, unit labour costs in Canadian manufacturing, expressed in United States' dollars, rose 56.8 percent, compared to only 9.8 percent in the United States (Bureau of Labor Statistics 1993). In relative terms, Canadian cost-competitiveness deteriorated 47 percent in that six-year period, an unprecedented development in Canadian economic history. Given the crucial importance of manufacturing exports to the United States for the Ontario economy, and the openness of the Ontario market to American competition, this loss of cost competitiveness contributed to the decline in output in manufacturing. Indeed, the fall in net exports accounted for around 40 percent of the decline in real output between 1989 and 1992.[10]

Weak domestic demand in the United States due to the recession also played some role in the fall in output. However, the fact that the downturn in the United States was less severe in 1990–91 than in 1981–82 suggests that developments in the American economy cannot account for the greater contraction in Ontario's manufacturing in the early 1990s than in the early 1980s.

This deterioration of Canadian cost-competitiveness in the American market is attributable to two key factors – the appreciation of the Canadian dollar and the virtual collapse of productivity growth in Canadian manufacturing. Between 1985 and 1991 the value of the Canadian dollar vis-à-vis the United States dollar rose 19 percent from U.S. $0.73 to U.S. $0.87 and accounted for about one-half of the deterioration. Output-per-hour growth in manufacturing advanced a meagre 1.3-percent between 1985 and 1991 in Canada, compared to 15.5 percent in the United States. This relative decline in productivity explains about 35 percent of the relative cost increase. Finally, slightly higher growth in hourly labour compensation in Canada relative to that in the United States (33.4 percent versus 27.0 percent) explains the remaining 15 percent of the decline.

The appreciation of the Canadian dollar in the late 1980s was a result of the tight monetary policy pursued by the Bank of Canada in its quest for price stability (see Fortin 1996; Osberg 1996). High interest rate differentials with the United States attracted funds to Canada and put upward pressure on the exchange rate. By 1991 the dollar was overvalued by around 10 percent, given estimates of the Organization for Economic Cooperation and Development of the purchasing power parity exchange rate in the U.S.$0.78 to $0.80 range.

The extremely poor productivity performance of Canadian manufacturing in the second half of the 1980s is harder to explain. Possible factors include the lagged effect of the low value of the Canadian dollar in the 1983–85 period, which had sheltered Canadian manufacturers from international competitive pressures and may have made productivity enhancement less of an priority; a low rate of innovation and diffusion of new technologies; and inadequate skill levels of the workforce. This issue merits much closer study.

The Construction Boom of the Late 1980s

In the late 1980s, Ontario enjoyed an unprecedented boom in the construction sector, particularly in commercial real estate and particularly in the Metropolitan Toronto area. This resulted in considerable overbuilding of office buildings and condominiums. Such a development set the scene for a major correction. This in fact happened in the early 1990s when the construction sector collapsed, with output in the sector falling 17.5 percent between 1989 and 1992 (Statistics Canada 1993). When measured on an expenditure basis, the collapse is even more dramatic, with real spending between 1989 and 1992 down 31.7 percent on non-residential construction and 27.8 percent on residential construction (Ontario Ministry of Finance 1994). This development alone accounted for around two-thirds of the total decline in expenditure.

CONCLUSION

This paper has provided a comprehensive analysis of the rise in unemployment in Ontario between 1989 and 1992. The main findings are that the rise in unemployment was largely a macroeconomic development stemming from the drop in demand for the output of the manufacturing and construction sectors. High interest rates and exchange rate appreciation played important roles in reducing demand and hence in the deterioration of labour-market conditions. The concentration of employment losses in manufacturing and construction meant that blue-collar men with low educational attainment, who are over-represented in these industries, suffered the largest increase in unemployment.

ACKNOWLEDGMENTS

Helpful suggestions were provided by Brian MacLean. The cut-off date for data used in the chapter was November 1994.

NOTES

1 This paper makes extensive use of a number of basic relationships between labour-market variables. For example, working-age or source population is determined by the number of persons reaching working age (fifteen years) minus deaths and net out-migration of the working-age population. The size of the labour force is determined by the size of the working-age population and the participation rate of that population. In growth rate terms, labour-force growth equals working-age population growth and participation rate growth. The unemployment rate is of course defined as the number of unemployed (the labour force minus employment) over the labour force. The unemployment rate rises when labour-force growth exceeds employment growth and falls when employment growth exceeds labour-force growth. The employment-population ratio (employment over working-age population) is determined by both the participation rate and the unemployment rate. For further discussion of these definitions and relationships, see any standard labour economics textbook, such as Gunderson and Riddell (1993).

2 It should be noted that since Ontario makes up such a large share of the Canadian total (well over one-third and up to one-half for some variables), comparison of Ontario to the national average tends to reveal significantly less discrepancy than would comparison to the rest

of Canada. For example, Ontario's unemployment rate in 1988 was 52.6 percent of that in the rest of Canada, compared to 64.1 percent of the national rate. The inclusion of Ontario's low rate in the national rate has the effect of dampening the differential. The importance of this point should be kept in mind throughout the paper when comparisons are made only between Ontario and the national average.

3 The decline in output has resulted in a massive gap between the actual and potential levels of output, as potential output has continued to grow. According to estimates made by the economic forecasting firm, WEFA Canada, in 1992, the Ontario economy was producing around 14 percent below potential. The value of this lost output is around $45 billion.

4 Productivity can be measured on either an output-per-hour or output-per-worker basis. Labour input is more accurately measured on a total-hours basis than on a persons-employed-basis because of variations in average weekly hours worked. For this reason, the output-per-hour measure is the preferred definition of productivity. However, the output-per-worker measure is widely used because employment data are often more readily available than hours data. In the postwar period up to 1980, output-per-hour growth was significantly faster than output-per-worker growth because of large declines in average weekly hours. Since 1980, average weekly hours have been stable so trend output-per-worker growth has been comparable to output-per-hour growth.

5 For example, Business Week (1993) and Midland Walwyn (1993) argue that there has been an upward shift in trend productivity growth in the United States and Canada respectively. Gordon (1993) and Sharpe (1994) take the opposing view that there has been no fundamental change in productivity behaviour in the two countries.

6 As noted in the fifth section of the chapter, however, poor productivity performance in tradeables is a factor in the decline of Ontario's international competitiveness, which in turn accounts for a portion of the output drop.

7 Because of changes in the educational attainment categories, consistent data are only available from 1990.

8 This pattern is almost identical for the average expected completed duration of unemployment (Corak 1993). Between 1989 and 1992, this measure of unemployment duration rose 9.1 weeks in Ontario, 4.8 weeks in Canada, and 2.8 weeks in Canada, excluding Ontario. The relative deterioration in the duration of completed spells of unemployment in Ontario is even more dramatic for workers permanently laid off, up 13.3 weeks between 1989 and 1992 compared to only 4.2 weeks for the rest of Canada.

9 The best summary statistic for analysing developments in a country's international cost-competitiveness is trends in unit labour costs in common currency in manufacturing. Trends in this variable reflect changes in the exchange rate and domestic currency unit labour costs. This latter variable in turn is determined by changes in labour productivity (output per hour) and hourly labour compensation. For a discussion of these concepts, see Sharpe (1990).

10 Total exports to all countries actually rose 7.1 per cent or $8.2 billion (in 1986 dollars) between 1989 and 1992, but total imports increased even more (11.8 per cent or $13.2 billion), so net exports fell $5.0 billion.

REFERENCES

Bureau of Labor Statistics. 1993. *International Comparisons of Manufacturing Productivity and Unit Labor Cost Trends.* 25 August.

Business Week. 1993. "The Technology Payoff: A Sweeping Reorganization of Work Itself is Boosting Productivity." 14 June.

Corak, M. 1993. "The Duration of Unemployment During Boom and Bust." Statistics Canada Analytical Studies Branch Research Paper No. 56.

Fortin, P. 1996. "The Unbearable Lightness of Zero-Inflation Optimism." This volume.

Gordon, R.J. 1993. "The Jobless Recovery: Does It Signal a New Era of Productivity-led Growth?" *Brookings Papers on Economic Activity* 1: 271–316.

Gunderson, M., and W.C. Riddell. 1993. *Labour Market Economics.* 3rd ed. Toronto: McGraw-Hill Ryerson.

Midland Walwyn. 1993. *New Economic Trends: Growth and Restructuring.* 6 January.

Ontario. Ministry of Finance. 1994. *Ontario Economic Outlook, 1994–1998.* November.

Osberg, L. 1996. "Digging a Hole or Laying the Foundation? The Objectives of Macroeconomic Policy in Canada." This volume.

Sharpe, A. 1990. "Measuring Canada's International Competitiveness." *Perspectives on Labour and Income.* Summer, cat. 75-001, Statistics Canada.

– 1994. "A Comparison of the Productivity Performance of the Canadian Economy Between the Early 1980s and 1990s." *Canadian Business Economics,* Winter, 2: No. 2: 27–41.

Shephard, R. 1993. "The Millions Living on Welfare." *Globe and Mail,* 24 March.

Statistics Canada. 1993. *Provincial Gross Domestic Product by Industry,* cat. 15-203.

9 Joblessness among Canada's Aboriginal Peoples

HELMAR DROST

Canadian Aboriginals have suffered from greater economic inequities than any other ethnic group in our society, as measured, for instance, in their relatively low earnings, low labour-force participation rates, high unemployment rates, and high dependency on social assistance. This paper addresses one of these inequities – the serious lack of employment among Aboriginal peoples. While widespread agreement exists about the severity of the employment problems of Aboriginals, no consensus has evolved regarding the relative importance of the various causes of the problem. Are the sources of the high unemployment to be found primarily on the supply side or the demand side? To what extent do the job-market problems result from a low level of general academic education, inadequate training, or limited knowledge of the job market and job-search techniques? How much of the unemployment, if any, is related to low work motivation related to unstable family structures or government transfer payments? Alternatively, how much of the unemployment is caused by the insufficiency of employment opportunities? What role do location barriers or employment discrimination play? Is there a decline in those jobs in which Aboriginals have traditionally worked?

The lack of consensus about the relative importance of various causes of high unemployment among Aboriginals arises because most empirical research on the labour-market experience of Aboriginals has been descriptive, not based on econometrics (see, e.g., Hull 1987; Hagey et al. 1989a, 1989b; Armstrong et al. 1990). No systematic research, to my knowledge, has been conducted that estimates quantitatively the impact of various socio-economic, demographic, and labour-market variables on the unemployment status of Canadian Aboriginals.[1]

The objectives of this paper are twofold. The first is to determine the relative impact of various supply- and demand-side factors on the overall incidence of unemployment among Aboriginals. The second is to analyse the differences in the unemployment experience between Aboriginals of single and multiple ethnic origin. Labour-market analyses that treat the Aboriginal population as a relatively homogeneous entity ignore the large differences in the extent to which various Aboriginal groups have become integrated into mainstream society.

Our focus on the degree of ethnic identity as a determinant factor of labour-market outcomes is guided by two assumptions. One is that Aboriginals reporting multiple ethnic origins, that is, Aboriginals who have intermarried mostly with other non-Aboriginal ethnic groups, are expected to have become more absorbed into the dominant Canadian culture than those who reported their ethnic background as exclusively Aboriginal.[2] Intermarriage, in particular with individuals of English or French descent, tends to accelerate linguistic assimilation and the weakening of Aboriginal values, social patterns, and life-styles. The other assumption is that a higher degree of integration or assimilation at the cultural level generally entails a higher degree of integration at the political and socio-economic level.

The labour-market implications of the first assumption are supported by the data. Aboriginals of single ethnic origin seem to be at a much higher disadvantage relative to Aboriginals of mixed ethnic background. Approximately 40 percent of Aboriginals of single ethnic origin, for example, were not active in the labour market as compared to 25 percent of Aboriginals who reported different ethnic origins. Those of single ethnic origin who were in the labour force experienced unemployment rates almost twice as high as their counterparts who reported multiple ethnic origin. Statistical tests confirm that there are marked differences in the structure of labour-force activities between Aboriginals of single and multiple ethnic origin.[3] Because of the marked differences in labour-market outcomes between Aboriginals of single and multiple ethnic origin, *ceteris paribus* analyses of the determinants of the unemployment/non-employment incidence are conducted for both groups separately. Estimations are also carried out for non-Aboriginals to provide a frame of reference to which the results for Aboriginals may be compared.

In using the conventional unemployment rate, one will understate the extent of under-utilization of Aboriginal labour and of the labour-market inequalities between Aboriginals and non-Aboriginals if the number of Aboriginals who display a marginal attachment to the labour force (for example, those who are available for and desire work but are not actively seeking work) is substantial. If the behaviour of this group, currently classified as out of the labour force, is functionally indistinguishable from the unemployed, the non-employment rate is the preferable measure.[4] However, neither the size of the marginal attachment group among Aboriginals nor the empirical question of whether this group is distinct from the unemployed can be determined with census data. We therefore analyse the incidence of both unemployment and non-employment.

DATA

The estimates in this study are derived from the individual records of the Public Use Sample Tape of the 1986 Canadian census. The tape contains information on 500,434 individuals of whom 14,299 (or 2.9 percent) reported either a single or multiple Aboriginal origin. Aboriginals, as defined in this study, include all individuals who identified themselves as either a North American Indian, Inuit, or Métis on both paternal and maternal sides (single origin) or reported one of the Aboriginal origins in conjunction with any non-Aboriginal ethnic origin or any other Aboriginal origin (multiple origin). Of the 14,299 Aboriginals, 8,192 individuals belonged to the age group fifteen to fifty-four, which we selected for our study.

Since we were interested in comparing Aboriginals of single and multiple ethnic origin, we restricted our analysis to the off-reserve population. This was done for several reasons. Almost all North American Indians living on reserves reported a single ethnic origin.[5] Merging the on- and off-reserve populations, therefore, would confound the effects of the degree of Aboriginal identification with the effect of being on a reserve. Furthermore, the socio-economic conditions under which Aboriginals live on reserves are generally very different from those of the off-reserve population. Approximately 70 percent of all reserves are located in rural, often geographically, remote areas.[6] Excluding all North American Indians living on reserves from the 8,192 Aboriginals in the sample group left us with a final sample of 6,372 Aboriginals, of whom 2,571 (40.3 percent) reported single Aboriginal origins and 3,801 (59.7 percent) reported multiple ethnic origin.

Estimates of an individual's unemployment probability are conditional on the individual's participation in the labour force. Those parts of our study that analyse the incidence of unemployment, therefore, are based on the number of Aboriginals who actually participated in the labour force. With an overall labour-force participation rate of 68.7 percent, this reduced our original sample of 6,372 Aboriginals to 4,380 labour-force members of whom 1,534 (35 percent) were of single ethnic origin and 2,846 (65 percent) were of multiple origin.

The total number of non-Aboriginals aged fifteen to fifty-four in our sample was 288,530. To avoid contamination of the results by possible discrimination against other Canadian visible minorities, we excluded visible minorities from the sample of non-Aboriginals. This left us with a total number of 268,696 non-Aboriginals, of whom 211,370 were in the labour force.

Two limitations involved in the use of census data are noteworthy in the context of this study. First, Aboriginal status in the census is based on ethnic self-identification. Ethnicity as a sociological concept has proven to be elusive. Both the objective cultural criteria used to define ethnic identity as well as the subjective awareness of ethnicity are highly variable (see, e.g., Anderson and Frideres 1981: 36–78; Elliott and Fleras 1992: 133–51). The legal criteria that determine Aboriginal status have changed several times over the last hundred years. Changes in the legal definition, most likely, have affected the self-perception and ethnic self-identification of Aboriginals, and vice versa.[7] Given the ambiguous meaning of ethnicity and the volitional nature of ethnic identification in general, estimates of the number of Aboriginals of single and multiple origin have to be viewed with caution.

Second, the 1986 census, contrary to previous censuses, did not include a question on school attendance. This makes it impossible to differentiate between those who are out of school and looking for work and those who are unemployed while attending school. The lack of data on school attendance also prevents us from determining how many of those reporting an incomplete schooling were no longer attending school, either on a full- or part-time basis.

Despite such limitations, the census is the most comprehensive and reliable source of information on various socio-economic, demographic, and labour-market characteristics of Canada's Aboriginal population.[8]

QUANTITATIVE DIMENSIONS OF THE ABORIGINAL EMPLOYMENT PROBLEM

To illustrate the striking differences in the labour-force status of Aboriginals and non-Aboriginals and of Aboriginals of single and

Table 1
Dimensions of the Aboriginal Employment Problem

Age	All		Female		Male	
	Aboriginals Off-Reserve	Non-Aboriginals	Aboriginals Off-Reserve	Non-Aboriginals	Aboriginals Off-Reserve	Non-Aboriginals
PERCENT OF POPULATION WITH JOB						
15–19	25.5	37.8	24.0	36.8	27.1	38.8
20–24	54.2	73.2	47.9	69.8	61.4	76.6
25–34	62.3	75.9	52.2	65.8	74.3	86.2
35–44	64.6	78.0	56.1	66.6	74.9	89.3
45–54	55.8	72.0	46.6	57.8	65.1	86.3
15–54	54.1	70.4	47.0	61.6	62.2	79.3
LABOUR-FORCE PARTICIPATION RATE						
15–19	38.6	47.5	35.5	46.0	41.8	48.9
20–24	73.9	86.0	64.4	81.5	84.7	90.5
25–34	77.4	84.4	65.8	73.9	91.2	95.1
35–44	77.4	84.1	66.4	72.7	90.5	95.5
45–54	66.3	77.6	52.5	62.9	80.2	92.3
15–54	68.7	78.6	59.3	69.3	79.4	87.9
UNEMPLOYMENT RATE						
15–19	33.9	20.4	32.3	20.2	35.2	20.6
20–24	26.6	14.9	25.6	14.3	27.5	15.4
25–34	19.5	10.1	20.6	11.0	18.6	9.3
35–44	16.5	7.3	15.6	8.4	17.3	6.5
45–54	15.8	7.1	11.2	8.1	18.8	6.0
15–54	21.3	10.4	20.8	11.2	21.7	9.8

Source: Special tabulations from the 1986 Census, Public Use Sample Tape.

multiple ethnic origin, we present statistics on three indicators commonly used to measure the utilization or under-utilization of labour: the employment-to-population ratio, the labour-force participation rate, and the unemployment rate. Each of the three measures has advantages and disadvantages for analysis, highlighting some aspects of the labour-market position while neglecting others. Comparing the three measures for the total sample of Aboriginals off reserves and non-Aboriginals in Table 1 and for Aboriginals of single and multiple ethnic origin in Table 2, the following picture emerges.

First, the *unemployment rate* of Aboriginals is more than twice as high as that for non-Aboriginals. The unemployment differential between the two groups is highest for young people. For those aged fifteen to nineteen and twenty to twenty-four years, the difference is 17.1 and 13.1 percentage points, respectively.

Table 2
Labour-Force Status of Aboriginals Off-Reserve by Degree of Aboriginal Identification

| Age | All | | Female | | Male | |
	Single Origin Aboriginals	Multiple Origin Aboriginals	Single Origin	Multiple Origin	Single Origin	Multiple Origin
PERCENT OF POPULATION WITH JOB						
15–19	14.7	33.1	12.3	32.8	17.4	33.3
20–24	40.8	64.7	36.2	57.3	46.2	73.0
25–34	48.8	69.9	39.6	59.1	59.2	83.1
35–44	53.4	72.1	47.5	62.4	61.6	82.7
45–54	46.4	64.3	38.9	53.7	51.1	74.9
15–54	41.7	62.5	35.7	54.7	48.7	71.2
LABOUR-FORCE PARTICIPATION RATE						
15–19	27.9	46.1	25.5	43.0	30.6	50.0
20–24	63.1	82.3	54.3	72.5	73.5	93.2
25–34	69.2	82.0	55.7	71.2	84.6	95.1
35–44	70.5	82.0	59.3	71.6	85.6	93.4
45–54	59.8	72.2	45.1	59.3	74.8	84.9
15–54	59.7	74.9	49.7	65.9	71.3	84.8
UNEMPLOYMENT RATE						
15–19	47.3	28.2	51.6	23.7	43.3	32.0
20–24	35.4	21.3	33.3	21.0	37.2	21.7
25–34	29.6	14.7	28.9	17.0	30.0	12.6
35–44	24.2	12.1	20.0	12.8	28.1	11.4
45–54	22.4	10.9	13.7	9.5	27.7	11.8
15–54	30.1	16.5	28.1	17.0	31.8	16.1

Source: Special tabulations from the 1986 Census, Public Use Sample Tape.

Unemployment is particularly severe among Aboriginals who reported a single ethnic origin. They are, on average, 1.8 times more likely to experience unemployment than Aboriginals of mixed ethnic background. While the incidence of unemployment is generally very high in the youngest age category, it is extraordinarily so among teenagers with single Aboriginal ethnic origin. The unemployment rate of this group is about 47 percent (i.e., 19 percentage points) higher than the rate of those aged fifteen to nineteen years who gave more than one ethnic origin response.

Unemployment rates of Aboriginal men exceed those of women in all age groups with the exception of the group aged twenty-five to thirty-four. The aggregate figures, however, disguise significant differences in gender patterns of unemployment between single-origin and multiple-origin Aboriginals. While female teenagers of single Aboriginal origin suffer considerably more unemployment than their male counterparts, the opposite pattern applies to Aboriginals with multiple ethnic origin. For single-origin Aboriginals, men experience higher unemployment rates than women, while for Aboriginals with multiple ethnic origins, women aged twenty-five and older show higher unemployment rates than men. The gender pattern in unemployment of those twenty-five and older in the multiple-ethnic-origins group is in line with the non-Aboriginal population where women in the higher age groups also experience more unemployment than men.

Second, *labour-force participation rates* (LFPRS) of Aboriginals are substantially lower than those of non-Aboriginals, in particular for those aged twenty to twenty-four and forty-five to fifty-four. The large discrepancy for the twenty to twenty-four-year-old group is mainly due to the relatively low participation rate of female Aboriginals in this age group. By subtracting the LFPR from 100 (which gives the non-participation rate), we see that 35.6 percent of Aboriginal women aged twenty to twenty-four were not in the labour force, as compared to only 18.5 percent of non-Aboriginal women of the same age. It would be important to know whether differences in labour-market behaviour of Aboriginal women in this age group arise from child-bearing and child-care competing in a different way with market work than is the case for non-Aboriginal women. In the age group forty-five to fifty-four, on the other hand, the difference in the LFPR between Aboriginals and non-Aboriginals is more the result of the relatively low LFPR of Aboriginal men.

Aboriginals with single ethnic origin have LFPRS that are, on average, 15 percentage points lower than Aboriginals who reported multiple ethnic origins. The relatively low participation rate, for example, that we observed for the twenty- to twenty-four-year-old Aboriginals in comparison to non-Aboriginals is to a substantial extent due to the large number of Aboriginal women of single ethnic origin who are not participating in the labour force. Almost 46 percent are not in the labour force compared to 28 percent of Aboriginal women of the same age who reported multiple ethnic origins. Note also the much higher LFPRS of male Aboriginals with multiple ethnic origin across the various age groups that either exceed or come very close to those of non-Aboriginals.

Third, disparities in labour-force activities between Aboriginals and non-Aboriginals are accentuated when *employment-to-population ratios* are compared, since the ratios show the combined effects of the lower LFPRS and the higher unemployment rates of Aboriginals.[9]

Focusing on the non-employment rate, i.e., the fraction of the population not working (100 minus the employment-population ratio), we find that approximately 46 percent of Aboriginals were not employed compared to 30 percent of non-Aboriginals.

A disaggregation of the non-employment differentials between Aboriginals and non-Aboriginals into the relative contributions of unemployment and non-participation in the labour force leads to the following conclusions. The relatively higher non-employment of Aboriginal teenagers reflects more their relatively higher unemployment than their relatively higher non-participation. This applies to both male and female teenagers. On the other hand, in the group aged forty-five to fifty-four, it is the relatively higher non-participation of both Aboriginal men and women rather than their relatively higher unemployment rates that plays the stronger role.

Within the Aboriginal population, the non-employment rate is far higher for women than for men, particularly in the prime age groups of those who are twenty-five to fifty-four. The higher rate reflects in all age groups the relatively lower LFPR of women, which more than offsets the generally higher incidence of unemployment among men.

The higher unemployment and lower participation rates of Aboriginals of single ethnic origin result in non-employment rates that are even less favourable than those reported earlier for the total Aboriginal population. The figures in Table 2 reveal that 58 percent of Aboriginals of single ethnic origin are not engaged in market work compared to 38 percent of Aboriginals with multiple ethnic origin. Particularly disconcerting are the figures for the youngest and oldest age group. Almost 88 percent of female and 83 percent of male teenagers, and about 61 percent of females and 49 percent of males aged forty-five to fifty-four who reported single ethnic origin were non-employed.

We should conclude this section with a caveat. A comparison of the labour-force status of Aboriginals of single ethnic and multiple ethnic origin is confounded by the fact that traditional native activities in the non-wage sector such as hunting, fishing, trapping, gathering, and farming are more likely to be pursued by Aboriginals of single ethnic origin (due to their relatively larger concentration in rural areas), and that non-market and market activities are asymmetrically treated in the official definitions of labour-force activities. Because of the hierarchical nature of labour-force statuses, Aboriginals who search for a market job while pursuing hunting, fishing, or trapping as subsistence non-market activities are counted as unemployed, whereas those who search for a job while employed in a market occupation are not. On the other hand, Aboriginals who are hunting, fishing, or trapping full-time on a non-commercial basis are not counted in the labour force and are thus excluded from the denominator of the unemployment statistic, while those engaged in market work are members of the labour force. As long as it is uncertain how viable subsistence non-market activities are for Aboriginals and to which extent they represent a preferential choice over market activities, the application of conventional labour-force categorizations must be treated with caution.

THE EMPIRICAL MODEL

An Aboriginal's likelihood to be unemployed or non-employed may be affected by a wide range of variables. We consider several variables reflecting individual attributes, socio-economic characteristics, and local labour-market conditions. For convenience, these variables are divided into four groups: age; family background, gender, and receipt of social assistance; educational attainment; and location of residence.

We have classified our sample into five age groups. The probability of unemployment/ non-employment is assumed to decline with age. After leaving the educational system, most of the young people are expected to gradually adopt more stable employment patterns.

For family background we consider the influence of marital status and the presence of children in the family. Social assistance is an alternative source of income that is more commonly received by Aboriginals than non-Aboriginals. The Public Use Sample Tape includes a series of government transfer variables: (1) federal child tax credits; (2) Canada and Quebec Pension Plan benefits; (3) family allowances; (4) old-age security payments and guaranteed income supplements; (5) unemployment insurance benefits; and (6) "other" government transfer payments. The position taken in this paper is that only social assistance payments constitute "welfare" payments, while other government transfers, such as items (1) to (5) are not. Our welfare variable, therefore, includes only those federal, provincial, and municipal transfer payments not reported in items (1) to (5). This measure corresponds most closely to the "social assistance" notion of government transfers. The welfare variable takes the value of one if government transfer payments are received by the individual, and zero otherwise.

The economic literature that examines the financial work incentives built into the welfare system would suggest that the receipt of government income transfers has a positive effect on the probability of unemployment. By providing income transfers that raise individual incomes, transfer payments lessen the need to work. A work disincentive may also arise from the experience of being on welfare. Gaining familiarity with the use of public income support may exert an impact that is distinct from the pure financial disincentives associated with income transfer payments. Another potentially important role played by government income transfers may be their effect on child-bearing by Aboriginal women, especially unmarried young women. If government income transfers increase child-bearing, the effect would most probably have negative consequences for the employment of Aboriginal women. Young women who become mothers and family heads at an early age often do not complete their education or gain experience in entry-level jobs because of their child-care responsibilities. This would likely have adverse effects on their employment prospects and would, in turn, reinforce their reliance on social assistance.

In empirical studies following the human capital approach, education is commonly introduced as a continuous variable, measured in years of full-time schooling. For analyses assessing the impact of education on labour-market outcomes, this measure has obvious shortcomings. Aside from not capturing part-time education, it fails to address the effect that different curricula may have on the labour-market position of individuals. Also, it does not permit one to identify the potentially different effects that educational credentials and years of schooling may have on labour-force status. Unless more years of schooling are associated with the completion of a higher degree or certificate/diploma, more years of formal education may not necessarily imply a lower risk of becoming unemployed. The measure chosen for education in this study is the highest level of schooling/training attained by the Aboriginal respondent.[10] This measure combines the time dimension, the credentialling effect, and to some extent the orientation of schooling.[11]

Researchers have traditionally stressed the supply side in explaining the inability of Aboriginals to find employment. A cursory examination of the labour-market experience of Aboriginals, however, suggests that substantial employment problems remain even when supply-side factors are accounted for. Clearly, any explanation of the relatively high unemployment or non-employment rates of Aboriginals has to consider the demand side of the labour market. Data from the census, unfortunately, are not easy to translate into estimates of demand parameters. Variation in wage *offers* for given qualities and quantities of Aboriginal labour are not available. Clearly, the wages *obtained* reflect a mixture of supply and demand factors. Measuring a wage variable for Aboriginals that is exogenous to their labour supply is particularly difficult. A wage from the census data that is defined as reported earnings in 1985 divided by the reported hours worked in 1985 is particularly error-laden when part-time jobs are common, as they may be among Aboriginals. Restricting the wage to full-time, year-round workers reduces the error, but jobs for these workers tend to be in manufacturing and certain service industries at relatively high wages; such jobs may not be widely available for Aboriginals. We settle in this paper for indirect evidence of demand-side causes of the labour-force status of Aboriginals. Region and residence in a census metropolitan area act as a crude proxies for the industrial structure and labour requirements in the labour markets in which Aboriginals seek work. They can be assumed to be largely exogenous with respect to the supply of Aboriginal labour.

RESULTS

In Tables 3 to 6 we provide the following statistics: columns 1 and 3 in each table show the percentage of Aboriginals and non-Aboriginals with a particular characteristic; columns 2 and 4 report the average unemployment and non-employment rate of the groups who have that characteristic; and in the last two columns we calculate the unemployment/non-employment differential that can be attributed to the particular characteristic. The procedure used to calculate the differentials from the logit coefficients in Tables 7 and 8 is explained in the Appendix.[12] The relation between the computed unemployment/non-employment differentials and the observed differentials is as follows.

Taking the age variable in Table 3 as an example, we find that Aboriginal teenagers had an unemployment rate of 33.9 percent, whereas young adults aged twenty to twenty-four years experienced an unemployment rate of 26.6 percent. The observed unemployment differential between the two age groups was thus 7.3 percentage points. Clearly, this 7.3-percentage-point differential could be due to factors other than age, such as education or marital status. The computed unemployment differential in the second-last column states that when the unemployment effect of all the variables, except for age, is removed, there remains an unemployment differential between the two groups of 4.9 percentage points. This fraction of the observed unemployment differential reflects the pure age effect, the remainder of the differential (i.e., 2.4 percentage points) is due to other factors. We now examine our results in terms of the original four groups of variables.

Table 3
Age and Unemployment/Non-employment

Age Group	Percent in Sample	Sample Unemployment Rate	Percent in Sample	Sample Non-employment Rate	Differential Due to Age	
					Unemployment	Non-employment
ALL ABORIGINALS						
15–19	9.9	33.9	17.6	74.5	+4.9	+27.8
20–24	19.5	26.6	18.2	45.8	–	–
25–34	37.7	19.5	33.5	37.7	–6.1	–9.1
35–44	22.6	16.5	20.1	35.4	–9.2	–13.9
45–54	10.3	15.8	10.6	44.2	–12.1	–9.3
ABORIGINALS OF SINGLE ETHNIC ORIGIN						
15–19	8.4	47.3	17.9	85.3	+11.3	+23.5
20–24	21.0	35.4	19.7	59.2	–	–
25–34	34.6	29.6	30.0	51.2	–6.9	–11.1
35–44	23.5	24.2	19.9	46.6	–12.4	–19.3
45–54	12.5	22.4	12.5	53.6	–16.2	–16.7
ABORIGINALS OF MULTIPLE ETHNIC ORIGIN						
15–19	10.7	28.2	17.4	66.9	+2.7	+28.3
20–24	18.8	21.3	17.1	35.3	–	–
25–34	39.4	14.7	35.9	30.1	–5.9	–6.8
35–44	22.1	12.1	20.2	27.9	–8.4	–9.5
45–54	9.0	10.9	9.4	35.7	–10.9	–3.6
NON-ABORIGINALS						
15–19	7.8	20.4	12.8	62.2	+3.3	+31.3
20–24	16.6	14.9	15.1	26.8	–	–
25–34	32.6	10.1	30.1	24.1	–4.0	–5.1
35–44	25.9	7.3	24.3	22.0	–7.2	–8.8
45–54	17.1	7.1	17.5	28.0	–7.9	–3.9

Source: Special tabulations from the 1986 Census, Public Use Sample Tape, and own calculations.

Age

In accordance with prior expectation, unemployment rates decline with age. The relation between non-employment and age instead appears to be u-shaped. The differentials in the last two columns show that age exerts a strong independent effect on unemployment and non-employment. The effect appears to be more important for Aboriginals than it is for non-Aboriginals. For example, age contributes 4.9 percentage points to the increase in the observed unemployment rate of Aboriginal teenagers relative to Aboriginals aged twenty to twenty-four, whereas it accounts for 3.3 percentage points of the unemployment differential between the two corresponding non-Aboriginal age groups. Likewise, the contribution of age to the decline in unemployment of the older group aged forty-five to fifty-four relative to young adults was 12.1 percentage points for Aboriginals, compared to 7.9 points for non-Aboriginals. The pure age effect is particularly pronounced for Aboriginals of single ethnic origin. For this group, the observed unemployment differential between teenagers and twenty- to twenty-four-year-olds of 11.9 percentage points can be attributed almost entirely to age effects, and for the other age categories the computed unemployment differentials exceed the observed differentials. The implication is that the other variables included in our regressions have no relevance in explaining the observed age-specific unemployment differentials of Aboriginals of single ethnic origin. This is not the case for Aboriginals of multiple ethnic origin.

Gender, Family Background, and Social Assistance

Turning to the unemployment/non-employment differentials associated with gender, family background, and social assistance in Table 4, we find that gender plays a significant independent role only in the determination of unemployment of Aboriginals of single ethnic origin. Being female reduced the unemployment differential for this group by 7.6 points, whereas for both Aboriginals with mixed ethnic background and for non-Aboriginals, gender appeared to have no independent effect on unemployment. The pattern is reversed in the case of non-employment. Not surprisingly, being a woman increased the likelihood of being non-employed in all groups. The pure gender effect in the non-employment equation is much stronger for non-Aboriginals and Aboriginals of mixed ethnic background than for Aboriginals of single ethnic origin.

The presence of children at home had a significant positive effect on the likelihood of unemployment and non-employment for all three groups. The picture is more complicated in case of marital status. Overall, the negative effect of marital status is weaker on unemployment than on non-employment. For Aboriginals of single ethnic origin, only a relatively small part of the observed unemployment and non-employment differential between married and single individuals can be attributed to marital status. The large remainder may be accounted for by other factors such as age and education, both of which have a significant effect on the labour-force status of this group and both of which are likely to be different for married and single

Table 4
Family Background, Gender, Social Assistance, and Unemployment/Non-employment

Attribute	Percent in Sample	Sample Unemployment Rate	Percent in Sample	Sample Non-employment Rate	Differential Due to Attribute	
					Unemployment	Non-employment
ALL ABORIGINALS						
Female	45.7	20.8	53.0	53.0	-2.7	+6.9
Male	54.3	21.7	47.0	37.8	–	–
Children	23.9	21.5	29.2	55.7	+7.9	+24.8
No Children	76.1	21.2	70.8	41.8	–	–
Married	56.3	17.1	51.0	37.1	-6.8	-9.4
Divorced/Separated	10.2	21.0	10.2	45.7	-3.1	-7.2
Single	33.5	28.3	38.8	57.5	–	–
Social Assistance	11.8	50.1	15.4	79.2	+26.4	+30.9
No Social Assistance	88.2	17.8	84.6	38.7	–	–
ABORIGINALS OF SINGLE ETHNIC ORIGIN						
Female	44.9	28.1	53.9	64.2	-7.6	+2.7
Male	55.1	31.8	46.1	51.2	–	–
Children	25.2	28.5	30.9	65.3	+8.2	+18.8
No Children	74.8	30.7	69.1	55.2	–	–
Married	53.3	25.6	10.7	49.4	-4.8	-4.6
Divorced/Separated	10.6	29.0	46.7	58.2	-1.9	-1.9
Single	36.1	37.1	42.6	68.1	–	–
Social Assistance	15.6	56.4	20.8	83.9	+30.0	+31.4
No Social Assistance	84.4	24.8	79.2	48.7	–	–

ABORIGINALS OF MULTIPLE ETHNIC ORIGIN

Female	46.2	17.0	52.5	45.3	−0.4	+8.9
Male	53.8	16.1	47.5	28.8	–	–
Children	23.3	17.4	28.0	48.6	+7.2	+28.0
No Children	76.7	16.2	72.0	33.1	–	–
Married	57.9	12.9	53.9	29.9	−6.8	−11.4
Divorced/Separated	10.0	16.4	9.9	36.6	−2.5	−10.0
Single	32.1	22.9	36.2	49.0	–	–
Social Assistance	9.8	42.5	11.7	71.6	+15.9	+26.8
No Social Assistance	90.2	14.4	88.3	33.1	–	–

NON-ABORIGINALS

Female	43.9	11.2	49.9	38.7	−0.00	+9.8
Male	56.1	9.7	50.1	20.4	–	–
Children	21.3	11.0	26.0	42.6	+5.8	+27.1
No Children	78.7	10.2	74.0	24.9	–	–
Married	62.1	7.8	59.7	24.6	−5.4	−10.3
Divorced/Separated	7.3	12.2	7.1	29.3	−0.6	−10.4
Single	30.6	15.3	33.2	38.5	–	–
Social Assistance	5.4	37.2	6.6	68.0	+13.9	+27.9
No Social Assistance	94.6	9.2	93.4	26.7	–	–

Source: Special tabulations from the 1986 Census, Public Use Sample Tape, and own calculations.

individuals. On the other hand, in case of Aboriginals with mixed ethnic background and non-Aboriginals, being married reduced significantly the likelihood of unemployment and non-employment. Interestingly, being divorced or separated had only a minor independent effect on the unemployment differential of all three groups.

The single most important variable in our unemployment and non-employment regressions is found to be social assistance. The magnitude of the effect of this variable, however, differs substantially between the three groups considered in this study. A much higher proportion of Aboriginals of single ethnic origin received social assistance than Aboriginals with mixed ethnic background or non-Aboriginals and it is in the former group where the welfare variable has the strongest impact. After controlling for the effect of all other variables, Aboriginals of single ethnic origin who received social assistance had an unemployment rate 30 points higher compared to those who received no income transfer payments. The corresponding figure for non-employment was 31.4 points. Aboriginals of mixed ethnic background as well as non-Aboriginals were less likely to be found unemployed because of being on welfare. Although 42.5 and 37.2 percent of welfare recipients in these two groups, respectively, were unemployed, close to half of them were unemployed for other reasons.

Educational Attainment

Official policy documents and much of recent research have considered the relatively low level of general education and occupational skills of Aboriginals as the main barrier to stable native employment (see e.g., Employment and Immigration Canada 1981: 95; Economic Council of Canada 1982: 89; Sharzer 1984: 563; Employment and Immigration Canada 1991: 8). The results in Table 5, however, indicate that there are substantial differences in educational attainment levels between Aboriginals of single and multiple ethnic origin. Among individuals of single ethnic origin, more than one-half (i.e., 56 percent) had not completed secondary schooling as compared to 36 percent of those of multiple ethnic origin. At the other end of the educational spectrum, 13 percent of single origin Aboriginals had graduated from community colleges, Collèges d'enseignement général et professionnel (CEGEPs), institutes of technology, and similar institutions, and 8 percent had an incomplete or complete university education. This compares with 20 percent and 19 percent, respectively, for Aboriginals who reported multiple ethnic origins.

Similarly large are the unemployment and non-employment differentials between groups with the same educational qualification. For instance, 17.7 percent of Aboriginals of single ethnic origin who had completed a university education were found to be unemployed compared to 7.5 percent of Aboriginal degree-holders of mixed ethnic background.

Unemployment and non-employment were most adversely affected by an incomplete elementary school education. There is a sharp decline in unemployment/non-employment when we move from the group with less than Grade 9 education to the group who reported a high school certificate as their highest educational attainment. As the last two columns of Table 5 show, the pure effect of education remains strong once the other variables are controlled for, especially in case of Aboriginals of single ethnic origin.

Investment in post-secondary vocational education and training appears to have a different pay-off for Aboriginals of single and multiple ethnic origin in terms of influencing their unemployment as well as their non-employment probability. For Aboriginals of single ethnic origin, neither the attainment of a trade certificate nor of a college certificate or diploma reduced the likelihood of unemployment or non-employment when compared to the attainment of a secondary school certificate. On the contrary, vocational education and skill training that extend past the secondary school level worsened their employment prospects.[13] Holding a trade school or college certificate contributed 7.7 or 11.2 points, respectively, to the observed increase in unemployment. Aboriginals of mixed ethnic background, on the other hand, appeared to realize some economic benefits from obtaining a trade school or college certificate/diploma. The same holds for non-Aboriginals, though in their case the positive effect is minimal.

Another startling difference in the schooling variable is found at the university level. While the possession of a university degree or certificate was strongly significant for Aboriginals of multiple ethnic origin – degree-holders in this group had on average 7.1 points less unemployment than high school graduates – a university education had no independent effect on the unemployment probability of Aboriginals of single ethnic origin.

Our estimates of the schooling/training coefficients, however, ought to be considered with some caution because the nature of the selection into the various educational categories may create biases for which we have not corrected. For example, the group of Aboriginals of single ethnic origin who enrolled in vocational programs may be disproportionately composed of individuals who are less

Table 5
Education and Unemployment/Non-employment

Educational Qualification	Percent in Sample	Sample Unemployment Rate	Percent in Sample	Sample Non-employment Rate	Differential Due to Educational Qualification	
					Unemployment	Non-employment
ALL ABORIGINALS						
< Grade 9	11.5	35.1	16.7	69.3	+16.7	+33.8
Grades 9–13	31.6	25.8	36.5	55.8	+6.4	+16.4
High school certificate	11.0	17.5	9.5	34.7	–	–
Trade certificate	3.8	15.2	2.9	25.3	+0.2	–2.3
Some post-secondary	9.5	23.7	8.4	41.0	+5.9	+7.3
College	17.6	16.1	13.9	26.5	–0.1	–4.2
Some university	4.8	11.6	4.2	31.5	–6.3	–1.1
University	10.2	9.3	7.9	18.6	–6.0	–10.1
ABORIGINALS OF SINGLE ETHNIC ORIGIN						
< Grade 9	20.3	38.5	28.1	73.4	+21.4	+34.7
Grades 9–13	36.3	33.2	38.6	62.5	+10.6	+16.9
High school certificate	8.9	20.6	7.0	40.0	–	–
Trade certificate	4.3	22.7	3.0	32.9	+7.7	+1.5
Some post-secondary	8.6	27.2	7.7	51.3	+7.6	+13.5
College	13.2	27.1	9.5	40.0	+11.2	+4.2
Some university	3.2	18.4	2.6	42.9	–2.7	+2.4
University	5.1	17.7	3.5	27.0	–0.0	–9.6

ABORIGINALS OF MULTIPLE ETHNIC ORIGIN

< Grade 9	6.7	29.5	8.9	60.7	+12.6	+29.2
Grades 9–13	29.1	19.7	35.0	50.8	+4.0	+15.6
High school certificate	12.1	16.2	11.3	32.5	–	–
Trade certificate	3.4	10.2	2.9	20.0	–4.6	–5.9
Some post-secondary	9.9	21.9	8.9	35.1	+5.8	+4.3
College	20.1	12.2	16.8	21.4	–3.1	–7.1
Some university	5.6	9.5	5.2	27.4	–7.2	–2.1
University	13.1	7.5	10.9	16.8	–7.1	–10.0

NON-ABORIGINALS

< Grade 9	7.6	15.8	9.5	23.1	+9.0	+23.1
Grades 9–13	23.8	13.4	28.0	42.3	+3.6	+12.4
High school certificate	14.9	9.9	14.7	28.2	–	–
Trade certificate	3.6	9.0	3.1	18.9	–0.2	–4.2
Some post-secondary	7.9	12.1	7.5	26.7	+1.7	–0.4
College	18.6	8.5	16.6	19.0	–0.5	–4.5
Some university	5.2	10.3	4.7	22.1	–0.2	–2.7
University	18.4	6.1	15.9	14.4	–2.5	–7.9

Source: Special tabulations from the 1986 Census, Public Use Sample Tape, and own calculations.

Table 6
Region, City, and Unemployment/Non-employment

Residence	Percent in Sample	Sample Unemployment Rate	Percent in Sample	Sample Non-employment Rate	Differential Due to Residence	
					Unemployment	Non-employment
ALL ABORIGINALS						
Region A	4.7	33.3	4.7	54.4	+8.0	+6.0
Region Q	11.6	18.9	11.4	43.8	−6.4	+0.1
Region O	30.0	12.0	26.7	34.0	−15.5	−15.1
Region P	31.6	22.6	33.4	49.7	−7.1	−4.4
Region BC	23.0	29.8	23.8	53.2	–	–
City	41.7	17.3	39.2	50.0	−1.9	−2.7
Non-City	58.3	24.0	60.8	39.5	–	–
ABORIGINALS OF SINGLE ETHNIC ORIGIN						
Region A	2.9	36.4	2.8	61.1	+7.3	+5.5
Region Q	14.5	21.2	13.7	50.1	−13.9	−4.4
Region O	16.1	17.8	14.4	45.3	−16.2	−10.6
Region P	36.4	32.4	38.9	62.2	−6.9	−2.4
Region BC	30.1	37.7	30.2	62.9	–	–
City	32.3	28.2	30.8	59.8	+3.9	+4.1
Non-City	67.7	31.0	69.2	55.0	–	–

ABORIGINALS OF MULTIPLE ETHNIC ORIGIN

Region A	5.5	32.5	5.9	52.2	+10.6	+10.0
Region Q	10.1	17.2	10.0	37.9	-2.2	+3.5
Region O	36.2	10.6	34.9	30.8	-11.8	-12.3
Region P	29.0	16.0	29.6	38.6	-7.4	-6.2
Region BC	19.2	23.1	19.5	43.0	–	–
City	46.8	13.2	44.9	41.7	-3.1	-4.2
Non-City	53.2	19.4	55.1	32.3	–	–

NON-ABORIGINALS

Region A	8.8	18.4	9.5	40.4	+4.2	+6.1
Region Q	26.1	13.1	27.5	35.4	+0.3	+4.3
Region O	36.6	6.8	35.4	24.1	-5.9	-9.0
Region P	17.6	6.9	16.9	24.9	-4.4	-6.7
Region BC	10.9	12.6	10.7	29.8	–	–
City	49.4	8.5	48.0	32.8	-1.8	-2.2
Non-City	50.6	12.2	52.0	25.9	–	–

Source: Special tabulations from the 1986 Census, Public Use Sample Tape, and own calculations.

motivated or lack other employment-related attributes that are unobservable to the researcher. In this case, negative self-selection of single origin Aboriginals into vocational versus non-vocational programs could lead to estimates that potentially understate the true effect of trades school or college training on the likelihood of being unemployed.

Region and City

Regional labour-market conditions play an important role in determining the probability of Aboriginals being unemployed. Again, we find significant differences in the unemployment experience of the two Aboriginal groups. As is evident from Table 6, unemployment and non-employment differentials decline from the Atlantic provinces to central Canada and increase as one moves further west. However, the central-west unemployment differential is substantially larger for single origin Aboriginals than for those of mixed ethnic background. The "unexplained" part of the differentials are rather small for both groups. Admittedly, important factors that may explain regional unemployment differentials, such as the occupational and industrial distribution, are not included in our analysis. Nevertheless, our findings allow us to conclude that possible differences in the regional distribution of personal characteristics (e.g., education and age) do not account for much of the observed differentials.

Of interest is also our finding regarding residence in one of Canada's nine metropolitan areas. Aboriginals who reported a multiple ethnic origin appear to do much better in urban labour markets. Living in a metropolitan area reduced their probability of unemployment whilst the opposite applied to their counterparts of single ethnic origin. The question why Aboriginals of single ethnic origin seem to be far less integrated into urban society requires further research.

CONCLUSION

Our results indicate that receipt of social assistance is the variable most strongly correlated with the incidence of unemployment. The interpretation of this result, however, warrants caution. It would be premature to interpret our finding as clear evidence that the poor labour-market outcome of Aboriginals is caused by being on welfare. Reliance on government income support may merely be associated with unfavourable conditions resulting from unemployment. Since the transfer payments variable refers to social assistance received

Table 7
Probability of Unemployment (Logit Regression)

Variable	All Aboriginals Estimate	Aboriginals of Single Ethnic Origin Estimate	Aboriginals of Multiple Ethnic Origin Estimate	Non-Aboriginals Estimate
Constant	−0.8613***	−0.8901***	−.8721***	−1.492***
	(−5.1637)	(−3.2894)	(−3.9444)	(−45.0876)
Age 15–19	+0.2371	+.4709*	+.1554	+.2381***
	(+1.7045)	(+2.0617)	(+0.8548)	(+9.0884)
Age 25–34	−.3395***	−.3160*	−.3976**	−.3579***
	(−3.0124)	(−1.8799)	(−2.5553)	(−15.9067)
Age 35–44	−.5447***	−.6064***	−.5673***	−.7342***
	(−3.9759)	(−3.0396)	(−2.9424)	(−27.2937)
Age 45–54	−.7607***	−.8335***	−.8467***	−.8366***
	(−4.4073)	(−3.4315)	(−3.3295)	(−27.5197)
Sex	−.1698	−.3759**	−.0285	−.0008
	(−1.6110)	(−2.2536)	(−0.2055)	(−0.0428)
Children	+.4247***	+.3664*	+.4661**	+.4893***
	(+3.2544)	(+1.8219)	(+2.6352)	(+19.8902)
Married	−.3665***	−.2099	−.4365***	−.4979***
	(−3.5756)	(−1.3993)	(−3.0292)	(−23.5972)
Divorced/Separated	−.1590	−.0826	−.1476	−.0432
	(−1.0044)	(−0.3524)	(−0.6737)	(−1.3211)
Welfare	+1.1767***	+1.3040***	+0.9823***	+1.0890***
	(+11.3144)	(+8.5007)	(+6.6778)	(+45.1867)
< Grade 9	+.8971***	+1.0247***	+.7386**	+.7547***
	(+5.4205)	(+3.8581)	(+3.1497)	(+24.4326)
Grades 9–13	+.3926**	+.5580**	+.2698	+.3477***
	(+2.7648)	(+2.2711)	(+1.5157)	(+14.6092)
Trade certificate	+.0113	+.4189	−.3827	−.0182
	(+0.0434)	(+1.0881)	(−1.0045)	(−0.3965)
Some post-secondary	+.3655**	+.4136	+.3804*	+.1813***
	(+2.0898)	(+1.3529)	(+1.7709)	(+5.8109)
College	−.0098	+.5130*	−.2448	−.0553*
	(−0.0603)	(+1.8256)	(−1.2047)	(−2.0558)
Some university	−.5201*	−.1773	−.6715*	−.0276
	(−2.0159)	(−0.3922)	(−2.0997)	(−0.7282)
University	−.4917**	−.0021	−.6604**	−.3124***
	(−2.3292)	(−0.0054)	(−2.5677)	(−10.6258)
Region A	+.3609*	+.3033	+.5248**	+.3384***
	(+2.0611)	(+.8666)	(+2.4696)	(+11.5102)
Region Q	−.3317**	−.6599***	−.1302	+.0278
	(−2.3392)	(−3.2111)	(−0.6517)	(+1.1347)
Region O	−.9307***	−.7925***	−.8627***	−.6911***
	(−7.9751)	(−3.8886)	(−5.7246)	(−27.4246)
Region P	−.3691***	−.3108**	−.4746***	−.4740***
	(−3.6400)	(−2.1390)	(−3.2229)	(−16.8683)
City	−.1070	+.1764	−.2123*	−.1757***
	(−1.2243)	(+1.2591)	(−1.8317)	(−10.9130)
Log L	−2025.96	−847.44	−1144.34	−64831.50
χ^2	479.83	182.30	258.68	11325.81
	N = 4380	N = 1534	N = 2846	N = 211370

Note: t-values in parentheses; *, **, *** indicate significant at the 10-, 5-, and 1-percent level respectively.

Table 8
Probability of Non-employment (Logit Regression)

Variable	All Aboriginals Estimate	Aboriginals of Single Ethnic Origin Estimate	Aboriginals of Multiple Ethnic Origin Estimate	Non-Aboriginals Estimate
Constant	−.7343***	−.5925***	−.9275***	−.3113***
	(−5.6790)	(−2.8187)	(−5.3799)	(−13.6535)
Age 15–19	+1.1951***	+1.4656***	+1.1634***	+1.3303***
	(+11.5692)	(+8.3653)	(+8.5987)	(+73.6328)
Age 25–34	−.3751***	−.4481***	−.3141**	−.2758***
	(−4.2240)	(−3.3242)	(−2.5788)	(−16.6145)
Age 35–44	−.5933***	−.7823***	−.4528***	−.5123***
	(−5.6829)	(−5.0212)	(−3.1554)	(−27.5430)
Age 45–54	−.3865***	−.6752***	−.1609	−.2064***
	(−3.1628)	(−3.7616)	(−0.9526)	(−10.6392)
Sex	+.2841***	+.1097	+.4044***	+.5234***
	(+3.7137)	(+0.8853)	(+4.0521)	(+42.097)
Children	+1.0215***	+.8375***	+1.1558***	+1.1830***
	(+11.3248)	(+5.8444)	(+9.7536)	(+79.9324)
Married	−.3785***	−.2040	−.4684***	−.4650***
	(−4.6442)	(−1.6776)	(−4.1451)	(−30.3922)
Divorced/Separated	−.2905**	−.0905	−.4083**	−.4729***
	(−2.4168)	(−0.5006)	(−2.4912)	(−20.2094)
Welfare	+1.2875***	+1.4465***	+1.1066***	+1.1951***
	(+15.0761)	(+11.2568)	(+9.3700)	(+66.3944)
< Grade 9	+1.4111***	+1.4861***	+1.2072***	+.9871***
	(+11.5474)	(+7.4678)	(+7.0227)	(+51.1451)
Grades 9–13	+.6778***	+.6828***	+.6557***	+.5521***
	(+6.4799)	(+3.6928)	(+5.0788)	(+37.3041)
Trade certificate	−.1044	+.0610	−.2820	−.2179***
	(−0.5110)	(+0.1933)	(−1.0122)	(−6.7046)
Some post-secondary	+.3108**	+.5447**	+.1891	−.0185
	(+2.3263)	(+2.3703)	(+1.1283)	(−0.8685)
College	−.1898	+.1713	−0.3478**	−.2362***
	(−1.5244)	(+0.7776)	(−2.2643)	(-13.2697)
Some University	−.0497	+.0983	−.0956	−.1397***
	(−0.2893)	(+0.3098)	(−0.4605)	(−5.3118)
University	−.4900***	−.4250	−.5038**	−.4308***
	(−3.1922)	(−1.3821)	(−2.7849)	(−22.5550)
Region A	+.2493	+.2294	+.4034**	+.2771***
	(+1.6902)	(+0.7819)	(+2.2663)	(+13.1952)
Region Q	+.0048	−.1921	+.1413	+.1996***
	(+0.0458)	(−1.2849)	(+0.9567)	(+11.7412)
Region O	−.6134***	−.4861***	−.5324***	−.4802***
	(−7.3198)	(−3.2956)	(−4.9024)	(−28.5833)
Region P	−.1762**	−.1044	−.2574**	−.3459***
	(−2.2474)	(−0.9078)	(−2.3168)	(−18.3016)
City	−.1156*	+.1677	−.1989**	−.1197***
	(−1.8320)	(+1.5866)	(−2.4465)	(−11.7353)
Log L	−3528.93	−1428.09	−2044.14	−134107.38
χ^2	1732.14	636.74	939.52	57779.14
	N = 6372	N = 2571	N = 3801	N = 268696

Note: t-values in parentheses; *, **, *** indicate significant at the 10-, 5-, and 1-percent level respectively.

during the previous calendar year, the variable may capture the effect of past unemployment on present unemployment rather than the effect of being on welfare. Sample-selection bias may be another problem. Individuals who receive income transfer payments may systematically differ from other Aboriginals in terms of various characteristics, some of which are difficult to measure. To the extent that these unmeasured attributes exert an impact on the unemployment probability, one might find strong welfare effects on unemployment that actually represent differences in unmeasured personal characteristics. Whatever the biases connected with the welfare variable may be, they do not, however, seem to affect our findings regarding the other determinants in the unemployment equation.[14]

Among the personal attributes having a positive effect on the incidence of unemployment, an incomplete elementary school education was the most significant one. This finding suggests that large gains in lowering the risk of unemployment for Aboriginals may be achieved by raising their elementary school completion rates.

Region is another variable that significantly affects the probability of Aboriginals of being unemployed. Living in Ontario as opposed to British Columbia, for instance, reduced considerably the likelihood of unemployment. This result points to the important role demand-side factors appear to play in the determination of unemployment.

Considering the incidence of non-employment, we find that the highly significant variables in the unemployment equation are also the ones that strongly affect the probability of non-employment. The two characteristics that have a considerably bigger effect on non-employment are being a teenager and having children at home. The presence of children can be assumed to have a large negative effect on labour-force participation, especially in the case of women. This is in line with our finding regarding the opposite effect gender has on unemployment and non-employment. While being female reduced the probability of unemployment, it increased the probability of non-employment.

Finally, our results stress the importance of differentiating between various degrees of ethnic identification when analysing the labour-market outcomes for Aboriginals. The unemployment/non-employment incidence of Aboriginals of single ethnic origin differed considerably from that of Aboriginals with a mixed ethnic background. The differences were particularly pronounced in terms of the effects of gender, schooling/training, and location of residence. Overall, Aboriginals of multiple ethnic origin showed more similarities in their unemployment patterns with non-Aboriginals than with their counterparts of single ethnic origin.

APPENDIX

The logistic regressions presented in Tables 7 and 8 estimate the probability that individuals will be observed in state j (i.e., unemployment or non-employment) as a function of a set of explanatory dummy variables X_i. Assuming that the function takes the logistic form, the estimated probability, which is the unemployment or non-employment rate of all individuals with characteristics X_i, is given by

$$(1) \qquad P_j = \left[1 + \exp\left(-\sum_i \beta_i X_i \right) \right]^{-1}$$

or taking natural logs

$$(2) \qquad \log\frac{P_j}{1 - P_j} = \sum_i \beta_i X_i \;.$$

The differential propensity to experience state j of all individuals with a specific characteristic from set X_i and of the default group for each variable is

$$(3) \qquad \log\left(\frac{P_{ij}}{1 - P_{ij}}\right) - \log\left(\frac{\bar{P}_j}{1 - \bar{P}_j}\right) = \beta_i(1 - 0) = \beta_i$$

where P_{ij} denotes the probability of the group of individuals with characteristic i to be observed in state j, and $\bar{P}_j$ is interpreted as the probability of the default group dummy variable to be in state j; $X_i = 1$ denotes to have characteristic i, and $X_i = 0$ not to have it. Solving (3) for P_{ij} we obtain

$$(4) \qquad P_{ij} = \left[1 + \frac{1 - \bar{P}_j}{\bar{P}_j} e^{-\beta_i} \right]^{-1}$$

where β_i is the logistic regression coefficient of the characteristic i and $\bar{P}_j$ is given by the sample mean of the dependent variable of the default group.

In calculating the unemployment differential attributable to a specific characteristic we assume that individuals with that characteristic are identical to the default group except for the particular characteristic. We estimate P_{ij} from (4) and calculate the specific unemployment differential as the difference between P_{ij} and the unemployment rate of the default group.

ACKNOWLEDGMENTS

I would like to thank Lars Osberg, George Tourlakis, and seminar participants at the University of Toronto, Scarborough Campus, and Laurentian

University for helpful comments and suggestions. John Tibert from the Institute for Social Research at York University provided excellent research assistance. I am grateful to Multiculturalism and Citizenship Canada for financial assistance. The views expressed in this article are mine and do not necessarily reflect those of the sponsors.

NOTES

1 The little statistical analysis that exists has mostly focused on the relative earnings performance and the welfare dependency of Aboriginals (see Kuo 1975/76; Alam and De Civita 1990; Wright 1991; George and Kuhn 1994; Patrinos and Sakellariou 1992).

2 The application of the single/multiple ethnic origin classification seems inappropriate in case of the Métis, since this Aboriginal group comprises the offspring and descendants of mixed unions, traditionally between Indians and Europeans of English or French ancestry. In spite of their mixed ethnic background, the Métis regard themselves as a separate social entity, as an indigenous group with a distinct history and culture.

3 The statistical tests are F-tests on interaction terms.

4 This is the position taken, for instance, by Clark and Summers (1982), Corcoran (1982), and Ellwood (1982) in the context of an analysis of youth unemployment in the United States. However, Flinn and Heckmann (1983) take the opposite view, while Gönül (1992) finds mixed evidence for the hypothesis that being unemployed and being out of the labour force are distinct states.

5 In our sample, only seventy-nine Aboriginals of multiple ethnic origin lived on reserves. This small number is the result of legislation that restricts the right to live on reserves to status Indians.

6 According to Indian and Northern Affairs Canada, Indian reserves or settlements are defined as being remote if their location is over 350 kilometres from the nearest service centre with a year-round access road. "Special access" reserves or settlements are even more remote than that.

7 A recent example is Bill c-31 which, in 1985, changed the legal definition of who is and who is not Indian by providing for the partial reinstatement of those people who had lost their Indian status or who were denied it as a result of the discriminatory clauses in the Indian Act. This amendment to the Indian Act not only changed the number of registered Indians – one year after the bill was passed, nearly 21 percent of the 41,000 applicants who had requested registration in that year had been reinstated as Indians – but most likely also increased the number of Aboriginals who identified themselves as North American Indians in the 1986 census.

8 Most of the major government surveys, such as the Labour Force Survey, the Labour Market Activity Survey, or the Survey of Consumer Finances, contain only very small sub-samples of Aboriginals. The resulting large sampling errors reduce confidence in the estimates of statistical analyses, especially if they are conducted on a disaggregated geographical level.

9 The interrelation between the three indicators can be shown by decomposing the identity that links the employment (E) to population (P) ratio to the labour force (L) participation rate (L/P) and the unemployment rate (U/L). The identity is $E/P = (L/P)(1 - U/L)$.

10 The qualifications listed in our tables can be considered to be in ascending order with the exception of the attainment of a post-secondary trade school certificate. Entrance into many of the vocational programmes offered in trade schools does not require a secondary school graduation certificate. For the purpose of econometric estimation, a set of eight binary dummy variables describes the hierarchy of educational qualifications for our samples.

11 In Canada, since the early 1970s, vocational and academic programs are difficult to differentiate at the secondary school level, since the streaming into the two types of programs has become hidden in the wide variety of courses chosen by students as their electives. Statistics on the type of courses selected by students in high school are not collected in the census, nor are they through any other source at the national level, for that matter. In using census data, the possession of a high school diploma as such, therefore, does not allow us to analyse the question of whether vocational and academic streaming of Aboriginals in high school has a differential effect on labour-market outcomes. Trade schools, community colleges, and technical institutes at the post-secondary level, on the other hand, focus on the provision of occupation-specific skills. Relating census data on the possession of certificates/diplomas from these institutions to labour-force status enables us to investigate the impact of vocational education or training at the post-secondary level on the unemployment/non-employment probability of Aboriginals.

12 A binomial logit model is chosen to estimate the factors that influence the probability of an Aboriginal to be unemployed or non-employed. Since the logit regressions are non-linear, the actual regression coefficients are not particularly meaningful. We, therefore, translate the estimated coefficients into unemployment/non-employment differentials by following a two-step procedure. We first calculate the unemployment/non-employment differential for Aboriginal groups with a certain characteristic vis-à-vis a reference group and then determine with

the use of the regression coefficients the fraction of the differential that is due to the characteristic. Our procedure is a slightly altered version of the one proposed by Pissarides and Wadsworth (1990).

13 The same was found to hold for Aboriginals on reserves (see Drost 1994).

14 Maximum likelihood estimation of the unemployment and non-employment equations excluding the welfare variable yields coefficients that are not significantly different from those shown in Tables 7 and 8, both in terms of their signs and statistical significance.

REFERENCES

Alam, J., and P. De Civita. 1990. "Wage Gap Between Natives and Non-Natives: An Empirical Analysis." Indian and Northern Affairs Canada. Mimeograph.

Anderson, A.B., and J.S. Frideres. 1981. *Ethnicity in Canada: Theoretical Perspectives*. Toronto: Butterworths.

Armstrong, R., J. Kennedy, and P.R. Oberle. 1990. *University Education and Economic Well-Being: Indian Achievement and Prospects*. Ottawa: Indian and Northern Affairs Canada.

Clark, K.B., and L.H. Summers. 1982. "The Dynamics of Youth Unemployment." In R.B. Freeman and D.A. Wise, eds., *The Youth Labor Market Problem: Its Nature, Causes and Consequences*, 199–234. Chicago: University of Chicago Press.

Corcoran, M. 1982. "The Employment and Wage Consequences of Teenage Women's Nonemployment." In R.B. Freeman and D.A. Wise, eds., *The Youth Labor Market Problem: Its Nature, Causes and Consequences*, 391–425. Chicago: University of Chicago Press.

Drost, H. 1994. "Schooling, Vocational Training and Unemployment: The Case of Canadian Aboriginals." *Canadian Public Policy* 20: 52–65.

Economic Council of Canada. 1982. *In Short Supply: Jobs and Skills in the 1980s*. Ottawa: Minister of Supply and Services.

Elliott, J.L., and A. Fleras. 1992. *Unequal Relations: An Introduction to Race and Ethnic Dynamics in Canada*. Scarborough, Ontario: Prentice-Hall.

Ellwood, D. 1982. "Teenage Unemployment: Permanent Scars or Temporary Blemishes?" In R.B. Freeman and D.A. Wise, eds., *The Youth Labor Market Problem: Its Nature, Causes and Consequences*, 349–90. Chicago: University of Chicago Press.

Employment and Immigration Canada. 1981. *Labour Market Developments in the 1980s* [The Dodge Report]. Ottawa: Minister of Supply and Services.

– 1991. *Pathways to Success: Aboriginal Employment and Training Strategy*. Ottawa: Minister of Supply and Services.

Flinn, C.J., and J.J. Heckman. 1983. "Are Unemployment and Out of the Labour Force Behaviorally Distinct Labor Force States?" *Journal of Labor Economics* 1: 28–42.

George, P., and P. Kuhn. 1994. "The Size and Structure of Native-White Wage Differentials in Canada." *Canadian Journal of Economics* 27: 20–42.

Gönül, F. 1992. "New Evidence on Whether Unemployment and Out of the Labor Force are Distinct States." *Journal of Human Resources* 27: 329–61.

Hagey, N.J., G. Larocque, G., and C. McBride. 1989a. "Highlights of Aboriginal Conditions 1981–2001: Part II, Social Conditions." Indian and Northern Affairs Canada Quantitative Analysis and Socio-demographic Research Working Paper No. 89-2.

– 1989b. "Highlights of Aboriginal Conditions 1981–2001: Part III, Economic Conditions." Indian and Northern Affairs Canada Quantitative Analysis and Socio-demographic Research Working Paper No. 89-3.

Hull, J. 1987. *An Overview of the Educational Characteristics of Registered Indians in Canada*. Winnipeg: The Working Margins Consulting Group.

Kuo, C.Y. 1975/76. "The Effect of Education on the Earnings of Indian, Eskimo, Metis and White Workers in the Mackenzie District of Northern Canada." *Economic Development and Cultural Change* 24: 387–98.

Patrinos, H.A., and C.N. Sakellariou. 1992. "North American Indians in the Canadian Labour Market: A Decomposition of Wage Differentials." *Economics of Education Review* 11: 257–66.

Pissarides, C., and J. Wadsworth. 1990. "Who are the Unemployed?" Centre for Economic Performance Discussion Paper No. 12.

Sharzer, S. 1984. "Native People: Some Issues." In R.S. Abella, Commissioner, *Equality in Employment: Report of the Commission on Equality in Employment*. Ottawa: Commission on Equality in Employment.

Statistics Canada. 1989. *Census Data 1986: A Data Book on Canada's Aboriginal Population from the 1986 Census of Canada*. Ottawa: Minister of Supply and Services.

Wright, R.E. 1991. *Welfare Dependency Among Canadian Aboriginals*. Unpublished manuscript. Ottawa: Institute for Research on Public Policy.

10 Unemployment Persistence in France and Germany

DOMINIQUE M. GROSS

For more than a decade, European unemployment has been a puzzle. After the second oil price shock, it showed no sign of receding for several years, even though European economies were growing. Traditional theories of the business cycle could not explain why the labour market was taking so much time to adjust, and identifying the reasons for persistence of high unemployment became the focus of attention.

At first, it would appear that such a problem would not be of much concern in the more flexible Canadian labour market. However, recently the Canadian unemployment rate has exhibited a growing gap with its American counterpart. During the second part of the 1980s, the unemployment rate in Canada was slow to decrease, despite growth in the economy. Using both a microeconomic and macroeconomic perspective, several studies have already analysed the phenomenon (see, e.g., McCallum 1987; Milbourne et al. 1991). This chapter examines European unemployment as it appeared earlier in the decade, provides suggestions as to the sources of its persistence, and develops policy implications for France and Germany that should also be of relevance for Canada.

Out of the large body of literature devoted to European unemployment came two important concepts: first, the *flow approach* to the labour market (see Nickell 1982; Pissarides 1985; Junankar and Price 1984; Gross 1993a, 1993b), and second, *hysteresis* or *persistence* in its extreme form (see Blanchard and Summers 1986; Cross 1988). Several arguments have been put forward to explain persistence, one of which is the role of the long-term unemployed in the job allocation process (see Layard and Bean 1989; Franz 1987). This chapter uses the flow framework to gain insight into the role of the long-term unemployed in explaining persistence in unemployment in France and Germany (former West Germany only). It also provides reasons why long-term unemployment was a growing problem throughout the 1980s in the two countries.

The *flow* framework offers at least two appealing features. First, the flows of workers and jobs are large and variable compared to the stock, and the aggregate level of unemployment represents only the net impact of the various forces acting at any point in time. Second, the flow framework allows for the distinction between *incidence* (the rate at which people become unemployed) and *duration* (which depends on the rate at which individuals leave unemployment). This differentiation between two aspects of unemployment is necessary to study the relationship between long-term unemployment and hiring by firms.

In this chapter it is shown that the hiring process (and therefore duration of unemployment) has been affected by different factors in France and Germany. In Germany, duration of unemployment has increased because the unemployed offer the wrong type of skills to the market. This is true regardless of the length of time they have been unemployed. In France, high labour costs induce employers to discriminate on the basis of the length of unemployment, and individuals unemployed for more than six months have greater difficulty finding jobs. However, the high cost of labour does not slow down the hiring of individuals who have been unemployed for less than six months. These results show that the reasons for persistence can differ widely, as will the policies needed to address the problem of long-term unemployment. In Germany, the situation calls for policies that aim at improving the mismatch between jobs newly created and the skills of the unemployed. In France, policies that would reduce the cost of hiring the long-term unemployed may help alleviate the problem.

The chapter is organized as follows. Section two, which follows, describes important features of unemployment in France and Germany. In the following section, the methodology used in the study is described and the results are analysed. The final section offers some concluding comments.

UNEMPLOYMENT IN FRANCE AND GERMANY

Because most European countries measure unemployment differently from Canada, information on the movement of people into and out

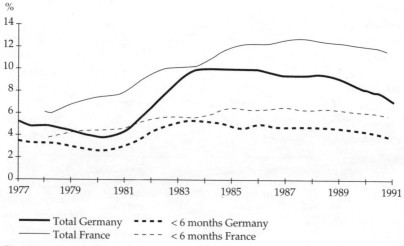

Figure 1
Unemployment Rates

of unemployment is readily available. Unemployment statistics come from administrative data through registration at regional labour offices. Thus, direct information on the inflow into unemployment and the level of unemployment is available through newly accepted claims and beneficiaries. The outflow can be computed as the residual from the inflow series and the change in the unemployment level.[1] The difference in the source of information also implies small differences in the definition of unemployment. European data cover people who collect unemployment benefits or unemployment assistance, provided they are readily available for work. Thus, a person who has been unemployed for more than a year, who is not actively looking for a job but is available for work, is considered unemployed. Collecting benefits requires a relatively long period of past employment; therefore, young people and people re-entering the labour market are likely to be underrepresented.[2] As it will be seen later, these differences in definitions have some implications for the development of the analysis.

Figure 1 clearly shows that, throughout the 1980s, unemployment in France and Germany was relatively high and exhibited persistence.[3] The average rate of unemployment is higher in France than in Germany. Moreover, the gap between the two national rates remains when only people unemployed for six months or less are considered. The trends in the unemployment rates are quite different in the two countries. In France, the unemployment rate rose steadily over most of the period, whereas in Germany, a large step-like increase occurred over a three-year period in the early 1980s and from then on, the rate remained relatively constant. Again a similar profile can be observed

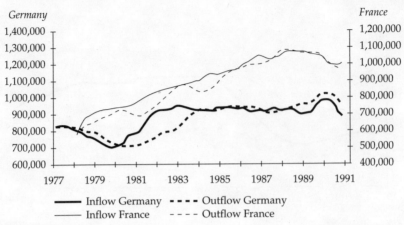

Figure 2
Total Flows

when only short-term unemployment is considered. One common characteristic is that, in both countries, the share of long-term unemployed has risen steadily throughout the 1980s.

Even more significant differences occur when the flows into and out of unemployment are considered separately, as in Figure 2. Also, a simple look at the behaviour of unemployment inflows and outflows provides some insight into the reasons why stocks have evolved differently. In France, both flows show a clear upward trend that is, however, more steady for the inflow than the outflow. Thus, a steady rise in the inflow coupled with regular slowdowns in the number of people leaving unemployment account for the continuous rise in unemployment over most of the period. In Germany, there is a large increase in the inflow relative to the outflow in the early 1980s (leading to the step-increase in unemployment) and then the two flows are constant and almost equal, except in 1989–90. These observations lead us to believe that different reasons lie behind the persistently high unemployment in France and in Germany.

The next section is devoted to the definition of unemployment inflow and outflow. The model underlying the estimated equations is briefly sketched and the results of the estimations are analysed in the light of the role of the long-term unemployed.

ESTIMATION AND RESULTS

Unemployment Flows

The flow into unemployment and the flow out of unemployment can be defined as follows:

$$I^u \equiv L + QU + YU,$$
$$O^u \equiv HU + RU.$$

The inflow (I^u) is the sum of lay-offs (L), quits ending in unemployment (QU), and new entrants who do not find a job immediately (YU). The outflow from unemployment (O^u) is the sum of people newly hired (HU) and people who drop out of the unemployment registry.

Given the characteristics of the two unemployment insurance schemes, QU and YU are likely to be small. In effect, the requirement of a relatively long period of work prevents most new entrants (YU) from registering for unemployment insurance benefits. Furthermore, it is assumed that employed people who reach retirement age are replaced through promotion and young people are hired at the bottom of the ladder. This is consistent with the well-developed apprenticeship system that exists especially in Germany. Also, people who leave their job voluntarily and end up unemployed (QU) are penalized with a disqualification period of twelve weeks in Germany and with complete disqualification in France. Finally, RU represents people who lose eligibility mostly because of age, since the "discouraged worker" effect is not likely to be present in this data as the unemployment insurance and assistance schemes are integrated.[4]

The underlying model defining the flows is an aggregate equilibrium search model developed in Nickell (1982) and Pissarides (1988, 1985) where firms respond to shocks that hit them randomly in every period. It is a partial equilibrium model where feedbacks from the labour market on wages are ignored and where instantaneous adjustments are ruled out by imperfect information. Firms hit by negative shocks lay off workers. Firms hit by positive shocks open vacancies and unemployed job-seekers apply to fill these vacancies. Unemployed workers contact firms and some of them receive a job offer.[5] Of those who receive a job offer, some decide to accept it. In this search process, firms make decisions about the lay-off rate and the job-offer rate based on a number of factors in addition to the size of the shock they face. Similarly, an unemployed worker decides to accept a job offer and an employed worker decides to quit by comparing various alternative possibilities.

The factors affecting firms' and individuals' decisions can be classified into three broad categories: long-term, medium-term, and short-term factors. The following two equations summarize the relevant factors and their expected impact:

(1) $I^u/N = A[CL,UIC,CV,LABC,ENERG,STRUCT,LF,VAR,AD]$,
                  $-$? $-$ $+$ $+$? $+$ $+$ $-$

$$O^u/U = G[CL,UIC,CV,LABC,ENERG,STRUCT,VAR,AD] \; .$$
$$\quad\quad\; - \quad ? \quad + \quad - \quad\quad - \quad\quad ? \quad\quad + \quad +$$

The signs below each equation indicate whether the factor is expected to have a positive (+) or a negative (−) impact on the flow rates or if the effect is uncertain (?). Note that the flows are defined in terms of rates: I^u/N is the incidence of unemployment, and O^u/U is the exit rate from unemployment or the inverse of average duration.

There are four long-term factors that are considered in this study; two of them are legislative factors. The first, CL, is the cost of laying off workers. A change in the legislation on employment protection is expected to exert a negative influence on both flow rates, because the lay-off rate and the job-offer rate are expected to decrease with the degree of protection offered. This variable is relevant only for Germany, as the legislation for protection against lay-offs was reinforced in 1978.

Second, changes in characteristics of the unemployment insurance scheme (UIC) will affect firms' and individuals' behaviour. A more generous scheme increases incidence (higher lay-off and quit rates) and decreases the outflow rate (lower job-acceptance rate). In 1984, the French government totally reorganized the system of unemployment insurance because the UNEDIC, the institution in charge of running it, was registering large deficits. The direct participation of the state was introduced and several criteria for eligibility were changed (see ILO 1984). As a consequence, the scheme became more generous in some respects and less generous in others. At this level of aggregation it is not possible to measure every parameter that has changed independently and therefore, the expected sign on an aggregate variable is uncertain. In Germany, no major change in the unemployment legislation has taken place during the period and the benefits are indexed to inflation, allowing for little change in the opportunity cost of being unemployed.[6] As a consequence this factor is not introduced.

Thirdly, CV is the cost of opening a vacancy or the opportunity cost of idle capital. As CV rises, the lay-off rate decreases and the job-offer rate increases. Thus the inflow rate and the outflow rate move in opposite directions. Finally, LF accounts for the effect of changes in the composition of the labour force. In this study it is approximated by the participation rate of women which is expected to affect the inflow positively.

The medium-term factors are the real labour costs (LABC), and the real energy price (ENERG). Rising labour costs and supply-shocks such as energy price increase are expected to have adverse effects on the labour market. Thus, both will be positively related to incidence and negatively related to the outflow rate. Another medium-term factor is structural changes (STRUCT) such as technological changes that affect firms' lay-off and hiring policies. Two aspects are relevant. The first one is the degree to which employment is shifting across sectors. As some sectors are growing faster and some are declining faster, more lay-offs and more hiring take place and both flow rates increase. The second aspect is the discrepancy between the characteristics offered by the unemployed and the ones demanded by growing firms during periods of structural changes. If unemployed workers laid off from declining sectors do not have the "right" characteristics (i.e., skill or geographical location), growing firms will have difficulty hiring. Thus, an increasing degree of mismatch affects both flows adversely.

Finally, the short-term variables are aggregate demand factors (AD). Business cycles can be generated by domestic factors, foreign factors, or expectations of firms and individuals. An improvement in the business cycle will decrease the inflow and increase the outflow rates. Note that the impact of these factors on the flows is expected to be small since short-time work and temporary lay-offs are registered separately from unemployment (see footnote 2).

The strategy for identifying the role of the long-term unemployed is as follows. First, we estimate each of the two equations in (1) over the sample including all the unemployed. Second, we test whether the results for the outflow rate are altered when people unemployed for more than one year or six months are excluded. The behaviour of the coefficients gives a first insight into the role of the long-term unemployed. Third, we run simulations to measure the actual responsibility of the some factors in changing the flow. In particular, we want to identify whether the key factor affecting hiring is labour costs or structural changes.

Two factors have been identified in the literature as possible sources for increasing the share of the long-term unemployed and therefore generating persistence. The insider-outsider model (see Lindbeck and Snower 1988) predicts that persistence occurs in unemployment because outsiders (the unemployed) do not have the same power as insiders (the employed) or new entrants in the bargaining process. Because of fixed costs such as those for hiring and firing, the insiders can negotiate higher wages without being threatened with lay-offs. Thus, in expansion, rising wages lower the probability of the unemployed being hired. The mismatch model (see Layard and Bean 1989, Franz 1991) predicts that structural changes have an adverse effect on the job-matching process between the unemployed and firms, because the unemployed supply what growing firms perceive as inadequate characteristics.

The simulations allow us to identify which case is relevant in each country. They can be seen as the answer to the following question: "What would have happened to incidence and duration if a given factor had been constant over the period?" If the simulated flow rate is lower, then the factor is responsible for increased incidence and/or duration of unemployment.

The equations in (1) are estimated dynamically using quarterly data from 1978.1 to 1990.4 for France and 1977.1 to 1988.1 for Germany. The reader interested in the details and the technical aspects of the estimations is referred to the Appendix. General comments are made separately below about each country. Comparisons between the two countries are made in the conclusion.

France

The results of the estimations for France in Table 3 show that both flows exhibit hysteresis, implying that shocks have permanent effects. However, when the sample of unemployed for six months or less is considered, the degree of persistence in the outflow rate is lower. Also, when only the short-term unemployed are considered, the labour-cost and the energy-cost variables have no significant impact. Since most of the outflow is related to hiring, the disappearance of the cost variable suggests that employers are reluctant to hire unemployed workers unless they have been unemployed for a very short period of time (i.e., less than six months). This is consistent with the fact that firms may use the duration of unemployment as an indicator for the quality of skills offered by the unemployed. The structural change variables exhibit relatively stable coefficients across the experiments with the various groups of unemployed. In each case, hiring is slowed down by structural changes. In other words, regardless of the duration of their unemployment, some workers tend to be in the "wrong place at the wrong time."

The simulations in Figures 3a to 3c provide an evaluation of the actual impact of the factors during the period 1978–90. In Figures 3a and 3b, it is clear that, first, labour cost is mostly responsible for the rise in incidence and duration in France (i.e., the simulated curve at constant labour costs lies below the reference curve). Second, structural shifts and mismatch have had very little impact on either incidence or duration. In Figure 3c, when average duration is simulated for unemployed workers for less than six months, the wage effect has disappeared and structural shifts still have very little impact. Thus,

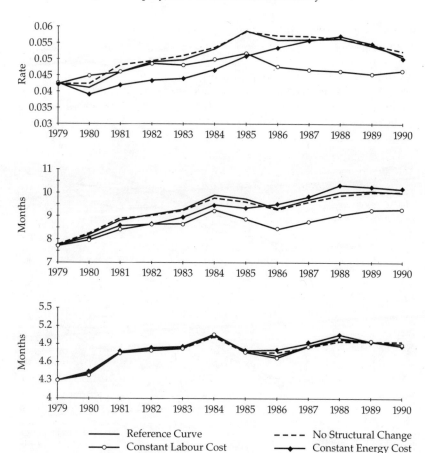

Figure 3
France. a: Incidence; b: Duration (Total Unemployed);
c: Duration (Unemployed < 6 months)

our results suggest that the long-term unemployed are at the source of persistence. This is so because hiring by firms is strongly influenced by labour costs and energy costs when applicants have been unemployed for more than six months. These factors become irrelevant when applicants have been unemployed for less than six months. Finally, the effect of structural shifts has been minimal in France.

Germany

The results of the estimations for Germany in Table 4 show a much lower degree of persistence. The inflow rate is free from any persis-

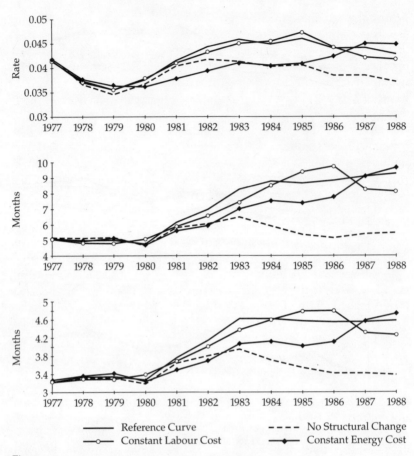

Figure 4
Germany. a: Incidence; b: Duration (Total Unemployed);
c: Duration (Unemployed < 6 months)

tence and the outflow rate exhibits a relatively low level of persistence. As the long-term unemployed are gradually eliminated from
the sample, the impact of the labour cost remains highly significant.
The coefficient on the energy-cost variable hardly changes. Thus costs
have a significant impact on hiring that is independent of the duration of unemployment. However, the structural-shift variable loses
significance across experiments. Shifts in the rate of growth of sectors
penalize the hiring of long-term unemployed but not that of people
unemployed for less than six months. The mismatch factor remains
significant in equations.

In the simulations (Figures 4a to 4c), the labour-cost variable plays
a relatively minor role in explaining incidence and duration over the

period 1977 to 1988. The energy-price variable has a similar impact as it does in the French case. Most of the increase in incidence and duration is due to structural shift and mismatch (i.e., the simulation line lies below the reference line). The effect varies relatively little when only those unemployed for less than six months are considered. In other words, structural changes and their consequences on mismatch of skills play a major role in explaining the slowdown in the exit rate from unemployment. Thus, in Germany, the slowdown in hiring (or increased duration) can be attributed to skill mismatch and there is evidence that all workers, regardless of the length of their stay in unemployment, are affected. Some unemployed typically supply the wrong type of characteristics to the market. A simple computation shows that, in 1988, average duration would have been back to its 1977-level had mismatch been unchanged. Because of the increased mismatch, the average duration for people unemployed for less than six months was about one month higher.

To summarize, in France, labour costs act against the long-term unemployed and there is little structural unemployment. In Germany, the increased share of long-term unemployment is more likely to be the consequence of an increase in mismatch between the skills demanded by employers and those offered by the unemployed.

CONCLUSION

During the 1980s, average unemployment duration has been increasing in Canada as the unemployment rate showed some difficulty in returning to its pre-1980 level. This phenomenon, called persistence or hysteresis, has plagued European unemployment for the past fifteen years. Using France and Germany as examples, we have analysed the degree of persistence in unemployment flows and have tried to identify the role of the long-term unemployed in explaining persistence. Simulations were run to establish the responsibility of the two most likely causes of persistence in unemployment: high cost of labour and mismatch generated by structural changes. We found evidence that in France, rising labour costs have influenced firms' hiring decisions. Given the high labour costs, firms appear reluctant to hire workers who have been unemployed for more than six months. This result is consistent with the argument that firms may use the length of unemployment as a measure for the "quality" of workers. If so, policies aimed at monitoring the search of jobs by the unemployed can reduce duration (see, for example, OECD 1990). Also subsidies that are conditional on hiring long-term unemployed workers may induce firms to do so since their labour costs are lowered.

It must be noted that such a policy, in the form of a reduced contribution to social security, has been implemented in France (OECD 1990: 105). In Germany, skill mismatch is the main culprit for increased duration and it affects all the unemployed, regardless of duration. In that case, gathering information on the types of skill required by growing sectors and organizing training programs would be an appropriate response.

Increased duration can have widely different sources that influence unemployed individuals differently and thus, will call for different policies. There are many reasons why individuals would spend more time unemployed and this paper has looked at only a few possibilities. However, it has also suggested one approach that leads to a more in-depth macroeconomic analysis of the sources of unemployment. Such an approach may help define more targeted and thus more efficient policy responses to the unemployment crisis in Canada.

APPENDIX

Empirically, the estimated equations in (1) are specified as auto-regressive distributed lag forms such that

$$Y_t = C + a_0 Y_{t-1} + \sum_{j=1}^{n} \sum_{i=1}^{6} a_{ji} X_{jt-i} ,$$

where the lagged dependent variable accounts for possible persistence or hysteresis. If $a_0 = 1$, there is hysteresis, and if $0 < a_0 < 1$, there is persistence (see Wyplosz in Franz 1987). Unit-root tests are often used as a basis for empirical specification in time series. Because of their low degree of reliability in small samples (see Campbell and Perron 1991), we chose to consider only the results of the Durbin-Watson (DW) tests as indicators. If DW is close to zero, the series is non-stationary and there is a unit root. In our framework, it would indicate the presence of hysteresis. In both countries, the DW-values for the unemployment rate and the outflow rate increase as unemployed with lower duration are considered. However the values remain below one. Also, in both countries, the DW-values on the inflow rates are much higher. It is 1.7 in Germany, suggesting little persistence and it is around 1.1 in France, leaving doubt about stationarity. The detailed results of the tests are not reproduced here but are available on request.

The results of the estimations are presented in Table 3 for France and Table 4 for Germany. The reported coefficients are the sum of the coefficients on any given lagged variable in the final specification. Thus, they represent the short-run impact of any given shock. Absolute t-values are in parentheses.

Table 1
Main Characteristics of Unemployment, France 1978.1–1990.4

	Mean	Maximum	Minimum	SD
LEVELS				
Unemployment	2,101,800	2,688,911	1,039259	508,183
Unemployment < 1 year	1,517,610	1,877,059	819,746	307,849
Unemployment < 6 months	1,067,997	1,399,885	583,786	219,230
Inflow into unemployment	910,294	1,262,320	556,445	178,706
Outflow from unemployment	880,129	1,132,511	568,667	154,470
Outflow < 1 year	891,105	1,106,880	591,594	146,414
Outflow < 6 months	896,078	1,132,097	580,922	150,577
RATES				
Unemployment rate	10.5	13.2	5.7	2.2
Unemployment rate < 1 year	7.9	9.7	4.5	1.4
Unemployment rate < 6 months	5.7	7.4	3.3	1.1
Incidence	0.0513	0.0713	0.0327	0.0095
Outflow rate	0.4294	0.5681	0.3481	0.0539
Duration*	7	5.3	8.6	–
Outflow rate (unemployment < 1 year)	0.5956	0.7217	0.4853	0.0578
Duration* for unemployment < 1 year	5	4.2	6.2	–
Outflow rate (unemployment < 6 months)	0.8495	0.9951	0.7050	0.0697
Duration* (unemployment < 6 months)	3.5	3	4.3	–

Source: Computed from information from Ministère du Travail, de l'Emploi et de la Formation profes-sionnelle, Statistiques du Travail. Bulletin mensuel. Service des Études et de la Statistique. Various years.
* Average number of months. Maximum outflow rate corresponds to minimum duration and conversely.

All the variables and statistical sources are defined in detail in Gross (1993a, 1993b) and only a brief description is given here. The variables appearing in the final specifications are the following:

Dependent variables
(I^u/N) Inflow rate (Δ indicates first difference).
(O^u/U) Outflow rate (Δ indicates first difference).
$FLOW_{t-1}$ Lagged dependent variable in level.

Business cycle variables (AD):
DM   Domestic aggregate demand. Deviations of the rate of growth of money from target in Germany. Deviation from twelve-month real growth rate in France because the target was shifted on different aggregate during the period.

Table 2
Main Characteristics of Unemployment, Germany 1978.1–1990.4

	Mean	Maximum	Minimum	SD
LEVELS				
Unemployment	1,767,656	2,474,451	736,809	577,442
Unemployment < 1 year	1,301,421	1,833,547	627,246	349,189
Unemployment < 6 months	934,542	1,250,585	499,207	210,227
Inflow into unemployment	882,985	1,107,154	589,843	139,885
Outflow from unemployment	869,649	1,125,747	580,532	132,817
Outflow < 1 year	876,559	1,105,299	594,225	110,645
Outflow < 6 months	878,748	1,106,347	614,796	108,903
RATES				
Unemployment rate	7.8	11.0	3.4	2.4
Unemployment rate < 1 year	5.9	8.4	2.9	1.5
Unemployment rate < 6 months	4.3	5.9	2.3	1.0
Incidence	0.0424	0.0541	0.0288	0.0066
Outflow rate	0.5446	0.9456	0.3587	0.1794
Duration*	5.5	3.2	8.4	-
Outflow rate (unemployment < 1 year)	0.7136	1.0963	0.5245	0.1646
Duration* for unemployment < 1 year	4.2	2.7	5.7	-
Outflow rate (unemployment < 6 months)	0.9754	1.3695	0.6947	0.1762
Duration* for unemployment < 6 months	3.1	2.2	4.3	-

Source: Computed from information from Bundesantalt für Arbeit, *Amtliche Nachrichten der Bundes-anstalt für Arbeit. Arbeitsstatistik-Jahreszahlen*. Various years.

* Average number of months. Maximum outflow rate corresponds to minimum duration and conversely.

DT   Foreign demand. Change in the terms of trade.
SHORT-T   Temporary layoffs used for expectations about the state of the economy.

Cost variables (LABC, ENERG)
LAB COST   Ratio of real wage augmented for employment taxes and productivity per employed.
ENERG COST   Real energy price in domestic currency.

Structural change variables (STRUCT)
SECT SHIFT   Lilien (1982)'s dispersion index corrected for aggregate demand effect (see Abraham and Katz, 1986).
GEOG MATCH   Mismatch index based on individual U-V curves for regions in France.

Table 3
Results of the Estimations for France, 1978.1–1990.4

	1 Δ(I/N)_t	2 Δ(O/U)_t total	3 Δ(O/U)_t < 1 year	4 Δ(O/U)_t < 6 months
ΔDM	−0.661*	1.325**	1.340**	0.551*
	(2.4)	(3.2)	(3.4)	(1.7)
ΔDT	–	1.430**	1.268**	1.095**
		(3.8)	(3.6)	(3.7)
ΔLAB COST	1.422**	−0.430**	−0.452**	−0.109
	(5.0)	(5.9)	(6.6)	(1.3)
ΔENERG COST	0.155*	−0.070*	−0.045	−0.028
	(2.5)	(1.9)	(1.3)	(1.0)
ΔSECT SHIFT	13.76**	−6.602**	−7.924**	−9.001**
	(2.7)	(2.6)	(3.3)	(4.5)
ΔGEOG MATCH	–	−0.021*	−0.024*	−0.023**
	(2.0)	(2.4)	(2.7)	(2.0)
ΔWOM PART	0.074	–	–	–
	(1.7)			
ΔVAR	0.736*	1.049**	0.991**	0.800**
	(1.8)	(3.5)	(3.3)	(3.2)
ΔUIC	0.064	0.089*	0.082**	0.083**
	(1.5)	(2.4)	(3.8)	(2.7)
(O/U)_{t−1}	–	–	–	−0.132*
				(1.9)
R²	0.975	0.776	0.893	0.942
F	93.79	7.68	18.50	32.75
	(13,31)	(14,31)	(14,31)	(15,30)
N	44	45	45	45
RSS	0.0433	0.0323	0.0289	0.01926

Note: Δ indicates first difference. Absolute t-values are in parentheses.
Both * and ** are significant at 5 percent, 1 percent, one-tail test. All the variables are described in detail in the Appendix.

SKILL MATCH   Mismatch index based on individual u-v curves for skill categories in Germany.

Labour force (LF)
WOM PART   Participation rate of women.

Legislative variables (CL,UIC)
LAYOFF LEG   Dummy variable for Germany with value 1 starting 1978.1, 0 otherwise.

UIC   Dummy variable for France with value 1 starting 1984.1, 0 otherwise.

VAR   Changes in the level of new orders in Germany, in retail sales in France.

Table 4
Results of the Estimations for Germany, 1977.1–1988.4

	1 $(I/N)_t$	2 $(O/U)_t$ total	3 $(O/U)_t$ < 1 year	4 $(O/U)_t$ < 6 months
C	−6.121**	2.604**	1.567**	1.553**
	(7.2)	(6.1)	(4.8)	(3.7)
FLOW$_{t-1}$	−	0.566**	0.669**	0.534**
		(6.7)	(8.1)	(4.2)
DM	−	3.737*	3.174*	1.257
		(1.9)	(2.3)	(0.7)
DT	−0.283	−	−	−
	(0.8)			
LAB COST	0.572**	−1.121**	−0.897**	−0.661**
	(3.3)	(5.3)	(5.9)	(3.1)
ENERG COST	0.147**	−0.090**	−0.078**	−0.077*
	(7.7)	(2.5)	(2.9)	(2.2)
SECT SHIFT	−	−7.033**	−2.930*	−0.064
	(3.4)	(2.0)	(0.1)	
SKILL MATCH	0.058**	−0.097**	−0.048**	−0.059**
	(3.2)	(4.3)	(3.3)	(3.4)
WOM PART	0.039	−	−	−
	(1.5)			
VAR	0.051	0.187*	0.088	0.003
	(0.8)	(2.2)	(1.4)	(0.1)
SHORT-T		−0.043*	−0.013	0.010
		(1.7)	(0.7)	(0.4)
LAYOFF LEG	−0.149	−	−	−
	(6.1)			
R^2	0.943	0.977	0.977	0.932
F	61.35	136.8	137.2	43.95
	(10,37)	(11,35)	(11,35)	(11,35)
N	48	47	47	47
RSS	0.0717	0.1155	0.0586	0.1125

Note: All variables are in levels. Absolute *t*-values are in parentheses.
Both * and ** are significant at 5 percent, 1 percent, one-tail test. All the variables are
described in detail in the Appendix.

Note that the opportunity cost of capital (CV), measured by the real interest
rate, never appeared significantly in the estimations.

In Tables 3 and 4, column 1 provides the final estimation for the inflow
rate; column 2, the final estimation for the outflow rate, including all the
unemployed; column 3 is the outflow rate with people unemployed for less
than one year and column 4 with people unemployed for less than six
months. The symbols * and ** indicate that the coefficients are significant at
the 5-percent and 10-percent level. Because of non-stationarity, the equations
in Table 4 are estimated in first difference. Overall, the coefficients are
remarkably stable across the changes in the definition of the outflow rate.

They all have the expected sign except the sectoral-shift variable in the outflow rate in both countries. The negative sign indicates that an increase in the variance of the rates of growth of sectors slows down the hiring even when mismatch is controlled for (see also Gross 1993a, 1993b).

Finally, the simulations are dynamic or recursive simulations where some factors are alternatively held constant. The benchmark value for each factor is the average value of the first year of the sample. The exceptions are the sectoral change variable and VAR (average over the whole sample) and DM, DT (zero). All the simulations are run for neutral aggregate demand.

ACKNOWLEDGMENTS

I would like to thank B. MacLean, Lars Osberg and Mark Setterfield for their comments.

NOTES

1 More precisely, if U_t represents unemployment in the current period, U_{t-1}, unemployment in the previous period, and I_t, the inflow into unemployment, then the outflow from unemployment (O_t) is calculated as $O_t = U_{t-1} - U_t + I_t$.

2 It must be noted that both countries have well-developed unemployment-insurance-assisted work-sharing schemes. Workers on temporary lay-off are registered in a different category and are not included in the unemployment numbers. For more details on unemployment insurance schemes in Europe, see Gross (1994).

3 Moving averages over four quarters have been computed to eliminate seasonal variations. The main characteristics of the level of unemployment, the flows, and the average duration of unemployment are summarized in Tables 1 and 2.

4 In Canada, the survey data do not include unemployed people who have stopped looking actively for a job ("discouraged worker effect"). Our definition of unemployment is different because these people are included in the sample since they get financial support from the government. Availability for work is the characteristic that defines an unemployed person. Both countries have special early retirement schemes for the unemployed. Also, in both countries labour offices act as placement offices and monitor the search by the unemployed (see Gross 1994 for details). The Canadian and European definitions of unemployment are not directly comparable (see OECD 1987, chapter 5 for a detailed explanation of the differences).

5 In equilibrium, firms make job offers to employed as well as unemployed applicants. However, they do not discriminate between the two

types and the search by the employed is not endogenous (see Burgess 1993).
6 There is evidence that variations in the replacement rate (i.e., the ratio of unemployment benefits to wage) that can be observed are due to the changing proportion of the long-term unemployed. After twelve months, the benefits drop from 67 percent of past wage to 57 percent (see Franz 1991; Gross 1994).

REFERENCES

Abraham, K.G., and L.F. Katz. 1986. "Cyclical Unemployment: Sectoral Shifts or Aggregate Disturbances." *Journal of Political Economy* 94 (June): 507–22.

Blanchard, O.J., and L.H. Summers. 1986. "Hysteresis and the European Unemployment Problem." In S. Fischer, ed., NBER *Macroeconomics Annual*, 15–78. Cambridge, Mass.: MIT Press.

Burgess, S.M. 1993. "A Model of Competition between Unemployed and Employed Job Searchers: An Application to the Unemployment Outflow Rate in Britain." *Economic Journal* 103 (September): 1190–1204.

Campbell, J.Y., and P. Perron. 1991. "Pitfalls and Opportunities: What Macroeconomists Should Know about Unit Roots." In O.J. Blanchard and S. Fischer, eds., NBER *Macroeconomics Annual*, 141–201. Cambridge, Mass.: MIT Press.

Cross, R., ed. 1988. *Unemployment, Hysteresis and the Natural Rate Hypothesis.* Oxford: Basil Blackwell.

Franz, W. 1987. "Hysteresis, Persistence, and the NAIRU: An Empirical Analysis for the Federal Republic of Germany." In R. Layard and Lars Calmfors, eds., *The Fight against Unemployment: Macroeconomic Papers from the Centre for European Studies*, 93–138. Cambridge: MIT Press.

– 1991. "Match and Mismatch on the German Labor Market." In F. Padoa-Schioppa, ed., *Mismatch and Labor Mobility*, 105–39. Cambridge: Cambridge University Press.

Gross, D.M. 1993a. "Equilibrium Vacancy and Unemployement: A Flow Approach to the Beveridge Curve." *Journal of Macroeconomics* 15 (Spring): 301–27.

– 1993b. "The Causes of Unemployment in France: A Flow Approach." *Applied Economics* 25: 495–504.

– 1994. "Unemployment and UI Schemes in Europe." In *Unemployment Insurance: How to Make It Work*, 160–93. Toronto: C.D. Howe Institute.

ILO (International Labour Office). 1984. *Bulletin d'Informations Sociales*, No. 3/4: 606–10.

Junankar, P.N., and S. Price. 1984. "The Dynamics of Unemployment: Structural Change and Unemployment Flows." *Economic Journal* 94 (Conference Papers): 158–66.

Layard, R., and C. Bean. 1989. "Why Does Unemployment Persist?" *Scandinavian Journal of Economics* 91, No. 2: 371–96.

Lilien, D.M. 1982. "Sectoral Shifts and Cyclical Unemployment." *Journal of Political Economy* 90 (August): 777–93.

Lindbeck, A., and D.J. Snower. 1988. *The Insider-Outsider Theory of Employment and Unemployement*. Cambridge, Mass.: MIT Press.

McCallum, J. 1987. "Unemployment in Canada and in the United States." *Canadian Journal of Economics* 20 (November): 802–22.

Milbourne, R., D. Purvis, and D. Scoones. 1991. "Unemployment Insurance and Unemployment Dynamics." *Canadian Journal of Economics* 24 (November): 804–26.

Nickell, S. 1982. "The Determinants of Equilibrium Unemployment in Britain." *Economic Journal* 92 (September): 555–75.

OECD (Organization for Economic Cooperation and Development). 1987. *Employment Outlook*. Paris: OECD.

– 1990. *Labour Market Policies for the 1990s*. Paris: OECD.

Pissarides, C.A. 1985. "Short-Run Equilibrium Dynamics of Unemployment, Vacancies, and Real Wage." *American Economic Review* 75 (September): 676–90.

– 1988. "The Search Equilibrium Approach to Fluctuations in Employment." *American Economic Review* 78 (May): 363–8.

11 Low Unemployment in Japan: The Product of Socio-economic Coherence

PATRICE DE BROUCKER

In Japan, as elsewhere, the unemployment rate is an indicator that receives considerable attention. Upward movements periodically make the newspaper headlines, with editors speculating about signs of the Western disease penetrating Japan. For several months following the Plaza Accord[1] of September 1985, the spectre of unemployment haunted even the most qualified observers of the Japanese labour market, such as Japan's Economic Planning Agency, the Ministry of Labour, and the business federations. We even saw, at the beginning of the summer of 1986, forecasts of a Japanese unemployment rate at 5 percent by the year 2000, after it had just reached its postwar peak of 3.1 percent in May, and forecasts were made of 2.2 million jobs lost from manufacturing by 1993.

These sudden surges of fear illustrate that unemployment is a phenomenon largely unknown in contemporary Japanese society. The Japanese have been living with an environment of close to full employment since the late 1950s, with an unemployment rate below 2 percent from 1960 to 1976, and never higher than the 3-percent range since then.

Nevertheless unemployment does exist and we should not ignore it completely. Beginning in the 1970s, an intense debate arose on the international comparability of unemployment rates. Measurement differences were alleged by some to account for extremely low Japanese rates that have been, moreover, largely insensitive to fluctuations in economic activity. But all serious attempts to standardize unemployment rates altered only marginally the disparities between Japan and the other industrialized countries. It is now widely acknowledged that the essence of the disparities does not lie in measurement differences, but in differing labour-market mechanisms.

Unemployment in Japan does not play the role of reallocating human resources according to conventional "market" rules. Major changes in the employment structure – by industry as well as by occupation – do occur, but the dynamics of change do not bring about massive unemployment. Companies and their personnel management practices are driving forces at the heart of labour-market operations.

The following section deals with the visible reality of Japanese unemployment. But one must not stop there; one must search for its hidden face – under-employment of various forms, a topic taken up in the following section. For although there is a hidden face to Japanese unemployment, a very large real gap exists between the unemployment rate in Japan and that in most other countries of the Organization for Economic Cooperation and Development (OECD). This gap calls for explanation and cannot be fully accounted for by standard macroeconomic factors. The fourth section of this chapter evaluates the impact on Japanese unemployment of structural change and personnel management practices, while the following section focuses on the role of government policies in labour-market adjustment. The implications of Japan's low unemployment experience for Canadian policy making are discussed in the final section.

THE VISIBLE REALITY OF UNEMPLOYMENT

In the monthly labour-force survey of Japan, an unemployed person is defined as one who did not work at all (or did so for less than an hour) during the reference week, who actively searched for a job or waited for the results of past search, and who was available for work. This section will examine the main features of Japanese unemployment so defined. For the sake of comparison, mention is made of corresponding features of Canadian unemployment.

A Sustained Growth of Salaried Employment

It is necessary, first of all, to recall that Japan has faced a situation generally favourable to containing any large increase in unemployment: not even once since 1955 has salaried employment declined,

228   Patrice de Broucker

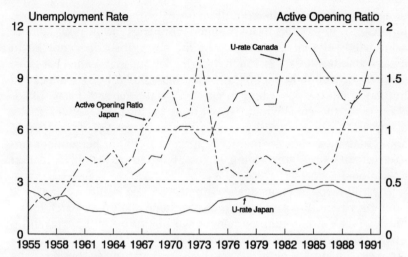

Sources: Year Book of Labour Statistics, various issues, Policy Planning and Research Department, Minister's Secretariat, Ministry of Labour, Japan; Historical Labour Force Statistics, 1992, Statistics Canada, 71-201.

Figure 1
Japan-Canada: Unemployment Indicators

while total employment – which includes self-employed and family workers – has decreased only once, in 1974.

Unemployment and the "Active Opening Ratio"

The unemployment rate has constantly been low, by Canadian standards, for close to four decades (see Figure 1). The Japanese rate (measured along the left axis of Figure 1) decreased from 2.5 to 1.1 percent between 1955 and 1964; it stabilized at this low level until 1973, averaging only 1.3 percent in that year. In 1974, a slow but consistent growth trend started with the annual unemployment rate reaching 2.1 percent in 1979, then 2.8 percent in 1986 and 1987. A quick decline followed to 2.1 percent in 1990, a level that has been unchanged until recently when the recession pushed it up again to 2.3 percent.

Figure 1 also presents another indicator that is often used to assess the state of the Japanese labour market – the "active opening ratio," the ratio of the number of active job vacancies to the number of active applications for jobs. Note that the unemployment rate corresponding to an "equilibrium" in the labour market – the rate corresponding to an active opening ratio equal to one – has risen from 1.3 percent in 1967 to around 1.5 percent in 1974–75 and to 2.5 percent in 1988.

Significant Regional Disparities

Regional unemployment disparities are large: the two geographical extremes of the country (Hokkaido in the north, Kyushu in the south) record unemployment rates double that of the highly urbanized centre of the country (Kanto). But, again, these geographical disparities are significantly less important than in Canada. Considering the same number of geographical divisions (ten regions in Japan and ten provinces in Canada), the standard deviation of the unemployment rate in recent years has been well over 3 percentage points for Canada against less than 1 percentage point for Japan.

No Differences in Unemployment Rates for Men and Women

Male and female unemployment rates show minimal differences: the gap between the two almost never exceeds 0.3 percentage points. The growth of the female labour force accelerated significantly after 1975. While from 1955 to 1975 only 21 percent of the growth in the labour force was due to women, from 1975 to 1990 this proportion jumped to 57 percent. But this cannot explain the growing trend in the female unemployment rate that seems to have taken place at the same time, since, during the same period, women contributed 57 percent of total employment growth (22 percent between 1956 and 1975) and 56 percent of salaried employment growth (34 percent between 1956 and 1975).

A Common Pattern of Unemployment Rate by Age

The composition of unemployment by age is similar to that observed in most OECD countries, including Canada: higher rates – although still comparatively low – for the youth (both male and female) and for men aged fifty-five years or more. Actually, Japan and Canada show a fairly similar ratio of youth-to-adult unemployment rates (between 1.5 and 2 times) but both Canadian rates are at a much higher level. For the young, the transition from school to work is always a period of relative employment mobility. But one has to acknowledge that the specific, efficient organization of this transition period helps a great deal, minimizing the risk of unemployment among the young people. The situation of older workers reflects a weakness of the Japanese employment system: hiring and other personnel management practices generally best protect young and middle-aged workers against the risk of unemployment, to the detriment of older workers who, once unemployed, have relatively greater difficulties landing a new job (de Broucker 1992).

A Low Average Duration of Unemployment

The low unemployment rate also reflects its low average duration: Japan is one of the OECD countries where the proportion of unemployed for a long period (in excess of six months or a year) is the lowest. In 1991, 17.9 percent of the unemployed were in that situation for more than a year (7.2 in Canada, 6.3 in the United States), and 38.1 percent for more than six months (23.6 and 13 percent respectively in Canada and the United States). All countries with a better score in this respect (with Sweden to be added to Canada and the United States) present a much higher incidence of unemployment. For the same reasons as those just outlined, the duration of unemployment tends to rise with age.

Quits: The Dominant Reason for Separation

Not surprisingly, the relative importance of the reasons for separation varies with the business cycle. But the importance of so-called "voluntary" unemployment (i.e., not related to the employer's decision, but to the individual's) remains a key characteristic of Japanese unemployment. About 70 percent of new claims for unemployment benefits are assessed by the Public Employment Service as following *voluntary quits*; this is in line with indicators obtained through household or employer surveys. The pattern is quite the reverse in Canada, where typically *job-leavers* represent less than 20 percent of the unemployment pool, while *job-losers* form between 50 and 60 percent, depending upon economic conditions.

A Higher Incidence of Unemployment for Workers in Small Firms

The incidence of unemployment, as measured by the probability of entering unemployment from an employment situation, tends to rise as the size of the employing organization diminishes. Both voluntary and involuntary separations act in the same direction to explain this phenomenon. However, it is worth noting that the phenomenon is significant for men but not for women, whose incidence of unemployment, although generally higher, is not very sensitive to the size of the employing organization.

THE HIDDEN FACE OF UNEMPLOYMENT

For a deeper understanding of unemployment in Japan, it is necessary to go beyond the examination of unemployment rates by age, sex, region, and sector to look at other labour-market indicators. These indicators show that Japan's labour markets exhibit somewhat more "slack" than the unemployment rate might suggest.

The Structure of Employment by Labour-force Status

The structure of employment (with a large share of self-employment) provides one clue to explain the low unemployment rate: the self-employed have a much lower probability of becoming unemployed. In 1990, 11.5 percent of the non-agricultural civilian employment were self-employed and an additional 5.5 percent were unpaid family workers. These figures are much larger than the Canadian ones, which show 7.4 percent self-employed and 0.2 percent unpaid family workers. If one restricts the definition of the labour force (the denominator in the calculation of the unemployment rate) to those really facing the risk of becoming unemployed, the unemployment rate [unemployed/(wage and salary earners + unemployed)] would not have been 2.3 percent in 1989, but rather 2.9 percent. Indeed, the gap between these two rates is now much lower than it used to be (in 1956, the observed unemployment rate was also 2.3 percent, but it would have been 4.9 percent under the restricted definition of the labour force), as salaried employment has become the dominant form of employment. But, as we shall see later, one should not conclude too quickly from this phenomenon that Japan will soon experience significantly higher, more volatile unemployment.

Non-salaried Employment to Absorb Employment Growth Fluctuations

Still very large, even if decreasing, non-salaried employment plays an important role in moderating unemployment growth. Between 1973 and 1979, while economic growth was reduced to an annual average of 4 percent, after two decades of almost 10-percent annual growth, salaried employment increased by only 440,000 annually (1,060,000 between 1956 and 1964; 950,000 between 1964 and 1973), but non-salaried employment diminished by only 70,000 a year (280,000 and 460,000 for the two similar previous periods). When, after 1979, growth in salaried employment picked up at a higher pace

(730,000 annually until 1985), the diminution in non-salaried employment also happened at a faster pace (200,000 annually until 1985). This is part of the explanation for the somewhat limited rise in unemployment, from 1.3 to 2.1 percent between 1973 and 1979. It is clear that the non-salaried sector can retain human resources when economic conditions are less favourable.

Labour-force Participation Behaviour

The labour-force participation behaviour provides a complementary explanation: without a decline in participation rates when economic growth slows down, unemployment rates would increase significantly more. This phenomenon, which reflects discouragement on the part of some unemployed confronted with a lack of job opportunities, is frequently observed everywhere, but it seems to be more pronounced in Japan. When economic growth slowed down after the first oil price shock, the male participation rate declined 1.8 percentage points in five years (from 1973 to 1978), while a continuation of the trend would have posted a decline of only 1.2 percentage points over the same period; the incidence on the unemployment rate can be estimated at 0.6 percentage points, i.e., one-fourth of the unemployment rate recorded in 1978.

The incidence is even higher for women. If between 1973 and 1976 the participation rate had behaved according to the previous trend, it would have been as high as 47.4 percent in 1976, compared with the actual 45.8 percent, and the unemployment rate – considering no change in the relative employment situation – would have been 5.1 percent, i.e., three times the official rate.

A similar phenomenon occurred in 1985–87, but it was much attenuated. Without any change in the participation rate, the unemployment rate for men would have been 3.2 percent in 1987 (compared with the official 2.8 percent), and 3.6 percent for women (also compared with an official 2.8 percent rate). As observed in most other industrialized countries, labour-force participation has become less and less sensitive to the slowdown of economic growth; hence, in the future, major economic shocks could have a much more negative impact on the unemployment rate.

In Canada, too, participation rates are affected by the economic conditions (see, e.g., Sharpe 1996). But what one observes is most often a bend in the trend rather than a temporary reversal. The female participation rate typically exhibits a slowdown in its long-term upward trend when economic conditions worsen, while the male participation rate exhibits an acceleration of its downward trend, sometimes partly compensated for when the economy recovers. The most recent recession is, however, a case in which the female participation rate in Canada actually dropped significantly for the first time since 1966.

Regional Unemployment Disparities Hiding Under-employment

A comparison of unemployment-rate disparities and labour-force-participation disparities is also revealing. Unemployment rates are highest where participation rates are lowest, and vice versa. It points to the existence of a substantial under-employment not recorded in those high unemployment regions, and to real disparities that are even higher than those observed. This phenomenon, of course, is also observed in Canada.

UNEMPLOYMENT, STRUCTURAL ADJUSTMENT, AND PERSONNEL MANAGEMENT PRACTICES

Japan's low unemployment is not a statistical illusion. At times the Japanese labour market exhibits considerably more slack than the unemployment rate indicates, but the same is true for Canada and other countries. Conventional analysis of unemployment from a macroeconomic perspective can explain in part the low unemployment situation experienced in Japan, but only *in part*. Additional hypotheses therefore attract attention.

At this point, we will examine questions related to two such hypotheses. First, could Japan's low unemployment rate possibly arise in part because the intensity of structural change experienced by Japan has been different from that experienced by other industrialized countries such as Canada? Second, have management practices played an important role in maintaining low unemployment rates in Japan?

Intensity of Structural Change

The underlying assumption is that the higher the intensity of structural change in the economy, the higher will be the unemployment rate. We adopt here a measure of structural change proposed in the literature (Samson 1993), an index of dispersion in employment by industry:

$$\sigma_t = \left[\sum_{i=1}^{N} (E_{it}/E_{Tt})(\Delta \ln E_{it} - \Delta \ln E_{Tt})^2 \right]^{\frac{1}{2}}$$

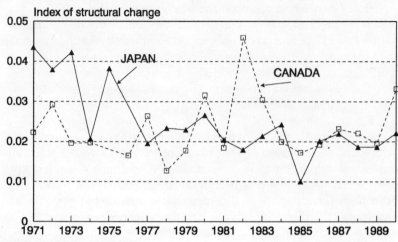

Source: OECD Labour Force Statistics.

Figure 2
Index of Structural Change, Employment by Industry

The computation is conducted for employment in nine industrial sectors. One series of index values is calculated for Japan and one for Canada. The results are graphed in Figure 2.

Clearly, from the observation of the twenty-year period from 1970 to 1990, it appears that the Japanese economy underwent structural change of a magnitude comparable to that experienced in Canada. Even if it is conceivable that a more disaggregated analysis would alter this result, we can rule out that an allegedly smoother structural change would be a *major* explanation for the low Japanese unemployment rate. The result that Japan is affected by structural change of a magnitude similar to what is happening in other developed countries is confirmed by other analysis (see, e.g., Samson 1991).

The Importance of Management Practices

Probably more important than all the elements mentioned above is the effect of specific Japanese management practices. We cannot review in detail all the various aspects of these practices. We will therefore focus on two such examples: one directly related to the management of personnel resources in periods of economic slowdown; the other related to strategic management (business diversification) with a clear preoccupation for employment.

*Personnel Management Practices and Employment
Adjustment*

If quantitative adjustment in terms of employment occurs when economic conditions worsen, in Japan as in any other country, the ways
to achieve such an adjustment are notably different. The analysis of
firms' reactions to the *endaka* (the sharp rise in the international value
of the yen during the 1985–88 period, which seriously challenged
Japan's export industries) provides a good example. In September
1986, when the need for adjustment was taken most seriously, a large
number of firms had adopted measures to adjust the level of employment. By that time, more than half of the firms in the manufacturing
industries had adopted some measures. These were the following, in
decreasing order of mention[2]: control of overtime (adopted by 58
percent of firms), reduction of hiring (40 percent), retraining (36.3
percent), reduction in part-time jobs (35.2 percent), bonus reduction
(32.3 percent), reduction in wage increase (31.6 percent), training in
preparation of future needs (26.1 percent), and reallocation of personnel in affiliated companies (25.9 percent). Lay-offs came in ninth
among the measures with only 21 percent of firms resorting to lay-
offs. Moreover, 44.1 percent of firms rejected even the possibility of
resorting to lay-offs in the future; only lower wages was rejected by
a larger proportion of firms.

It may be difficult to measure the effect of these preferred Japanese
practices on unemployment, but no one would doubt their significance. In April 1987, when the unemployment rate reached an historical high, the indicator of relative excess in personnel (the
difference between the proportion of firms that estimate having an
excess of personnel and that of firms that estimate a lack of personnel) reached 20 percent in manufacturing and 25 percent among large
manufacturing firms.

It is thus really within the firm, among the measures developed as
personnel management practices, that we find keys to explaining the
success in fighting unemployment. According to Ito and Weitzman
(1987), "an ounce of microeconomic prevention is worth a pound of
macroeconomic medicine." Undoubtedly, one key to Japan's low
unemployment is the mix of (1) active micro-policies aimed explicitly
at stabilizing the workforce and (2) macroeconomic policies oriented
judiciously towards stable growth objectives.

Figure 3, borrowed from Kosai and Ogino (1984), adequately represents this essential difference in employment adjustment between
Japan and the United States (the Canadian situation in this respect is

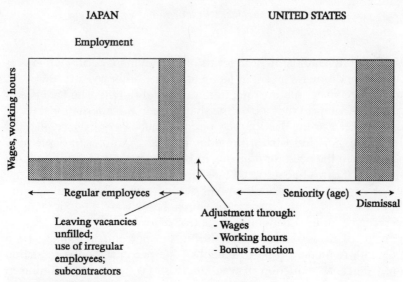

Source: Kosai and Ogino (1984), 81.

Figure 3
A Comparison of the Adjustment of Wages and Employment in Japan and the USA

most likely better reflected by the latter). In North America, external flexibility – lay-offs in bad times, hiring in good times – is the essential adjustment mechanism, with seniority playing a key role in the lay-off line-up. In Japan, this type of adjustment is very rarely used against regular workers; external adjustment affects the peripheral workforce of companies (temporary or part-time employees, subcontractors). The bulk of adjustment is borne internally by regular employees through reduced overtime, possibly lower wages and bonuses, and by job transfers within the company.

It is important to relate the favoured adjustment mechanisms to the degree of worker participation at the firm level. After an extensive review of the available empirical evidence, Levine and Tyson (1990) suggest that participatory institutions foster higher productivity. They state that such institutions are much more prevalent and effective in Japan than in the United States. The underlying cooperative behaviour rests, according to these authors, on four mutually supporting pillars that form the very rationale for the adjustment mechanisms used in Japan: (1) profit sharing or gain sharing, to make workers feel that cooperative behaviour is rewarded; (2) guaranteed long-term employment, to give workers lengthy time horizons so that they do not feel threatened by change; (3) relatively narrow wage differentials, apart from those attributable to seniority, to promote group cohesiveness and solidarity; and (4) guarantees of worker rights, such as dismissal only for just cause.

The performance of Japanese firms and their ability to navigate fairly smoothly through troubled economic waters demonstrate that participatory institutional settings make economic sense. But one has to recognize that these do not exist independently of a socio-economic context in which they can operate effectively. We have argued elsewhere that a key to global economic success rests largely on the *coherence* of the socio-economic environment (Economic Council of Canada 1992). If the specific country's institutional setting can be argued as being heavily marked by history and culture, the principle of coherence is one that can be borrowed and adapted to any national context with high potential return, as a principle for close scrutiny of national policies and practices.

In the present context, and adopting the Webster's definition of coherence – ("the quality of being logically integrated, consistent and intelligible"), the term refers to a socio-economic system in which the various elements and their respective players work towards the same goals, with the same underlying principles and understanding of each other's actions. The success of economies such as those of Germany and Japan has been shown to result in a large part from a high degree of coherence between their respective education systems, labour-market characteristics, and economic policies.

Japan's economic success owes much to the behaviour of employers, but that behaviour has been dependent upon the stance of public economic policy and the socio-economic structures that formed the business environment. Roles and responsibilities have been clearly defined and accepted with a high degree of social consensus: for example, to the schools and universities has been assigned the task of inculcating academic knowledge, and to the firms, the skills training needed to operate efficiently as a worker. No one questions the importance of a high level of education. Clear signals are given by employers to students as to the implications of their school performance and the subject choices they make within the education system.

Business Diversification

In Japan, having to declare involuntary redundancies is seen as a more serious sign of management failure than failure to pay dividends for two or three years. The latter may be an acceptable price for avoiding the former. Japanese firms value highly the reputation that they can guarantee stable employment, and generally make the great efforts that we have just described to avoid declaring involuntary lay-offs. This places a heavy premium on anticipating probable decline in existing markets and on planning to diversify into new products or services in order to use the personnel the firm is morally committed to employ (Dore et al. 1989).

Instead of proceeding through mergers and acquisitions to achieve diversification objectives, the Japanese firm typically sets up an internal task force to plan a new venture from scratch – including the necessary acquisition of skills by existing members of the organization. After plans have been developed and widely discussed within the company, including within union-management joint-consultation committees, targets for restructuring efforts are announced (for example, a major steel company announced in 1986 that 50 percent of its sales should be in non-steel products by 1995). These announcements serve to concentrate the collective mind of the company and to make manifest a sense of mild crisis that facilitates sacrifice of those comfortable niches that change will inevitably threaten.

In choosing directions to diversify, firms obviously have to balance the objectives of (1) getting into the most promising growth businesses; (2) capitalizing on the firm's existing comparative advantages by moving into fields close to their existing technologies or marketing skills; and (3) finding fields in which their existing employees can be absorbed.

The commitment to existing employees is high in the diversification objectives: at the end of the 1980s, more than 90 percent of diversifying companies used reassignment of their own employees out of the company's main business to secure personnel in their new ventures (Economic Planning Agency 1988). This has often required a major effort of retraining.

There is evidence that the pace of diversification has accelerated in recent years. The proportion of firms' Research and Development devoted to "fields other than their main business" has been rising in several industries such as textile, steel, precision instruments, engineering, and non-ferrous metals. Table 1 shows the progress of diversification in the first part of the 1980s. Although we cannot present data on more recent developments, there is evidence that diversification even accelerated after the strong appreciation of the yen in 1985.

Related to the above-mentioned finding that structural change is not less severe in Japan than in other countries such as Canada, the business diversification movement gives a clue to the different relationship that may exist between structural change and employment. In Japan, most of the change in industry employment happens within companies or within groups of companies, without any transition through the external labour market.

Table 1
Sales Shares of Core Business Areas

Industry	1979	1986
Textiles	66.3	57.1
Wood and wooden products	86.1	68.8
Publishing and printing	99.9	88.3
Chemicals	88.4	84.6
Iron and steel	85.8	78.6
Non-ferrous metals	89.1	60.8
Metal products	91.5	90.0
General machinery	75.9	73.1
Electric machinery	93.3	83.6
Transportation machinery	79.4	79.0
Precision machinery	59.1	37.6
Average manufacturing	86.7	80.2

Source: T. Amaya, *Recent Trends in Human Resource Development*, The Japan Institute of Labour, Japan Industrial Relations Series, N° 17, 1990.

THE ROLE OF GOVERNMENT POLICIES IN LABOUR-MARKET ADJUSTMENT

The government is not absent from the scene. Its role must be recorded and placed in proper perspective. Table 2 provides an international comparison of the financial involvement of national governments into labour-market-related matters. It shows that the Japanese government has only a limited financial weight in labour-market affairs, and its share of labour-market expenditures devoted to active measures is only slightly higher than the share for Canada, the worst performer in this respect (Canada).[3]

Nevertheless, government-initiated labour-market policies are diverse, and present about the same range of actions as in most industrialized countries. They do have, however, two special features (Dore et al. 1989). First, government policies can be divided into (1) those that are designed to assist the various processes by which an employer of an about-to-be redundant worker helps that worker obtain employment, and (2) programs that help those who are already unemployed and out in the open market. The Japanese system has a good deal more emphasis than most other countries on programs of the former type.

The second characteristic is that programs are targeted: there are special programs for special problem sectors. In the 1960s, such programs were established on an ad hoc and sector-by-sector basis. In 1978, a uniform system of intervention was established through

Table 2
Public Expenditure on Labour-market Programs as a Percentage of Gross Domestic
Product

Country		Public Expenditure on Labour-market Programs as a Percentage of GDP	Proportion of Public Expenditures devoted to "Active" Measures
Canada	(1991–92)	2.87	21.6
France	(1990)	2.68	29.9
Germany	(1991)	2.73	44.3
Great Britain	(1991–92)	1.91	29.3
Italy	(1988)	1.52	52.6
Japan	(1990–91)	0.44	29.5
Sweden	(1991–92)	3.75	55.2
United States	(1991–92)	0.84	29.8

Source: OECD, Employment Outlook, Paris, July 1992.

legislation to deal with "structurally depressed industries" in general. In a separate piece of legislation, in 1978, the government also established a uniform set of measures to deal with "structurally depressed areas."

Faced with the deterioration of the employment situation after the first oil price shock, the government put into place the Employment Adjustment Subsidy to be paid to employers in depressed industries or areas when they trained, transferred, or suspended their employees with pay, without interrupting the employment contract. The major thrust of the subsidy was to assist employers' efforts to maintain the level of employment while adapting smoothly and flexibly to changes that followed the oil crisis. At the same time, in a gesture full of significance, the government revised the Unemployment Insurance Law, and changed its name to the Employment Insurance Law. In the revision, conditions to access benefits are made less restrictive, especially for older workers, and emphasis is placed clearly on an active policy to stabilize employment and develop job opportunities.

In accordance with the legislation on the measures to assist industries and areas structurally depressed, the number of industries or areas covered by the measures would vary according to needs. For example, in August 1987, the number grew to thirty-six; in November 1988, it was down to thirty-one. Around the same time, thirty-two geographical areas were designated as structurally depressed and as such eligible to receive government assistance. A firm receives assistance after the employer has declared to the public employment service the measures taken to help the laid-off personnel find another job. Measures are then established to provide special assistance for job-search, training for workers changing jobs, an extension of unemployment benefits for workers forty-years-old and over, and mobility and housing subsidies.

Around the end of 1978 targeting measures to older workers became a high priority for the government, since those workers were the most susceptible to suffer from difficulties in finding new jobs. At the same time, the preoccupation of a rapidly aging population added to the effects of the economic conditions. A major reinforcement of the policies in this area occurred in 1987 when the Regional Employment Development Act was passed at the time that the economy faced the shock of *endaka*, the sharp appreciation of the yen.

But measures in themselves tell only one part of the reality. Their impact must be assessed. And the fact that the take-up was always below forecast is a clear indication that government-initiated labour-market policies are not driving adjustment in Japan. They accompany change. Employers' practices have, in effect, much more weight. As we have already mentioned, the microeconomy is essential in keeping unemployment down to low levels.

To say that labour-market programs have not had the essential role in keeping unemployment low is not saying that government policies have not been important. In fact, it is essential to emphasize that company policies have been operating in an especially favourable macroeconomic context. Whenever the economy was dropping into recession (e.g., post-1974, post-1985, and again recently), the government has always implemented traditional Keynesian anti-recessionary policies.

We cannot go into the detail of the macro-policies that formed the favourable context into which companies could operate, but it is relevant to emphasize three major characteristics of those policies. First, without having to worry about the trade balance – at least in the last twenty years – the Japanese government has always had sufficient room of manœuvre to increase significantly public spending when needed to support an ailing economy. Moreover, household savings have also been at a level high enough to finance both public deficits and companies' needs for investments, and even to ensure net outflows of capital.

Second, as a result of several specific structural factors, such as the relative isolation of the domestic market and high national savings, the Bank of Japan has been able to maintain low interest rates. Moreover, monetary policy actions are often prepared in consultation with banks and closely consider companies' performance. Low interest rates that could have affected savings negatively have not actually done so because the under-remuneration of savings was counterbalanced by the positive effects of the low interest rates on growth and incomes.

Finally, in analyses of economic growth in Japan, it is quite remarkable to note how little attention is paid in general to macroeconomic regulation operated by the government. Government interventions are meshed into private-sector actions through a close association in the definition of industrial strategies and economic policies. The symbiotic relationship that developed has been key to the success of both macro-policies and companies' management policies. This is essential to understanding the coherence of the Japanese socio-economic system.

CONCLUSION

Unemployment does exist in Japan. Yet it is well contained by Western standards, even when taking into account its hidden face. We have argued that the major agents of unemployment containment are the Japanese employers and workers themselves, through specific personnel-management practices and participatory institutions. These operate in full coherence with the whole socio-economic system, where government *fine tunes* macroeconomic policy and facilitates labour-market adjustment with targeted measures.

National cultural characteristics are often put forward as reasons for not transplanting the "Japanese model" in North America. But what would we say if Japan's success at achieving low unemployment were the result of combined macro-policies and micro-practices that always *make economic sense*? In that case, one has to search for the underlying principles of success, and to disregard superficial arguments. Japan teaches us an important lesson: the *coherence* of the socio-economic system is a necessary condition for sound economic performance. It is time for policies and practices in Canada to be reviewed and checked against this fundamental principle.

ACKNOWLEDGMENTS

This paper has been written under the sole responsibility of the author and does not engage in any way the organization where he works. The paper incorporates many of the detailed comments which Brian MacLean provided on an earlier draft.

NOTES

1 An agreement on exchange rate issues among finance ministers of the
  G5 countries (United States, Japan, Germany, France, and the United
  Kingdom). Following this agreement, the value of the yen rose steeply
  against other currencies.
2 From a Keidanren survey whose results were quoted in *Japon Économie*,
  N° 203, 31 mars 1987.
3 *Active measures* include public employment services and administration,
  labour-market training, youth measures, subsidized employment, and
  measures for the disabled. *Passive measures* include unemployment compensation and early retirement for labour-market reasons.

REFERENCES

Amaya, T. 1990. *Recent Trends in Human Resource Development*. Tokyo: The
  Japan Institute of Labour.
de Broucker, P. 1992. "Le vieillissement de la population: un défi à relever
  pour l'État et les entreprises." *Revue Française de Gestion*. November–
  December.
Dore, R., J. Bounine-Cabalé, and K. Tapiola. 1989. *Japan at Work: Markets,
  Management and Flexibility*. Paris: OECD.
Economic Council of Canada. 1992. *A Lot to Learn*. Ottawa: Minister of Supply
  and Services.
Economic Planning Agency. 1988. *Economic Survey of Japan, 1987–1988*. Tokyo:
  Printing Bureau, Ministry of Finance.
Ito, T., and M. Weitzman. 1987. "Unemployment: Lessons to be Learnt from
  Japan." *Financial Times*, January 21.
Kosai, Y., and Y. Ogino. 1984. *The Contemporary Japanese Economy*. London:
  Macmillan.
Levine, D.I., and L. Tyson. 1990. "Participation, Productivity, and the Firm's
  Environment." In A.S. Blinder, ed., *Paying for Productivity: A Look at the
  Evidence*, 183–237. Washington, DC: Brookings Institution.
OECD (Organization for Economic Cooperation and Development). 1992.
  Employment Outlook. Paris: OECD.
Samson, L. 1991. "Fluctuations in Employment Growth: National or Sector-
  Specific Disturbances?" *Japan and the World Economy* 3, No. 3: 271–83.
– 1993. "Aggregate Sectoral Shifts and the Last Two Canadian Recessions."
  Paper presented at the Statistics Canada/CERF Conference on "Labour
  Markets and the Last Two Recessions." March.
Sharpe, A. 1996. "The Rise of Unemployment in Ontario." This volume.

PART FOUR

Which Way Now?

12 A Macroeconomic Policy Package for the 1990s

MIKE McCRACKEN

We have a major problem in Canada. Our current forecast is for the unemployment rate to average about 10 percent over the balance of this decade. The output gap – using the 1988 level of the unemployment rate of about 7 percent as representing "potential output" – is about 10 percentage points. That gap continues for the balance of the decade.

What should we do about it? If there is an output gap and we want to close it, then we need more rapid economic growth. Growth at 4 percent per year between now and the year 2000 would roughly close the gap and bring us back down to 7 percent unemployment. In my view, the real output gap is much larger than 10 percent, because we should have as our objective about 3 or 4 percent unemployment, not 7 percent. I take the pragmatic view that, if the Department of Finance can initiate policies that help us arrive at an unemployment rate of 7 percent again, then we can begin a new debate about how to get down to a 3-percent or 4-percent unemployment rate.

No one is forecasting sustained economic growth rates of 4 percent, 5 percent, or 6 percent. The consensus view is for growth in the 2.5-percent to 3-percent range for the balance of the decade. This is not like the vigorous growth that has occurred on other occasions when the country has been coming out of a recession. The policy packages in place are unlikely to produce anything like the growth necessary to close the output gap.

In addition to the "minor" problem of a $70-billion or 10-percent output gap, we have a current account deficit, which at the present time is running about 4 percent of Gross Domestic Product (GDP). This is historically high for Canada. Unfortunately, it may take some time before the current account deficit narrows. We forecast that between now and the year 2000 we will cut only about two percentage points off the current account deficit, which is not enough to reduce our growing indebtedness to foreign economies. It also means that we will continue to run a larger net investment income deficit, in spite of the fact that we may achieve some improvement in our current account. A policy package must, therefore, consider the current account problem along with the output gap. Obviously, one of the key elements of the strategy must be to stimulate added growth through enhanced exports and import substitution.

The federal and provincial governments are currently running a combined deficit of about 6 percent of GDP, a figure that is almost as high as that in the 1981–82 period. There is no fiscal stimulus. At the federal level, the government has been running a more restrictive fiscal policy every year since 1985. At the provincial level, the cutbacks are more recent, but the governments are all marching in step like lemmings, moving towards restraint just when we need stimulus.

The current Informetrica forecast of slow growth shows only gradual improvement of the government balance. Of course, one reason is the large net interest payments on the outstanding debt, reflecting the explosive growth in the debt-to-GDP ratio since the late 1970s and early 1980s. The change in the debt ratio can be expressed as a first-order difference equation with a coefficient greater than one, when the interest rate exceeds the growth rate of the economy – which is a mathematical way of saying that we are in deep trouble. In essence, if interest rates exceed economic growth – either real interest rates relative to real growth or nominal interest rates relative to nominal growth – then there will be continued increases in the debt-to-GDP ratio, unless there is an offsetting primary surplus.

In considering policy packages, we cannot ignore the inflation targets of the Bank of Canada. They were well ahead of their target of 3 percent inflation for the end of 1992 (actual inflation was 1.5 percent). The target was 2.5 percent for mid-1994 and 2 percent for the end of 1995.

With all of the above as the context, let us consider a policy package that makes some sense. Such a package would require a few "minor" changes in four areas: monetary policy, fiscal policy, incomes policy, and structural policies.

First, for monetary policy, we need a real interest rate policy, which would set real interest rates at less that 3 percent, or basically lower than the real growth rate, or the growth potential of the economy. We also need a floating exchange rate. It has been said that monetary policy is exchange rate policy. This seems to be the way we have been operating, but it "ain't necessarily so." We should break that link. Indeed, the whole concept of a flexible exchange rate policy is that it can provide us with a tool to maintain our external balance while also giving us the flexibility of using interest rates for domestic policy. We should make strong efforts to encourage domestic lending via financial institutions to reduce credit gaps.

We can choose to run a regional monetary policy, provided we employ additional tools, such as selective credit controls, in a timely manner. All too often we fail to achieve any useful impact because we act too late. For example, we raised the Canadian Mortgage and Housing Corporation lending requirements in Alberta after the market overbuilt. But we could have done it before, preventing the boom-bust pattern.

Second, in terms of fiscal policy, the objective should be to stimulate demand until the output gap is closed. We may also be able to accomplish some other things out of that process. For example, we can accelerate the infrastructure program. Intriguing evidence exists of a link between public infrastructure and productivity growth in the private sector. Some people think this effect is large, others are less optimistic. But by spending on infrastructure, it is likely that longer-term productivity growth will be enhanced, along with job creation.

Certainly we can also encourage social employment. We have a literacy problem in Canada. We also have a number of students who are unemployed. We could put them to work teaching those who are illiterate, providing both employment for young people and training of others of value for both labour-force participation and society. Surely this is more useful than "make-work" projects to stimulate demand and increased employment.

As well, there is further room for stimulus to consumers through tax cuts and transfer increases. Real incomes of consumers are still declining. Any sustained increase in economic growth needs the support of the consumer sector.

Third, we should take the heat out of the economy as we approach full employment. The best way to accomplish this is to have a permanent incomes policy in place. Many would disagree with this statement. But in fact we have one today. Our incomes policy is an inflation target set by the Bank of Canada, enforced by interest rate changes. Since this policy works by raising unemployment – most recently from 7 percent to above 11 percent – it becomes a stick to beat us with if we are outside their targets. At the same time, it is a major income redistribution from debtors to creditors, and from poor to rich. Indeed, the income redistribution from this incomes policy has been more massive, and in the opposite direction, than that of all the social programs that have been put in place in the postwar period.

All actors in the economy have to understand what we are trying to do about inflation, and have some voice in the determination of the objectives. We should calculate a Consumer Price Index net of those shocks for which no one can compensate, such as indirect tax hikes or a commodity price shock. We should not be saying: "We are going to avoid the OPEC price shock because we're indexed." Such a statement is ludicrous when, as a country, we have had a relative price change that cannot be compensated for by indexing. More generally, exchange rate changes cannot be "indexed" away.

It would take a national accountant or statistician about a week to figure out a proper price index that would be within plus or minus half a point of what it should be. This would provide a starting point because it would say that there is some arbitrariness about fairness or indexing, and there are some rules.

We should have a consensus on national wage-and-price *guidelines.* We should encourage voluntary sectoral guidelines in the same spirit. And the enforcement side should be made clear. If we overshoot, that is a federal and provincial responsibility. Let governments face up to some of their responsibilities: this would be one of them. They can find some very easy ways of doing it, compared to the enormous losses associated with continued, high unemployment as at present.

Fourth, we should make a series of structural policy changes. These should aim at trying to raise the investment effort (investment as a share of GDP), improve productivity growth, promote trade, and deal with some of the market problems that we have with venture capital and initial public offerings.

The question is, can we do any of this in Canada? Or are our institutions so imperfect that all we can do is talk about it, since the capacity of anyone to deliver is poor?

At the federal and provincial levels, we need to change the way we do business. Right now, federal and provincial governments are shooting at each other through us. Can they move to the coordination/coordination role that is required – for incomes policy, for infrastructure planning and financing, for rationalizing the indirect tax system that is an abomination at both the federal and provincial levels? Can we go out and reduce our borrowing costs by some coordination in both domestic and international markets?

Can we begin thinking about how to develop some national institutions apart from the federal government? These would be groupings that would include governments, the private sector (business and labour), as well as some public interest groups.

Certainly, we had such an institution in the Economic Council of Canada. But the federal government conveniently destroyed it, leaving a major gap. Can the council be replaced? It would seem to me that, if nothing else, a National Economic Council could carry on some of the work necessary for underpinning a major policy package.

If we are going to make any progress with our mixed jurisdiction and with our desire to involve both business and labour, we need national institutions in training and education, science and technology, and in the health area (for drug prices and health promotion).

In some of these groups it is essential that the federal Department of Finance and the Bank of Canada be forced to sit together with others at the table. They now sit back in the weeds, watch what happens, and then, without any apparent consultation with anyone, determine that they will change policy. A good example of this is the "minor" change to the unemployment insurance system so that voluntary quits no longer need apply for benefits. Such intervention has got to stop. It causes problems, not only nationally, but within the federal government.

Elsewhere in this volume, Lars Osberg has questioned current policy with the provocative title, "Digging a Hole or Laying the Foundation?". One possibility is that the "holes being dug" are, in fact, graves. The question is whether they are for the policy-makers or for us.

ACKNOWLEDGMENTS

This chapter is based upon a speech I delivered to the "Which Way Now?" panel discussion of the "Unemployment: What is to be done?" conference held at Laurentian University. Brian MacLean prepared a transcript from a tape recording of the speech. As the editors suggested that the chapter should retain the "feel" of the speech, I have made but minor revisions to the transcript.

Index